DIE FIGHTING, OR JUST DIE

Holmes whipped out his .45 pistol and thrust the muzzle against his driver's temple. Sergeant Stevens wasn't the only tough, nasty maverick in Able Company.

"I'll blow your gawd damned brains out," Holmes snarled. "When I tell you to kill somebody, you kill him. Turn this gawd damned tank around and keep the main gun on the haystack. God, damn you, *go!*"

That settled the issue. Simmons charged the haystack like a monstrous knight. Sergeant Holmes took over the bow machine gun and chattered deadly streams of tracers into the hay.

Two unnerved Jerries in gray-green battle dress flew out of the hay with their arms stretched above their heads, shouting frantically in German and broken English: "*Kameraden! Kameraden!* No shoot! No shoot!"

Simmons stopped the tank directly in front of them. The steel monster crouched there, rumbling in a deep growl, with its main gun pointed directly at the Krauts' chests. Holmes cracked the turret hatch. These guys didn't look so fucking bad; one of them was no more than a kid.

"*Kameraden! Kameraden!*"

"Yeah, great," Holmes said. "Okay, you Kraut bastards, drop your gear. Understand? Drop everything."

THE AFRICAN-AMERICAN

761ST

TANK BATTALION IN WORLD WAR II

PATTON'S PANTHERS

CHARLES W. SASSER

POCKET BOOKS

NEW YORK   LONDON   TORONTO   SYDNEY

An *Original* Publication of POCKET BOOKS

 POCKET BOOKS, a division of Simon & Schuster, Inc.
1230 Avenue of the Americas, New York, NY 10020

ISBN-13: 978-0-7434-8500-5
ISBN-10:   0-7434-8500-9

First Pocket Books printing February 2005

10 9 8 7 6 5

Designed by Jaime Putorti

Manufactured in the United States of America

For information regarding special discounts for bulk purchases,
please contact Simon & Schuster Special Sales at 1-800-456-6798
or business@simonandschuster.com.

THIS BOOK IS DEDICATED TO
"PATTON'S PANTHERS,"
THOSE STILL LIVING AND THOSE HONORABLY DEAD.

*A colored soldier cannot think fast enough
to fight in armor.*

—General George S. Patton, Jr.

Author's Note

The purpose of this book is not solely to record a history of the all-black 761st Tank Battalion of World War II, the "Black Panthers," although I trust it will contribute in at least some minor way to a better understanding of the role black Americans played in the war. More important, what I hope to accomplish is to capture the essence of what it meant to these black men to be recognized and accepted as part of an *American* effort. It is not a book about race and racism—there are enough of those—although these topics must, of course, be addressed. It is, instead, a book about soldiers and uncommon valor in combat. Valor has no skin color.

The task proved to be a daunting one. To begin with, during particular periods of time in the United States, the achievements of black people were either officially ignored or downplayed. That means documentary trails tend to be faint or nonexistent. Also, with the passage of nearly sixty years, the memories of those who participated in such events have grown dim, recalled only episodically and incompletely. Time has a tendency to erode memory in some areas and selectively enhance it in others. I understand that. I served twenty-nine years in the military myself, combat time included. What I remember, and it was more recently than World War II, is merely highlights and snatches of events. I have long lost many of the details.

Therefore, in reconstructing the story of the 761st, I have had to rely on numerous sources to fill in gaps left by memory and official record. Also, using my own knowledge and experience with war and with men at war, I have had to improvise and to necessarily re-create scenes and dialogue in certain instances. Few of us can remember word for word conversations that occurred last year, much less sixty years ago. Where re-creation occurs, I strive to match personalities with the situation and the action while maintaining factual content. The recounting of some events may not correspond precisely with the memories of all involved. In addition, all data have been filtered through the author. I must therefore apologize to anyone omitted, neglected, or somehow slighted in the preparation of this book. To those of the 761st not named, I extend a particular apology. I do not intend to diminish your accomplishments or war records. It is simply that there are too many of you—more than one thousand, counting replacements—to list in a book. It would require a book of its own merely to name you individually and recount your exploits. I must therefore take complete responsibility for errors and omissions and ask to be forgiven for them.

The core of this book is built around interviews with surviving Black Panthers, gracious and kind men like Johnnie Stevens, Johnny Holmes, Bill Latimer, E. G. McConnell, William McBurney, John McNeil, Floyd Dade, Kenneth Hamm, and George Blake. Taffy Bates, the lovely widow of the commander of the 761st, Lieutenant Colonel Paul Bates, was gracious enough to give freely of her time not only to help me understand Colonel Bates's role in building the battalion but also to provide one of the warmest love stories to come out of the war. I would like to thank all these fine people who participated in reliving experiences, filling in the gaps of history, and sharing with me much of the drama that appears in these pages. Their help in the monumental task of researching and writing this book made a difficult project an enjoyable experience.

A variety of other sources also contributed in the building of this book: official U.S. military documents and After Action Reports; diaries; newspapers, books, and other published accounts; interviews with witnesses other than members of the battalion, and other authorities. I wish to thank all these sources for helping make this book possible.

I wish to particularly thank Joe Wilson, Jr., for his patience and time in directing me into this project, answering my questions along the way, and assisting in more ways than I can name. His friendship is something I have come to value.

Other particular thanks go to editor Kevin Smith at Pocket Books. It was he who clipped a newspaper article about a 761st reunion and encouraged me to begin this rewarding project. Also thanks to my longtime literary agent and friend, Ethan Ellenberg, who has guided and directed my writing career for some twenty years.

I would also like to express my gratitude to the following authors and published works, from which I drew in writing this book: *The 761st "Black Panther" Battalion in World War II*, by Joe Wilson, Jr. (McFarland & Co., Inc., North Carolina and London, 1999); *The 761st Tank Battalion*, by Kathryn Browne Pfeifer (Twenty-First Century Books, New York, 1994); *The Invisible Soldier*, compiled and edited by Mary Penick Motley (Wayne State University Press, Detroit, 1975); *The Deadly Brotherhood: The American Combat Soldier in World War II*, by John C. McManus (Ballantine Books, New York, 1998); *Death Traps: The Survival of an American Armored Division in World War II*, by Belton Y. Cooper (Ballantine Books, New York, 1998); *The Holocaust*, by Martin Gilbert (Henry Holt & Co., New York, 1985); *Come Out Fighting*, by Trezzvant W. Anderson (Advocate Press, Connecticut, 1979); *Tank*, by Patrick Wright (Penguin Books, New York, 2003); *The Second World War*, by Martin Gilbert (Henry Holt & Co., New York, 1989); *The Bedford Boys*, by Alex Kershaw (DaCapo Press, Massachusetts, 2003); *Patton's Third Army*, by Charles W. Province (Hippocrene Books, New York, 1992); *The World at War 1939–45*, by Reader's Digest (Reader's Digest, New York, 1998); *Across the Rhine*, by Franklin M. Davis, Jr. (Time-Life Books, Chicago, 1980); *Liberation*, by Martin Blumenson (Time-Life Books,

Chicago, 1978); *Total War,* by Peter Calvocoressi and Guy Wint (Pantheon Books, New York, 1972); *The Battle of the Bulge,* by Hugh Cole (Konecky & Konecky, Connecticut, 2003); *The Battle of the Bulge 1944: Hitler's Last Hope,* by Robin Cross (Casemate, Pennsylvania, 2002); *My Three Years with Eisenhower,* by Captain Harry G. Butcher (Simon & Schuster, New York, 1946); *Steel Victory,* by Harry Yeide (Ballantine, New York, 2003); "Down on Wall Street: Road Was Place to Go for Blacks in 1940s," *Killeen Daily Herald,* April 7, 2003; "The Maginot Line," *Smithsonian,* November 28, 2003; "I Saw the Walking Dead: A Black Sergeant Remembers Buchenwald," by Leon Bass/Pam Sporn, historymatters.gmu.edu, February 14, 2003; "Witness Who Won't Stay Silent," by Sue Fishkoff, *The Jerusalem Post,* February 3, 1998; numerous articles from *The Associated Negro Press* by Trezzvant Anderson; "Tanker Lets No One Down in Bloody Fight," by S. H. Kelly, *ArmyLINK News,* December 24, 2002; "The Army Nurse Corps in World War II," odedodea.edu/k, December 6, 2003; "Last Hero—Ruben Rivers," by Ann McDonald, *Tecumseh Countywide News,* October 5, 2002; "Allies Closing Rhine Ring," *Stars and Stripes,* November 27, 1944; "Trezzvant W. Anderson Papers 1932–1963," Robert W. Woodruff Library; "A Silver Star Comes Home," by Dorothy Wilhelm, *SeniorGlobe Media, Inc.,* February 14, 2003; "A Real American Hero," by Michael T. Lyle, Jr., *City News,* June 18–24, 2003; "The Men That Served with Distinction: The 761st Tank Battalion" by Craig A. Trice (U.S. School of Advanced Military Studies, 1997).

Finally, I would like to thank dozens of other people—military contacts, librarians, historians, retired military men, and others too numerous to list but whose assistance is gratefully acknowledged. Special thanks go to Dr. William J. Gregor, Professor of Social Sciences; William D. Smith, 761st tanker; Professor William M. Fishetti, Western Historical Manuscript Collection, University of Missouri–St. Louis; U.S. Army Center of Military History, Washington, D.C.; Robert W. Woodruff Library, Atlanta, Georgia; U.S. School of Advanced Military Studies, Ft. Leavenworth, Kansas; Gary L. Johnson, U.S. Army Heritage and Education Center.

Finally, an extra special thanks to my wife, Donna Sue, who has suffered my writing of books through the years.

Actual names are used throughout except in those rare instances where names were lost due to either imperfect memory or lack of documentation, where privacy was requested, or where public identification would serve no useful purpose and might cause embarrassment. I have almost certainly assigned the wrong ranks to men here and there and may even have placed them in the wrong companies and platoons. Such errors are understandable considering the passage of time and the numbers of men involved. Nonetheless, I ask to be forgiven.

While I am certain to have also made interpretational mistakes and other errors in a work of this scope, I am just as certain that the content of this book is accurate to the spirit and reality of all the brave men who participated in the events described.

—CHARLES W. SASSER

1

We are now in this war. We are in it all the way. Every single man, woman and child is a partner in the most tremendous undertaking of our American history. We must share together the bad news, the good news, the defeats, the victories, the changing fortunes of war.

—PRESIDENT FRANKLIN D. ROOSEVELT

A cold January rain drizzled onto the rolling red-dust hills of central Oklahoma the day Ruben Rivers walked to war. He had to walk to Tecumseh to catch the bus that would take him to join the army, because no vehicle could get down the road when it rained, not unless it was pulled by mules or horses. He seemed reluctant to take each step. He stopped and looked back down the muddy road that led past the ramshackle farmhouse behind the rusty barbed wire.

There were those in the little Negro community of Holtuka who insisted this was a white man's war and that Negroes didn't belong in it. The only reason Negroes were invited was so they could cook for the white man and clean up after him while he did the fighting. Ruben didn't see it that way. This was *his* country, too. Hadn't the Japs attacked Pearl Harbor? Ruben and the two other older boys in the large Rivers family, Robert and Dewey, had talked of little else but the war since the sneak attack five weeks ago. Ruben was the first of them to make up his mind to go.

He stood in the churned mud of the road looking back at the house. A gawky farm kid in faded overalls, brogans, and a raggedy old winter coat, seemingly stuck in a stage of growth that was neither boy nor fully man. Rainwater beaded on a smooth honey-brown face that showed traces, perhaps, of both slaves and slave owners. The jaw was strong and well defined, the eyes dark and so straight-staring they averted under no man's gaze. A lean young man going to war like millions of others from Los Angeles to Washington, D.C.

Little sister Anese stood alone on the front porch waving through the drizzle. A brown little girl wearing a faded feedsack dress Mama had sewn for her. Tears and rain in her eyes. Waving and waving. The others were out at the barn tending livestock or still inside because they couldn't stand the further heartbreak of actually watching Ruben leave home.

Ruben waved a last time at his baby sister. He then turned abruptly, batted his eyes, lowered his head into the cold rain, and resolutely trudged in the direction of Tecumseh. He would have to walk the whole distance. He never looked back again. He remembered hearing somewhere that the road away from home led in only one direction. Once you left home you could never go back again.

E. G. McConnell was sixteen years old when Moms went with him to the recruiting station in New York and lied about his age so he could enlist in the army. Moms went talking back to the recruiting sergeant, wagging her finger in his face and scolding, "Take care of my boy now, ya hear?"

"Yes, ma'am, we sure will do that."

The skinny kid with the wide boyish grin ducked his head in embarrassment. His brown face flushed even darker when Moms grabbed him and hugged him to her ample bosom, cried some more, and made sure he had his prayer book. Then she left him with the recruiter, her admonishment to "Take care of my boy" still hanging in the air.

E.G. was one green recruit, his first time away from home. Like most draftees or volunteers, he had little knowledge or understanding of the political and military machines that formed the war's "Big Picture." His only concern was with the narrow picture that affected him personally.

He traveled by rail from Camp Upton, New York, to Fort Knox, Kentucky, where he would attend basic training in the armored specialty. He understood that to mean tanks; Negroes had never been allowed to drive tanks before because they were not supposed to be smart enough.

The troop train swayed and rattled on its narrow steel tracks. It was stifling hot inside at times, what with all the black soldier recruits crammed into the cars talking and laughing and shouting and playing cards. Everyone seemed in high spirits, off to some great adventure. Soot and ashes from the steam engine blew in through the open windows. Sometimes a live ember sent men stomping and shouting and hooting with laughter as they frantically brushed it off their clothing and chased it down before it caused further chaos.

E.G. became acquainted with a tall, dark, sour man from Detroit.

"Man, you see how they put all us niggers in cars right behind the engine?" he asked.

"What you saying?" E.G. wanted to know, puzzled.

"The white boys' cars is back at the end of the train where they don't get ashes and stuff from the engine." He laughed bitterly. "The only time we ever go to the front of the line is when the white boys don't *want* to be there. It's gonna be the same thing when we go to the war. We only going to the front line when they don't want to be there."

E.G. had never realized before that there was so much country to the United States and that so much of it was mountains and forests. The heavily loaded train slowed as it climbed the northern Kentucky hills on its last leg to Fort Knox. Sergeants came through the cars.

"Pull down all the window shades," they ordered.

"What fo'?" the dark dude from Detroit asked.

"Do as you're told."

It got dank and silent in the cars. Was the train being attacked or what? Curious but not about to defy orders and mess with the shades, E.G. stepped out onto the platform between cars to see what was going on. The train had reduced speed as it always did to pass through one of those little rural towns that dotted the countryside. E.G. saw a paved main street lined by mom-and-pop stores, a few parked Ford pickups, some mule teams and wagons in the back alley. Nothing unusual.

Then, with a start, he realized the purpose for pulling the shades. White men and grown boys lined the track, standing almost shoulder to shoulder, each one armed with a squirrel rifle or shotgun. They glared at the train as it clack-clacked through town, as though daring it to stop or to lift a shade to reveal a black face. Rumors went around that several previous troop trains carrying Negroes had been fired upon.

The dude from Detroit laughed. "Yeah, and here we goes to fight fo' these crackers and the whole United States."

Fresh out of tanker training at Fort Knox, Eddie Donald was not overly surprised to find "white" and "colored" drinking fountains and latrines when he arrived at Camp Claiborne southwest of Alexandria, Louisiana. This was the Deep South. Claiborne was totally segregated. After all, it hadn't really been that long ago that slavery ended. Less than eighty years ago. There were still black folks living who had been born in slavery, others who had labored as kids in the massa's cotton fields.

White soldiers were quartered in newly painted white barracks on good ground near Headquarters, the sports arena, and the large Service Club near the front of the camp. Black soldiers were in the lowlands next to the swamp at the back of the camp.

They weren't allowed in the white areas, except to walk on through. That was fair enough, Donald thought wryly. After all, white soldiers weren't allowed in the black swamp either.

The tall, lanky black man shook his head, shouldered the barracks bag that contained his issued and personal items, and walked straightaway along the streets until black faces replaced white faces. The appearance of the camp changed drastically. Tents and one-story barracks lined the road, many of them old and sorely in need of repair and painting. They were miserable-looking quarters in comparison to those inhabited by white soldiers. Twelve bunks were lined up in each bay, enough for a squad. There was a coal-heating stove at each end. In the summer the windows were screened and mosquito nets installed.

Donald dropped his bag at his feet and looked up and down the road. Some Negroes were sitting on a barracks stoop talking trash and horsing around with guys on the stoops opposite them. Somewhere in the distance troops were being marched to the rhythm of a Jody call.

"You a new meat for the 758th Tank Battalion?" someone called out.

"I am that."

"Welcome home, boy. Let me show you where you bunking."

Donald sighed, slapped at a mosquito buzzing around his ears, and picked up his bag.

Corporal Leonard "Chico" Holland from Detroit drove freshly arrived Lieutenant David J. Williams from Camp Claiborne headquarters to the Negro section of the camp that quartered the all-black 758th. Lieutenant Williams, like all commanders from company level up, was a white man. About six feet tall, athletic-looking, early twenties, short, dark, wavy hair and even darker eyes. He sat on the passenger's side of the open quarter-ton Jeep, eagerly looking forward to his first command assignment.

Chico drove past the nice neat white barracks and officers' quarters on the hill, past the busy PX and the sports complex.

"Where are we going?" the lieutenant asked his driver, looking around and frowning.

"Lieutenant, you'll see," Chico said mysteriously, a half-grin on his face.

The Jeep slowed where the crest of the hill sloped off into lowlands that had once been a swamp. Williams stared, not immediately comprehending. Weather-beaten tents and raw one-story barracks presented a lithograph of a Civil War bivouac area. He had expected more.

"Officers are in the tents at the top of the row," Chico said. He seemed amused at the stunned expression on the green young officer's face.

The next morning, Lieutenant Williams went back up the hill to report in to the white commander of the 758th Tank Battalion. He saluted crisply. Captain Barnes looked him over with a disapproving eye and told him to sit down on the hard chair in front of his desk. From a folder he extracted a newspaper clipping from the front page of the *Pittsburgh Courier*. He shoved it across the desk. Williams recognized his own photo in uniform above the headline "Pittsburgh Industrialist's Son and Politician Goes with Race Troops."

"It looks like your daddy has money and influence," Barnes said with a dismissive flip of the hand. "Is that why you're here? Your old man put you in a safe place away from the war?"

"Sir, if you've looked at my file you'll see I was drafted as a private in January 1941, then attended Officers Candidate School after Pearl Harbor. I volunteered to come here. It had nothing to do with my father or his money."

"Humpf," Captain Barnes said, as though he didn't believe it. "Be that as it may, you've ended up in a safe place to ride out the war. These negras aren't ever going to fight. We're just marking time down here in these swamps until the war is over."

Lieutenant Williams didn't know what to say. He sat with his hands clasped between his knees.

"You're down here with Eleanor Roosevelt's niggers, Lieutenant," Captain Barnes continued. "These people are different and you've got to handle them different. You're from up east and you don't understand that yet. Boy, I'm going to teach you about negras."

Williams stared mutely at his commander, who seemed to expect some sort of reply. A light knock on the door saved him. A handsome black sergeant entered on Barnes's permission. Williams stood up.

"Turley," Barnes said to the sergeant, "I want you to meet our new second lieutenant from up east. From that uppity college, Yale University. Lieutenant Williams, Turley is one of our company first sergeants."

Williams shook hands. Immediately, Barnes sprang to his feet, his face reddening as if he were about to have a stroke. A thick finger jabbed toward the door.

"Turley, get out of here."

As soon as the first sergeant was gone, Barnes leaned heavily across the top of his desk, his voice low and menacing.

"Boy, don't ever do that again."

"Sir?"

"Shake hands with no negra. Don't ever put yourself on the same level with a nigger."

The venom in Barnes's voice stunned Williams. "Sir, with all due respect, first sergeants run the army. They deserve respect."

"You don't know nothing, Lieutenant. You've been up in that uppity college and the only negras you see up there are sheltered. Dismissed, Lieutenant. Get out of here."

Two weeks later, Captain Barnes summoned Williams to his office.

"We're getting a new negra tank battalion, the 761st," he said. "I'm getting rid of you. You have done ruined my best first sergeant."

On April Fool's Day 1942, the all-Negro 761st Tank Battalion was activated at Camp Claiborne, Louisiana. Captain Williams and First Sergeant Sam Turley were both kicked out of the

758th and reassigned to the 761st. Charlie Company's commanding officer, Captain Charles Wingo, took the boot lieutenant aside. Wingo was a soft-looking officer with a pale face.

"You are going to learn, Lieutenant," he said, "that you have got to have a mean coon to keep these boys in line."

2

A wind is rising throughout the world of free men everywhere, and they will not be kept in bondage.

—ELEANOR ROOSEVELT

Assumptions about the inferiority of black soldiers as combat troops dominated military thinking and supported a policy of segregating blacks into support and service units to provide cooks, stevedores, truck drivers, orderlies, and other noncombat personnel. Only five black commissioned officers served in the army in 1940; three of them were chaplains.

Such thinking had developed through a long history. General John J. Pershing penned a secret communiqué outlining how black troops should be treated in France during World War I: "We may be courteous and amicable . . . but we cannot deal with them on the same plane as white American officers without deeply wounding the latter. We must not eat with them, must not shake hands with them, seek to talk to them, or to meet with them outside the requirements of military service."

Colonel James A. Moss, commander of the 367th Infantry Regiment, 92nd Division, held a poor opinion of black soldiers.

"As fighting troops, the Negro must be rated as second-class material, this primarily [due] to his inferior intelligence and lack of mental and moral qualities."

"In a future war," said Colonel Perry L. Miles before World War II, "the main use of the Negro should be in labor organizations."

Even Colonel George S. Patton, Jr., had little confidence in black soldiers. In a letter to his wife, he wrote, "A colored soldier cannot think fast enough to fight in armor."

On the other hand, General Leslie J. McNair, chief of U.S. Army ground forces, was a main advocate of allowing blacks to serve in combat. He believed the nation could not afford to neglect such a large potential source of manpower. He, along with the black press, the NAACP, the Congress on Racial Equality, and Eleanor Roosevelt pressured the War Department and the Roosevelt administration to permit black soldiers, "Eleanor's Niggers," to serve on an equal footing with whites.

With war looming on the horizon, Congress passed into law the Selective Training and Service Act of 1940. It stated, "In the selection and training of men under this act, there shall be no discrimination against any person on account of race or color."

Three months later, however, in October 1940, the White House issued a statement saying that while "the service of Negroes would be utilized on a fair and equitable basis," segregation in the armed forces would continue. All-Negro units were to be formed, including the 5th Tank Group with its three battalions of armor—the 758th, the 761st, and the 784th.

In March 1941, ninety-eight black enlisted men reported to Fort Knox, Kentucky, for training and assignment in the first of these three activated battalions, the 758th. They trained in light tank operations, mechanics, and related phases of mechanized warfare.

Ranks swelled until a cadre and a core of enlisted men were sifted from the 758th to form the second of the three battalions, the 761st. The 761st was activated at Camp Claiborne,

Louisiana, on April 1, 1942, under the command of Major Edward R. Cruise.

"Probably the most important consideration that confronts the War Department in the employment of the colored officer," the War Department General Staff submitted in a memorandum to General Dwight D. Eisenhower, "is that of leadership qualifications. Although in certain instances, colored officers have been excellent leaders, enlisted men generally function more effectively under white officers."

3

When I went down to the induction center, they separated us. They sent me one way and they sent all my white friends another way, because all the armed forces were segregated.

—SERGEANT LEON BASS

When Major Paul Bates assumed command of the 761st Tank Battalion (light) in May 1943, he ordered a battalion dress formation in front of HQ. Rumor had already gone around that the major was a mover and a shaker, a hard-ass whose first action upon arrival at Camp Claiborne was to hang his motto on a wall above his desk: *Never leave to chance anything that hard work and intelligent application can reduce to a certainty.*

Tall, rangy, athletic, with wavy light brown hair and features that appeared chiseled from Michelangelo marble, Paul Bates had grown up in a small town near Los Angeles. He left California to attend Rutgers University, where he was an All-American in football. He enlisted in the army after college, was commissioned as a first lieutenant, and subsequently received his armor training under "Old Blood 'N Guts himself," General George S. Patton, Jr.

Patton insisted on excellence, a trait the young lieutenant from Rutgers soon adopted. Every man in Patton's division, starting with cooks and clerks and extending to staff officers, had to know how to drive every vehicle under his command, fire every weapon, operate every radio.

"As platoon leaders," he instructed his lieutenants, "you got to treat a platoon of tanks like a piece of spaghetti. If you want to go somewhere you can't get there by pushing it. You got to get in front and pull it. I can tell you that is one of the most unhealthy places you can be in your life."

After Major Bates called his first dress inspection on that sultry morning in May, he put the men at ease and climbed onto the hood of a Jeep so everyone would be able to see and hear him clearly. The black men listened cautiously to this new white officer, if for no other reason than that he controlled so much in their lives. In the ranks were Ruben Rivers, E. G. McConnell, Eddie Donald, Chico Holland, Johnnie Stevens, and nearly seven hundred others, all black except for a lean cadre of eight white officers in positions as company commanders and battalion staff.

"Gentlemen," Bates said in a firm voice that resounded across the parade ground, "I've always lived with the point of view that the rest of my life is the most important thing in the world. I don't give a damn about what happened before. Let's go from here. And if you're gonna go from here, if you're gonna make it, we got to do it together."

He paused to let the words sink in. The battalion waited in silence. The men had heard this kind of bullshit before. The Japs had attacked Pearl Harbor more than a year and a half ago.

President Roosevelt had rallied the nation with "Every single man, woman and child is a partner in the most tremendous undertaking of our American history. We must share together the bad news, the good news, the defeats, the victories, the changing fortunes of war."

Right. What "changing fortunes of war" were there at Camp Claiborne, Louisiana? There was no changing *anything*. Most of the guys—First Sergeant Sam Turley, Corporal Howard "Big Tit" Richardson, Sergeant Johnny Holmes, a bunch of the others—had been in the swamps since before the war even started. Waiting.

"We are gonna do it," this whitey major continued. "They say black troops can't fight, that you won't fight. Well, we're proving 'em wrong. Well, you guys are not supposed to be as clean as other people. There's a simple answer to that: Make damn sure you're cleaner than anybody else you ever saw in your life, particularly all those white bastards out there. I want your uniforms to look better, cleaner than theirs do. I want your shoes and boots to shine better. I want *you* to be better. Because, gentlemen, you must get ready. This battalion is going to war!"

After that, suddenly, things started getting intense. The whitey major trained his troops like they *really* might be going to war. The officers under him, both white and black, soon got with the program and began busting balls.

Lieutenant Charles "Pop" Gates, tall, balding, light-skinned, a former Buffalo Soldier and, at thirty-one years old, the "old man" of the outfit, blew up at the Assault Guns Platoon he commanded. Before Bates, the battalion was accustomed to being neglected. The men went to the field to "train," jumped out of their tanks and vehicles first thing, built fires, and sat around them talking trash and having a good time. That wasn't going to cut it anymore. Pop Gates called his platoon together.

"Now, gentlemen," he said in his soft but firm voice, "the first thing you do is concentrate on learning how best to use these things." His hand swept the area to encompass the battalion's light tanks, artillery, and mortars. "My first order of the day is: put out those damned fires and get in those tanks. When you see me working, that means you work. Any questions?"

Patton said you had to pull the spaghetti—and pull it Major Bates did. He was always out there with his black troops. He and Lieutenant Dave Williams and Lieutenant Phil Latimer and Captain Charles Wingo and the other white officers. Out there with the black officers, black NCOs, and black enlisted. Pale faces in a sea of dark faces. Humping on forced marches with full packs, fatigues salt-encrusted, wet with sweat, dusty, muddy . . . weather made no difference.

One mile, two miles, can't quit . . . three miles, four miles, won't quit . . .

"You stay alive in battle," Major Bates called out, "because you're better trained and tougher than the other poor sonsof-bitches."

Shoulder to shoulder on the obstacle courses, white officers and black officers and black soldiers. Training in the light Stuart tanks and on the half-tracks. Every man had to learn every other man's position—how to drive, how to load the main gun, how to be a bow gunner, how to shoot every weapon in the arms room.

"You win because you're good," the major said. "And, by God, you're gonna be good or we'll all die on the way to being good."

They went to the range every week to shoot .45 Colts, .50-caliber and .30-caliber machine guns. Carbines, grease guns, Thompsons. Major Bates out there with them, drawing and firing his .45 with such accuracy that the men watched in awe. "That motherfucker be Wyatt Earp."

"The object is to kill the other bastard before he can kill you," Bates said.

Tanks had to be kept clean and shining. The major and Battalion Sergeant Major Bob Jenkins inspected them to make sure not a speck of mud remained on the tracks.

It was training, training, training. In the swamps and in the mud and in the steamy Louisiana drizzle that made a man feel like he was out there boiling in a pot of Cajun shrimp. Bivouacking and eating rations out of cans, live-firing like in actual combat. When they returned from the field, a brief respite, the tankmen cleaned and serviced their steel war wagons before they cleaned and serviced themselves.

"Treat these tanks like they're your best friends," Major Bates said, "because they are."

The major was *visible*. Morale improved. A new *esprit de corps* infected the battalion. The men held their heads higher. They affected a cocky tanker's walk, wore their barracks caps tilted saucily over one eye, spit-shined their boots, and creased their khakis. Yet they still didn't know what to make of the major. Most still believed all their training was flash and polish toward no end.

One afternoon during a rest break in the field, tank commander Sergeant Johnny Holmes and some of the other men were practicing throwing knives into a tree. Private Leonard Smith's sheath knife ricocheted off the oak and flew into the grass. When he bent to retrieve it, a coiled timber rattler regarded him with its cold slitted eyes, black tongue flickering. Smitty jumped back.

"Shi-it!"

Although the tankers had been walking around the snake for the past quarter-hour, it hadn't offered to bite. Ruben Rivers killed it with a rock. Major Bates happened to be striding past. He paused and wiped sweat. A thin smile appeared at the corners of his mouth.

"That rattler had enough poison to drop all of you," he said, "except it didn't have the balls to use it. Learn that lesson. Bite when you get the chance, or you'll end up dead like that snake."

He walked on.

"Motherfucker," one of the men growled. "If *he* be that snake, he done bit all our asses."

"That man is hardcore," Smitty decided. "But what for? We ain't never going to fight nothing but snakes and mosquitoes and

spiders anyhow. The major need to lighten up and learn to sit
out the war right out here in the swamps with his niggers."

4

He put his men first, second, and third in his priorities.

—TAFFY BATES

Attachment to a Negro outfit in 1943 was considered to be
the most devastating thing that could happen to a white
officer's career. Bates's contemporaries commiserated
with his bad luck. He didn't look at it that way. He had had no
contact with Negroes growing up, nor had he known any blacks
all the way through college. As a result, he brought no baggage
about race with him to the 761st—no prejudices, no ideas about
Negroes one way or another. An athlete himself, the first
thought that crossed his mind when he laid eyes on his healthy
young tankers was *God Almighty, what a football team I could
make of them.*

Other white officers assigned to white outfits at Camp Claiborne viewed the tall, reticent major with a mixture of curiosity
and pity, which gradually mixed with envy and resentment as
the 761st shaped up and beat the behinds off other units during
war games. A loner by nature, Major Bates rarely patronized the
all-white Officers Club. Whenever he did, he was invariably
greeted with snickers and snide comments.

"Decide to come and join the white folk, Major?"

"How're the darkies doing down on the plantation?"

"It's awful white of you, Major, to come up and have a drink with us."

One time when he walked in, an impromptu trio broke into song, harmonizing "I'm Dreaming of a White Battalion" to the tune of Bing Crosby's "I'm Dreaming of a White Christmas." He stopped in the doorway, then turned abruptly and walked out. He swore never to go back again.

Bates was that rare sort of man who needed the approval of no other man to do the right thing, nor did he require outside encouragement to make up his mind about what the right thing was. Associating with his black officers while off-duty was verboten. It wasn't good form and good leadership to socialize with men you commanded, whether they were black or white, officer or enlisted. Most of the time when Major Bates went about business at Camp Claiborne, his tall frame and self-assured manner hard to overlook, he went about it alone.

Besides, his black tankmen had to endure a lot more than he. They were segregated on the worst section of the army post, down in "the swamp" where they were isolated from most facilities and had to walk a mile to the main gate and the bus station. They had to wait until last to get on the bus when they received a pass to go to town, and even then they always had to stand up at the back. Whites treated them with suspicion. Bus drivers wore pistols to enforce the rules and protect themselves from Negroes. If a Negro failed to obey or committed some minor infraction—such as not getting up to let a white soldier have his seat—the driver stopped at the nearest MP station or law enforcement office, and the offender was dragged off in chains.

One evening, alone as usual, Paul Bates attended a concert at the post theater. During intermission, he lit up a cigar and stood by himself at the end of the lobby to avoid offending anyone with his smoke. He became amused by the antics of a very young brunette nurse imitating ballet steps in front of a dance poster. She bounced up on her toes and awkwardly pirouetted with her arms arched above her head. She stumbled and, giggling, bounced off the wall. Major Bates caught her before she fell.

"Be careful, little girl, or you'll break your neck."

"No, I won't," the brunette replied, still laughing. "Taffy will show me how to do it. She's Russian."

"And who might I ask is Taffy?"

"I'm Melaney. That's Taffy."

She indicated her friend, a tiny slip of a nurse lieutenant with bobbed blond hair and a disconcerting way of looking straight into a man's eyes. By the time intermission ended, the three were in animated conversation. Paul accompanied the nurses back to their seats to sit with them until the end of the concert. He and Taffy kept exchanging looks. At curtain call, he invited them to the O Club for a nightcap. Melaney moaned. She couldn't go; she wasn't wearing a proper Class A uniform.

"I'd better go back to our quarters with Melaney," Taffy decided.

Melaney pulled her aside and hissed, "Don't be silly, Taffy. You go. Did you *look* at him? He's *gorgeous!*"

Paul and Taffy closed the club talking about music and books and finding out about each other. She was a nurse with the 14th Field Hospital. Paul told her that he had worked on a merchant ship and sailed to the Orient after college and before joining the army. She had never known *anyone* who had been to the Orient.

"Is it true," she asked, forward and impish, "what they say about Oriental women?"

He looked at her and blushed. She laughed delightedly.

"That *theirs* are crossways instead of up and down?" she elaborated.

He had never known a woman that forward and unconventional. She laughed more devilishly than ever while he went temporarily speechless.

"You're the first woman I've met in a long time who hasn't asked me if I'm married," he said.

"What a stupid question," she shot back. "The answer is obvious. Of course you're married. After all, nobody could be as handsome and exciting as you and not be hooked at your age."

He was thirty-four years old, Taffy ten years younger. He was indeed married and had a young son, but his wife had separated from him. They hadn't lived together for quite some time.

"We're waiting until the war is over to get divorced," he explained. He looked at her. "There was never a reason before—I mean . . ."

She was surprised to discover that he was the dashing white commander of an all-Negro tank battalion. Taffy detected a passion in this leadership role, in his association with his dark tankmen, that the tall major displayed for almost nothing else. He leaned across the table toward her, gripping his drink with both hands, as though to draw her into a complicity with him.

"I'm finding out they have a heritage of undeserved attributes that are all on the downside," he said. "I never look at them like that. I never have reason to because I make up my own mind. There is something that exists between men and men and women and men, and that is empathy. You can feel toward a person when you first meet him or her. It has nothing to do with words. You get a feeling between the two of you when you know you are on the same playing field."

They were on the same playing field, Taffy and this tall man. She knew it.

"We've learned not to depend on anyone else," he went on. "The tank destroyers—white guys—are taking their Army Ground Forces Tests to see if they are ready for combat. My men have defeated them so many times in training—and have thoroughly enjoyed it. That's because we've learned to respect ourselves and to respect our buddies. We've learned we can't exist unless we support each other. On maneuvers against the tank destroyers, it's ruled against you and you get a bad mark if a tank isn't maintained properly and falls out. I don't have to worry about my tankers. All I have to do is say, 'Men, if it's in combat, you're dead. So do it right.'"

He chuckled as he related a story of how he went to the tank shed where his companies were conducting equipment maintenance after a maneuver. He heard laughter coming from around one of the tanks. He asked First Sergeant Sam Turley about what was going on.

Turley grinned. "Sir, the tank destroyers have this logo: *Seek, Strike, and Destroy.* It don't work when we're around. That's when it becomes *Sneak, Peek, and Retreat.*"

There was a sober moment when the young nurse met Major Bates's eyes.

"Paul, will they ever be given the chance to fight?" she asked him.

He returned her gaze.

"Yes," he said forcefully, as though willing it. *"Yes."*

Her small hand reached across the table for his.

5

Machines will beat machines.

—WINSTON CHURCHILL

On September 5, 1943, the largest troop convoy yet assembled in World War II set sail from New York Harbor. It consisted of nine transports carrying the 3rd Armored Division, the 101st Airborne Division, and several separate artillery, medical, and service units; nine navy tankers and freighters loaded with fuel and supplies; and an escort of the battleship U.S.S. *Nevada* and nine destroyers.

The Allies were assembling and building up troops and equipment in preparation for an invasion of Europe by way of France.

On September 8, General Dwight Eisenhower broadcast the news of Italy's surrender. While the Italians had surrendered, the Germans hadn't. The German commander in Italy, Field Marshal Kesselring, rushed six full divisions to Salerno to repel an expected invasion landing.

On September 9, General Mark Clark's army hovered off the Italian coast to the south of Salerno. Harsh metallic voices boomed out of the darkness from loudspeakers providing the Germans a last chance: "Give up now, or you are dead."

German parachute flares responded, transforming night into day. Machine guns, mortars, and artillery opened up from all along the coast. The Salerno landing turned extremely bloody for the American invaders, and would become even more bloody during the next seven months as Germans dug in to conduct World War I–style trench warfare.

On September 15, the 761st Tank Battalion at Camp Claiborne packed up lock, stock, and tank and transferred from the Louisiana swamps to what Paul Bates, now promoted to lieutenant colonel, considered marvelous tank terrain in the hills, valleys, woods, and open grounds of Camp Hood, Texas.

Camp Hood had been officially opened on 218,000 acres of virtual wasteland in central Texas a year earlier, on September 18, 1942, as a tank destroyer tactical training and firing center. It quickly expanded to include armor training and a basic training site. As many as 100,000 soldiers were stationed there preparing to go to war.

The black tankers remained in the field on maneuvers most of the time, testing themselves and their skills against all comers. The War Department also upgraded the battalion from a light tank battalion to a medium tank battalion. Three of the battalion's four companies, A, B, and C, traded in their old M5 Stuart tanks with their 37mm guns for larger, tougher M4 Shermans with main 76mm cannon. Company D retained its Stuarts to operate as a light, fast reconnaissance unit.

While many considered these changes a signal that the battalion was getting ready for overseas movement, life for the black tankers remained little different from that at Camp Claiborne.

"The Paddy boys get ice for they water," Private Horace Evans protested. "We don't have any. It's them little petty things that really burns me up and makes you know what a vicious, scheming character Paddy is."

"We better'n all them Paddies," observed Private L. C. Byrd from Tuscaloosa, Alabama, "but we still ain't gonna see nothing but rattlesnakes in Louisiana and more rattlesnakes in Texas until this war be over."

6

One of the things I can say about the white man. They would watch ever damn thing you would do.

—SERGEANT JOHNNY HOLMES

Nearly seven hundred men of the 761st Tank Battalion had shouldered their barracks bags and swarmed off the troop train at Camp Hood, Texas, a hot, dry, dusty piece of real estate only one step short of the gateways to hell. They stood blinking against sunshine so hot it seemed to reach right down into a man's core to suck out his life's juices.

The kid of the outfit, E. G. McConnell, had looked forward to migrating out of the Deep South and escaping Camp Claiborne. Camp Hood proved to be another disappointment. Even German Nazi prisoners of war detained at the camp received more respect. They had full run of the post and the PX and, by virtue of their whiteness, enjoyed the privilege of cutting line at the checkout ahead of any black American soldier.

"Here we is, first-class Americans, never been in prison or anything," E.G. groaned. "We ain't even prisoners of war or nothing like that. Them POWs smirking at us because they know they can go in the PX on post and purchase whatever they want. Because they white—while us niggers has to stand outside and watch."

"It ain't gonna change none, boy," Harry Tyree said.

"That don't make it right."

"No. That don't for a fact make it right."

E.G., a northern boy who went south and confronted cultural shock, tried several times to get himself thrown out of the army. He missed muster, went AWOL, and in general made a nuisance of himself. "Take care of my boy now, ya hear?" Moms had admonished the recruiter. Colonel Bates was taking care of her boy, foiling his ploys to escape the army by denying him weekend passes and placing him on extra duty details. The boy was not going to get a Dishonorable Discharge if the colonel had anything to say about it. Moms's boy was going to war if the war didn't end.

"I am so dis-gusted with the U.S. Army and how they treating us," he complained, wearing his perpetual frown of disgust to prove it.

As at Camp Claiborne, the Camp Hood bus situation to town proved near intolerable for black soldiers. There was a white waiting line to catch the bus and a black line. When the bus pulled up, the driver got off and tapped off the first ten or so Negroes and allowed them to get on the bus.

"Y'all go to the back of the bus now, ya hear?"

White troops filled up the rest of the bus. It pulled away from the station—and, like as not, there stood E.G. and maybe Smitty and Big Tit Richardson and George Shivers in its exhaust, watching it leave, not enough room left on the bus for them because they were black and not among the first ten or so allowed to board. Waiting for the next bus and hoping to make that one before their passes expired.

"I am so dis-gusted."

"Private, what are you doing?"

"I ain't doing nothing, Sergeant."

"Then why you up here messing around in the white camp for?"

The white drivers seemed to take a vicious pleasure in overloading the last buses from town back to post at night. Black soldiers and their friends and wives either jammed themselves in the back or stood in the overcrowded aisles. Invariably, the bus would pull to the side of the road two or three miles short of camp and the driver would smirk. "Folks, this bus is overcrowded and I can't take y'all on post without getting in trouble. Some of y'all are going to have to get off and walk."

That meant *black* folks got off and walked. It got where they expected it. They grumbled, but there was little they could do. That was simply the way things were.

"I am so dis-gusted."

Black soldiers receiving passes from Camp Hood had few options on where to go for recreation. While Wall Street in New York was known as a place where financiers either made it big in the Stock Exchange or jumped out windows, Wall Street for the black soldiers at Camp Hood meant a couple of blocks of "nigger town" in nearby Temple.

Wall Street was one of only two spots in the area where blacks were allowed to set up their own businesses, to congregate, and to enjoy themselves socially. It branched off from the intersection at Avenue B and Second Street downtown. Near the corner, Herdon's Produce sold meats so fresh that chickens and turkeys were kept live in cages out back. Next door was a hole-in-the-wall café full of smoke, grease odors, and noise. Dr.

Thomas Edison Dixon, an M.D., and Dr. Atkinson, a dentist, had offices across the street and down a block. There were also a colorful variety of other cafés, juke joints, cinemas, barber shops, and pool halls. There was a USO, a cab company, a funeral home, and even a church down past the last juke joint.

Wall Street vibrated with energy from early Friday evening through Sunday, greatly expanding its weekend population with the arrival of the 761st and other black armor and artillery units at Camp Hood. There on any given weekend could be found Sergeant Warren G. H. Crecy, his wife, Margaret, and their best friends Horatio "Scotty" Scott and Aaron Jordan.

Should Crecy pull weekend duty, Scotty and Aaron escorted Margaret and took care of her.

Crecy's middle initials stood for Gamaliel Harding. Almost everyone called him Harding. Although he was a short little guy who looked almost meek in his thick eyeglasses, his core was steady and positive and wrought of pure steel. Anytime anyone said "Volunteer?" Crecy's hand went up first. Margaret liked to tell the story of how she and Harding were married.

They had grown up together in Corpus Christi, Texas. One afternoon following Sunday mass, twelve-year-old Harding showed up at Margaret's house carrying a bouquet of flowers and a carton of ice cream for Margaret's mother. He was all dressed out in pressed slacks and a bow tie. His face was scrubbed almost raw.

"Oh, Harding," Margaret's mother effused.

Crecy squared his shoulders. He always knew what he wanted.

"I come to ask for your youngest daughter in marriage," he announced grandly. "I'm going to marry her when she is eighteen."

Margaret was nine at the time. Nine years later they were married.

Passes were easy to come by at Camp Hood, and Colonel Bates granted liberal furloughs the rest of that summer and the winter and summer that followed. There was only so much training an outfit could endure without losing its edge—and what use was an edge anyhow to soldiers who were only marking time?

Tank commander Sergeant Johnny Holmes received a furlough to go home to Chicago. A strapping six-footer, he went into a café near the train station in Temple to buy sandwiches to take with him on the trip. He traveled in uniform. Khakis, garrison cap, black regulation tie tucked neatly between the buttons of his shirt, wearing his sergeant's stripes.

He paused at the front door, feeling uncomfortable. About twenty or thirty diners, all white, occupied tables or stools at the counter. At the back of the hall, stuffed between some overflowing garbage cans and a stack of Coca Cola crates, a few local blacks crowded around a pair of tables put there as an afterthought.

The sergeant squared himself and walked on in, the way he would have in Chicago. Whites glared at him. The man behind the counter eyed Holmes suspiciously. He was a beefy individual in a filthy T-shirt and apron, the tail of which he used to wipe both his utensils and the sweat from his florid face.

"What you want, boy?"

"I'm not a boy," Holmes flared. "I'm a United States soldier."

"So? What do you want?"

"I want a couple of sandwiches to go."

"All right. But you got to go around to the back door to get them."

"Back where the garbage cans is?"

A hush fell over the café. This was one uppity colored man, uniform or not.

"I don't want them then," Johnny snapped.

"Well, then, get the hell out of here, nigger."

The soldier froze as he fought to control the fury that damned near choked him. He felt hostile eyes boring holes into his back. This was enemy territory. Discretion being the better part of valor under the circumstances, Sergeant Johnny Holmes, U.S. Army, backed out of the café and rode the train all the way to St. Louis— fourteen hours—before getting anything to eat. He sat in his seat in the colored section glaring out the windows at the country he had volunteered to fight for and, if necessary, die for.

7

I just went along with the program. It was a horrible environment.

—CORPORAL FRANKLIN GARRIDO

When John Roosevelt "Jackie" Robinson attended the University of California at Los Angeles, he was the only man of his time to letter in four major sports, including football and baseball. After college, he attended Officers Candidate School and received a lieutenant's appointment to Fort Riley, Kansas, where he was asked to play football. The Fort Leonard Wood football team refused to play against a team with a Negro on it. Jackie was excluded from the game. Fort Riley lost.

"I will not play anymore unless you assure me this incident will never happen again in future games," Robinson told his coach.

"Jackie, you know I can't do that."

"Then I won't play."

The Special Services officer got with him. "Lieutenant Robinson, you either play or we'll transfer you to another post where you'll wish you had played."

"I'm not playing."

One of the most well-known athletes in the nation, black or white, was therefore shipped off to bake under a Texas sun with the 761st Tank Battalion at Camp Hood. It was an assignment Jackie could live with. The tankers were squared-away Joes, and the commander, Lieutenant Colonel Paul Bates, seemed a fair man well liked by the black soldiers under him.

Shortly after Lieutenant Robinson reported and assumed command of a tank platoon, Colonel Bates summoned him to headquarters. Robinson reported with a crisp salute and a disquieting voice murmuring in the pit of his stomach.

Uh oh. Something fucked up, blame the new nigger.

Colonel Bates stood up behind his desk. He was as tall as Robinson, but rather lean compared to the lieutenant's athletic bulk. He smiled and reached to shake hands.

"Robinson, I want to commend you and your outfit on your work down here," the colonel said. "You have the best record of all the outfits at the camp and I am singling you out for special mention."

That took the wind out of Jackie.

"Sir, if you'll pardon the expression," he stammered, "I didn't know shit about tanks when I got here. I owe it to my platoon sergeant. I put him in command and he's done a wonderful job of explaining things to me. I've learned as I went along."

Robinson felt as though he had managed to get to first base on an error and was now about to steal home.

"I don't care how you accomplished what you did," Colonel Bates continued, nonplussed. "The fact of the matter is, you found a way to make your outfit tops, and that's all I ask."

From that moment Robinson would have followed the tall white man to hell and back. Even stayed in hell with him if it were necessary. No wonder the 761st tankers spoke so highly of Bates, praise they lavished on few other white officers.

Somewhat later, on July 6, 1944, a day so hot Texans claimed you could bust an egg and it would cook before it struck the ground, Lieutenant Robinson emerged from the Negro Officers

Club into bright sunlight. Cadence and Jody calls from distant marching troops hung lazily in the somnolent air. Since it was a training-free day for the 761st tankers and Robinson had the day off, he strode to the nearest bus stop to catch a ride to the nearby town of Belton.

The wife of an officer friend of his sat near the front when Robinson got on. She was so fair-skinned that she could easily pass for white unless scrutinized closely for Negroid features. Jackie smiled and took the seat next to her.

The bus began to fill up after a few more stops around post. Several white soldiers shot hard glances at the big black man wearing lieutenant's bars who seemed to be sitting with a white woman. They got up and whispered to the driver. The driver pulled to the side of the street and made his way down the aisle, his eyes on Robinson.

"You know the rules," he said. "You have to go to the back of the bus."

"I'm comfortable where I am," Robinson responded.

The driver blinked and took a step back. He was a beefy man in his forties. Every eye in the bus turned toward him and the black passenger who had the audacity to sit in a whites-only seat. And with a white woman at that.

"Maybe you didn't hear what I said," the driver snarled.

"I heard."

"Then . . . ?"

"I'm an officer and I'm sitting where I am."

Jackie had reached the limits of his tolerance, this being only the latest in a series of racial insults. Only a few days before he had stopped at the white Officers Club to cash a check and was barred at the door because of his color. He had tried to avoid confrontation, but every man had his breaking point.

The driver glowered. "If you don't go to the back of the bus," he threatened, "I'm going to have to kick you off."

Robinson's great bulk slowly unfolded from the seat. His friend gripped his arm.

"It's all right, Jackie," she pleaded. "I don't mind moving."

"I do. You're a lady. You're not going to the back of the bus."

The short crop of his hair touched the ceiling of the bus. He towered over the driver.

"You were saying, friend, about kicking me off the bus?"

"I'll call the MPs."

"Do what you have to do. But you have a choice of either driving this bus—or I'll drive it for you."

The driver got on his radio and spoke loudly enough for all passengers to hear, telling his dispatcher that he had an "uppity kind of Negro." He drove to the MP station. Two white enlisted MPs came aboard and proposed to arrest Robinson. As an officer, Jackie refused arrest by enlisted men, as was his right.

"Looky here, nigger—"

By this time, Robinson's temper had grown dangerously short. "If you ever call me nigger again, I'll break you in two."

The enlisted MPs withdrew, blustering and nursing their wounded pride. They returned shortly with a captain of MPs, who arrested the upstart Negro and charged him with violating the 63rd and 64th Articles of War.

The first charge specified: "Lieutenant Robinson behaved with disrespect toward Captain Gerald M. Bear, Corps Military Police, by contemptuously bowing to him and giving several sloppy salutes while repeating, 'Okay, sir. Okay, sir, yassuh,' in an insolent, impertinent and rude manner."

The second charge stipulated: "Lieutenant Robinson having received a lawful order by Captain Bear to remain in a receiving room at the MP station disobeyed such order."

Word of the incident spread quickly around the post, especially among the all-black units. Jackie Robinson became an instant hero. Angry black soldiers swaggered about with their chests sticking out, daring anyone white to cross them. Tensions were as high at Camp Hood as they had been leading up to racial rioting in Detroit a year earlier. Colonel Bates was called back to his office to find Lieutenant Robinson waiting for him.

"Put in a request for a ten-day leave," the colonel suggested. "Go home to Pasadena where the entire atmosphere is different. Think about it, line up whatever you can to help yourself—because it looks like there's damn sure going to be a court-martial."

8

We left Camp Hood with a bitter taste in our mouths.

—COLONEL PAUL BATES

At the time of the Jackie Robinson bus incident, the 761st had already been placed on alert for overseas movement. Colonel Bates received the orders on June 9, 1944, only three days after the Allies made the Normandy D-Day landings on the French coast. The 761st had been in service and in constant training for more than two years. Few took the movement orders seriously. They were more interested in the pending Robinson court-martial than they were in something that would probably never happen.

The NAACP, Robinson's college fraternity, and the Negro press turned the episode into front-page news. Colonel Bates received a nervous telegram from the War Department: "We are being deluged with letters upholding the character and popularity of the man. Proceed in court-martial with great care."

Colonel Bates let it be known where his sympathies lay. He was called prejudiced for the first time in his life. The prosecuting attorney suggested that the colonel not be allowed to testify

in Robinson's behalf because he was obviously prejudiced in favor of the defendant.

"Isn't that a beautiful way to use that word?" the colonel dryly commented.

Still, in spite of the deluge of public support for Jackie Robinson, court-martial proceedings continued. JAG—the Judge Advocate General—appointed the defendant a white officer attorney. Robinson met with him in Colonel Bates's office.

"What chances do I have of getting out of this?" Jackie asked.

The attorney was a pudgy little major so pale he appeared to have been locked out of the sunlight for most of his life. He sighed expansively.

"To be frank," he said, "I think you have very little chance."

Lieutenant Robinson stood up, opened the door, and stepped aside for the lawyer to leave.

"I don't want you," he said. "I want somebody who believes in me."

Colonel Bates found the entire thing maddening, especially considering that his battalion was preparing for movement.

"It's bullshit," he agonized, slamming the meaty side of his fist against his desk. He sprang from his chair and stared out the window, chewing on his cigar. Camp Hood heat-wriggled in the July sun.

"You would think they would have dropped it by this time," David Williams said. Promoted to the rank of captain, the white Pennsylvanian now commanded Able Company.

"They won't do that, Dave," Colonel Bates said, tearing himself away from the window. "Don't you see? You can't let Negroes get out of place. Do that, and Lord only knows what will happen. Black folks might even start thinking of themselves as *real people*."

Robinson's second lawyer was a captain named Cline. Jackie asked him the same question about what chance he had.

"This is exaggerated beyond belief," Cline responded. "No doubt about it. I will defend you—and you will get off."

To the surprise of nearly every tanker in the battalion, an advance party from the 761st led by the executive officer, Major Charles Wingo, departed Camp Hood for Camp Kilmer, New Jersey, on August 1. Excitement rippled through the ranks. Kilmer was a debarkation point, the first stop for units on their way overseas. It appeared the black battalion would finally go to war after all.

The Robinson court-martial began the next day, on August 2. Robinson had been transferred from the 761st to a tank destroyer outfit that would be staying behind, since it was assumed his trial would interfere with his deployment. The court-martial was still going on when the main body of the 761st—36 officers, 2 warrants, and 767 enlisted—left for Camp Kilmer on August 9. Colonel Bates remained behind to see the trial to its conclusion.

At first, things looked bleak for the defendant. Witness after witness, all white, took the stand to accuse Lieutenant Robinson of defying and showing disrespect for authority. Finally, the enlisted MP who had called Jackie "nigger" took the stand. Captain Cline the lawyer looked him over and leaned over to whisper to his client.

"This guy," he said, "isn't the brightest penny in the piggy bank."

Cline, a slightly built man with a deceptively mild nature concealing his shrewd wit, began his cross-examination by casually asking, "Sergeant, during this incident did you ever refer to the defendant as 'nigger'?"

"Under no circumstances, sir."

"Did you ever use the word?"

"No, sir. None of us ever did."

Cline nodded as though in deep thought. "Sergeant, I want you to tell me the exact words Lieutenant Robinson used when he threatened you. This is very, very important so we can punish this man properly."

"Yes, sir," the witness responded with an aggrieved air, immediately adding without thinking about it, "He said to me, 'If you ever call me nigger again, I'll break you in two.'"

The stunned courtroom fell silent. That ended the trial abruptly after it had dragged on for seventeen days. The president of the court, a full colonel, and the rest of the court-martial board stood up. The colonel ordered the charges and specifications read. To each he announced in a stentorian tone, "Not guilty. Not guilty."

Afterward, Robinson shook hands with Colonel Bates.

"I don't reckon I'll be going overseas with you, sir."

"Jackie, this should never have happened."

"One of these days, sir, it won't happen. Sir, take care of the guys when you get over there. They need you."

By almost all accounts, the Sherman is not a match in one-on-one combat with the German Mark V or VI.

—JOHN C. MCMANUS, AUTHOR OF *TANK*

Tanks rumbled into the twentieth century like beasts from some future age, spitting streaks of death from their machine guns and hurling bolts of destruction from their main guns while they shrugged off counterfire and crushed enemies beneath their treads. The tank transformed the modern battlefield with its novel triad of mobility, protection, and firepower.

No single inventor produced the tank. Rather, it evolved

through centuries of dreamers and experimenters. There had been many previous incarnations—Boadicea's chariots; the Roman testudo; Hannibal's elephants; the medieval belfry; the armored knight. The Scottish used armored "war carts" against the English; Leonardo da Vinci sketched plans for protected chariots; Simon Stevin built two wind-blown "land ships" on wheels in the late sixteenth century; Napoleon was interested in steam-powered "automobiles of war."

In March 1838, John George and his son, of Cornwall, England, announced that they had invented a "modern steam war chariot . . . very destructive in case of war." It was described as a coke-burning chariot operated by three men, its side armored against "muskett and grape shot," and fixed with scythes and iron beaters that would beat an opening in enemy ranks twenty-three feet wide. The machine disappeared into oblivion and would not be recognized for another eighty years.

By 1915, the necessary mechanical ingredients were on hand to produce a tank—bulletproof armor, the internal combustion engine, and caterpillar tracks. These, and the need for such a war machine to break out of trench warfare and through enemy lines to end the stalemate of World War I's Western Front, produced the first "modern" tank and began the era of armored warfare. This "armed caterpillar" could go through and over anything and knock down trees.

On September 15, 1916, Mark I tanks of the Heavy Section of the British Machine Gun Corps went into action for the first time at the Battle of the Somme. Of the forty-nine machines available for attack, some broke down, some sank into crates and collapsing dugouts, and others lost their direction. Thirty-six actually engaged the Hun.

Although the results of these first tank engagements were modest, the tank had established itself as a permanent fixture of the world's militaries by the end of the Battle of the Somme in November. One of the earliest American advocates for the tank was none other than George S. Patton, Jr.

As World War II developed in Western Europe, it became primarily a campaign of movement, of armored conflict developed to a high art. On land, tanks were the supreme threat. Tools whose speed, firepower, and steel-clad massiveness allowed them to punch into rear areas to destroy command posts or supply depots, to roll over dug-in enemy, to move swiftly to cut off avenues of retreat, or to spearhead infantry attacks. Accompanied by lightly armored fighting vehicles such as half-tracks and armored cars, and by infantry doughboys, engineers, mobile artillery, and other forces, tank divisions and battalions formed the core of the armies fighting against Nazi Germany in Europe.

The medium M4 General Sherman main battle tank was the major U.S. weapon in this sustained engagement of armored titans. Its initial main armament was a short-barreled, low-velocity 75mm gun, later modified to the more powerful 76mm cannon. Two .30-caliber machine guns, one ball-mounted in front of the assistant driver and the other in the turret coaxial with the main cannon, and a heavy .50-caliber machine gun mounted on a ring on top of the turret completed the behemoth's array of defensive and offensive weapons. The .50-caliber could be fired only when the turret hatch was open.

The nimble Sherman's emphasis was on speed, mobility, and maneuverability, which meant compromising firepower and survivability. Weighing about thirty-five tons and powered by a 450-horsepower V-8 gasoline engine, it could reach speeds of nearly thirty miles per hour while exerting only seven pounds of pressure per square inch on its treads, about the same as a man walking on soft ground. It had a range of 100 to 150 miles, depending upon variables of speed and terrain.

A crew of five men operated the Sherman—the tank commander or TC; gunner; loader; driver; and assistant driver/hull gunner.

The TC sat in the turret directly above and behind the 76mm gunner. He was in charge of receiving radio communications from company or platoon commanders and carrying out their orders by coordinating the actions of his crew, of selecting targets, and of immediate command of his own machine. The .50-caliber attached to the top of the turret next to the hatch was his weapon. It could be moved in all directions, including upward as an antiaircraft gun. The drawback was that he had to open the hatch and stick up his head to operate it.

The gunner occupied a seat directly below the TC, his job to fire at anything the TC selected as a target. His weapons were the 76mm cannon and the coaxially mounted .30-caliber machine gun. Both cannon and machine gun moved together along the same axis and were zeroed in on telescopic sights to hit the same target. This made it possible to use machine gun tracers to target quickly, then fire the cannon to score. The gunner had two triggers: the machine gun trigger on the power traverse handles and the cannon trigger on the floor. A gyro-stabilizer compensated for the up-and-down motion of the tank and permitted the gun to be fired while the tank was moving, although with less accuracy than when it was stationary.

The loader below the gunner was in charge of loading shells into the tank's cannon, lifting them out of a rack in the turret floor and slamming them into the breech.

The driver had his own hatch at the left front of the tank. Steering was accomplished by pulling on brake handles, one left, the other right, while gunning the engine. The tank went backward when both brake handles were pulled and the transmission shifted into reverse.

The assistant driver/hull gunner also had his own hatch, at the right front of the tank. His weapon was the second .30-caliber machine gun. It moved freely in all directions and could be fired from the "buttoned-up" position, with all hatches sealed.

Although the M4 had more speed and a faster rate of fire than its enemy counterparts, the German Panthers and Tigers commanded greater accuracy and range with their main guns; the 128mm mounted on the huge Tiger could reach out nearly four times farther than the Sherman 76mm. In other ways, the German tanks were also decidedly superior to the Sherman—thicker armor, less vulnerability, wider tracks, and diesel-powered engines, which made them less likely to explode and burn when hit.

The Sherman's high profile made it an easy target for antitank guns. Because of its gasoline engine, it had an alarming propensity to "brew up" and incinerate the crew if a shot penetrated its hull. The British, who also used it, nicknamed the tank "Ronson" after the American cigarette lighter, because, in the words of a national ad, "It lights the first time." Americans often referred to it as a "Sears & Roebuck casket."

The M4's saving grace, in addition to its speed and maneuverability, was that it proved more mechanically reliable than German tanks. It could therefore spend more time in the field, providing it avoided being hit. Allied numerical superiority also became a decisive factor. The United States simply fielded more tanks faster than Krauts could knock them off. The Germans were unable to replace their losses.

Fully armed, the 761st Tank Battalion was equipped with fifty-four Sherman tanks and about fifteen smaller M5 General Stuart tanks for Dog Company's "Mosquito Fleet." The Stuart, equipped only with a 37mm main gun, was a smaller, lighter version of the Sherman.

The battalion organization consisted of Battalion Headquarters and a Headquarters Company composed of three platoons—Mortar Platoon, Reconnaissance Platoon, and Assault Guns Platoon; Service Company provided beans and bullets, communications and repairs; three fighting companies—Able, Baker, and Charlie, armed with Shermans—and the "Mosquito Fleet" of Dog Company that performed primarily reconnaissance and escort with their light Stuarts.

The 761st Battalion was officially known as the "Black Panther" Battalion when it departed Camp Hood for Camp Kilmer on August 9, 1944. Its patch and emblem was a black panther superimposed upon a silver shield, along with the battalion's motto: *Come Out Fighting*.

The motto came from a quotation by Joe Louis as he prepared to fight Max Schmeling for the second time. Asked about his fight plan, Joe said, "I'm going to come out fighting."

Brigadier General Ernest A. Dawley, commander of the Tank Destroyer Center at Camp Hood, delivered a short speech to the Black Panthers as they loaded up to leave for the East. He concluded with, "When you get there, put in an extra round of ammunition and fire it for General Dawley."

10

The post commander and his staff assure you that everything will be done for your comfort and pleasure during your short stay here.

—PAMPHLET DISTRIBUTED TO DEBARKEES AT CAMP KILMER

Charlie Company TC Sergeant Johnny Holmes had no idea Texas was so big. For a day and a half the troop train carrying the Black Panthers crawled across the arid flats before climbing into the hill and pine country of east Texas and finally breaking out into Louisiana. The battalion brought all its equipment except for tanks, which would be issued new later on. After a rest stop in New Orleans, the Panthers loaded up again and arrived at Camp Kilmer, New Jersey, two days later. Camp Kilmer and Camp Shanks, New York, were staging sites and ports of debarkation for troops bound for the ETO, the European Theater of Operations.

One of the primary functions of a staging area was to make sure each soldier left the United States fully equipped before crossing the Atlantic. For two weeks, the Panthers were herded and shuffled from place to place in a whirlwind of activity. Field inspections were conducted to identify equipment problems, make necessary repairs, or replace anything that could not be repaired. In between inspections were dental and medical checkups, immunization shot lines, *Know Your Enemy* movies, and always more training and accountability musters. Men groaned and cursed as reveille sounded before dawn in the cramped, summer-heated barracks, and they groaned and cursed again from exhaustion as they made their way back to their bunks for taps and lights out.

"I am so gawd damned tired," Corporal Ardis Graham complained. "I wisht they would just go ahead and throw me in that briar patch."

Sergeant Johnny Holmes burst into his barracks with the news that the 761st had been placed on "alert." That meant the unit would be shipping out within twelve hours. Ruben Rivers, Willie Black, Willie Devore, and a few other men were having a grabass session after the evening meal.

"I just now heard it," Sergeant Holmes exclaimed. "The colonel'll be coming soon with the official word. The Black Panthers is on *alert*."

Motel Johnson couldn't believe it. "Where you hear that at, Johnny?"

"It's all over camp. We are heading to New York in the morning to catch that big ole boat across the pond."

"New York?" marveled Kenneth Hamm, Able Company's clerk. "That's my home. Maybe I can go see my folks before we leaves."

"If we alerted," Willie Black said, "there ain't gonna be no time for that. We is gonna kick some German butt big time. The Nazis is gonna know the 761st has done arrived."

Excitement mixed with apprehension swept through the battalion. Sure enough, Colonel Bates called formation within the hour and passed the word. *Get ready!* That incited a last flurry of activity as soldiers removed their division sleeve patches and other markings in case spies were watching. Helmets were chalked with a letter and a number indicating the proper marching orders from the camp to the trains and the proper railroad cars for transportation. More than 70,000 troops a month were departing Camp Kilmer and Camp Shanks for overseas duty.

It seemed that after nearly two and a half years following its activation, the all-Negro 761st Tank Battalion was finally going to war.

11

I fell in love with his voice. Very deep masculine voice. Like I'm hearing music of some sort.

—TAFFY BATES

Colonel Paul Bates and Taffy had continued their wartime romance after their meeting during the concert at Camp Claiborne, sometimes over great distances. Taffy's 14th Field Hospital remained at Claiborne when the 761st moved to Texas. Several times Taffy caught a bus to Camp Hood and Paul likewise traveled to Claiborne so they could be together. It appeared they would soon be separated, would not be able to see each other for perhaps years.

"We'll be together when the war is over, permanently," Paul promised.

Nurses were governed by all types of regulations concerning proper behavior for women. Unlike soldiers, they even had strict curfews. As a liberated woman in a time not so liberated for women, Taffy chafed at the restrictions and blatantly defied them.

"You'll be late for curfew," Paul cautioned. "They'll write you up."

"Fuck 'em," she snapped saucily, boldly, for "ladies" never used such language. "I'm such a troublemaker anyhow that they don't know what to do with me. The chief nurse is a tyrant, but she doesn't have the balls to do anything about it. You'll bring me back in the morning. As long as I'm back by 0700 hours so I'll have time to shower and get dressed for work."

By some odd coincidence, by some luck of the draw, the 14th Field Hospital moved to Camp Shanks to prepare for overseas movement a week after Paul's battalion arrived at Camp Kilmer. Taffy was overjoyed at the prospect of seeing the man she loved before he left. Paul managed to get a full day to spend with her in New York. They could hardly let each other go for a minute. Hovering over them, as over other lovers during the war years, was the specter of a violent death in battle. There was always a chance they would never be together again.

"I won't be able to see you anymore before we go overseas," Paul said. "We're being alerted."

The young woman tossed her bobbed blond hair.

"How about tomorrow?" she asked. "I'll see you then."

He laughed. He didn't believe her.

All passes had been canceled, for the 761st as well as the 14th Field Hospital. Nonetheless, the indomitable Taffy sneaked off-post and caught a Trailways bus to New Jersey. She had no idea where Camp Kilmer was located, other than that it was near New Brunswick. When she got on the bus, the only available seat was next to a private. She sat down. Taffy's lieutenant bars made him nervous.

"You okay, young fella?"

"Yes, ma'am. I sure am, ma'am."

"Where are you going?"

"Camp Kilmer, ma'am."

"That's good. You can show me the way."

The private got off the bus at a stop before it reached the camp's main gate and guard shacks. Taffy followed him off. She was afraid she might have some difficulty getting on the post without a pass.

"Hey, soldier. You're in trouble, aren't you?"

"No, ma'am. You see . . ." He ducked his head, blushing. He couldn't have been any older than eighteen. Obviously, it wasn't in his nature to lie. "Yes, ma'am," he confessed. "I could get in trouble. I snuck off-post without a pass, ma'am. I had to see my girl before we shipped out."

Taffy's eyebrows arched. "How did you do that? Sneak off-post, I mean?"

"Through a hole in the fence, ma'am."

The nurse smiled brightly and slipped her tiny hand through the crook of his elbow.

"I'm your girl." She laughed. "Let's find that hole in the fence."

The hole wasn't there anymore. MPs had found and patched it. The private's face fell.

"Pick up your lip before you step on it," Taffy scolded, her quick mind already formulating an alternative plan. She steered the young GI back toward the main gate. "Listen to me and take your cue from that. Do whatever I tell you to do—or what comes naturally."

As they strolled within sight of the gate guards, Taffy wrapped herself around the young soldier. What the MPs saw was a lovely blond lieutenant hanging all over a happy, red-faced private. The couple was laughing and hugging, obviously very much in love.

"Aren't you absolutely thrilled for us?" Taffy purred. "We ran off and got married. We just had to before he went overseas. Jack didn't have time to get a pass or anything. There wasn't time."

She squeezed a pretty tear from one sad blue eye. Stranger things than a private marrying a lieutenant nurse occurred daily as soldiers prepared to deploy, perhaps never to return. The MP in charge hesitated. He looked at the blue eyes, the tears of joy on Taffy's cheeks, the blond hair, the shapely figure in the WAC uniform. What male could resist a picture like that? He shook his head and smiled.

"Congratulations," he said, stepping aside.

Taffy telephoned Paul from the Officers Club.

"Taffy! Where are you?"

Laughing, she told him.

"I don't believe it!" he exclaimed.

"But I am," she cooed. "Are you in the habit of keeping a lady waiting?"

12

You are a soldier of the United States Army. You have embarked for distant places where the war is being fought.

— PRESIDENT FRANKLIN D. ROOSEVELT, LETTER
HANDED OUT TO EMBARKEES

Specialist Kenneth Hamm, Able Company's clerk, almost missed movement the first time in the history of the United States that a Negro armored unit left American shores. Denied a pass—no passes were being issued so close to movement—he sneaked off anyhow and went home a last time. After all, he lived right there in New York. He returned to the docks at 0800 hours, just in time to be snatched up by MPs and escorted to the piers where the 761st was loading aboard the British troop transport H.M.S. *Esperance Bay.* Men were already filing up the gangplank, duffel bags on their shoulders.

"First thing they gonna do when we get back is they gonna court-martial your black ass," his buddies ragged him.

"What else can they do to me they ain't already done?" Hamm countered, grinning good-naturedly. "They already sending me over *there* where I might not come back from."

He looked around at the faces of men who had become his buddies and fast companions over the past two years.

"Might not none of us come back," he added.

"I ain't coming back," little Willie Devore flatly announced in a stentorian tone as bleak as a winter funeral. Devore was a small brown man with a round face and sad brown eyes. He had been brooding for days, thrown into a funk the moment the outfit was alerted for overseas movement. He had a premonition, he said, that he would be killed.

"That's all bullshit," Sergeant Ruben Rivers scolded. "Nobody can know something like that."

"*I* know it," Willie insisted.

Such dire predictions were rare, however, as the *Esperance Bay* pulled its lines and steamed down the Hudson Channel to the Atlantic. It was a clear, hot summer morning, 1040 hours, August 27, 1944. Hundreds of soldiers massed the stern deck to catch a last glimpse of the Statue of Liberty as her head disappeared behind the New York skyline. Young, virile men. Nothing could shake their high spirits for long. Few of them had traveled more than a hundred miles from their farms and neighborhoods before they enlisted—and now here they were embarking on the greatest adventure not only of their lifetimes but also of the century.

Even the teenager E. G. McConnell, who had devoted so much time and energy to attempting to get kicked out of the army, found himself caught up in the excitement and history of the moment. He actually felt privileged to be a part of it.

"They really need me over there," he exhorted. "I am one of only two in the battalion to get trained on the top-secret gyro-stabilizer. I am necessary to the team."

A member of Headquarters Company's vehicle maintenance section, he helped keep the steel behemoths running.

Captain David Williams, the white CO of Able Company, rested elbows on the rail next to his friend, Captain Irvin McHenry, Charlie Company's CO and the first Negro to command a company in the 761st. They stood together in companionable silence, momentarily unable to find words to express the emotions they experienced. Neither had thought this day would ever come.

Over the past years they seemed to have simply marked time on the sidelines, as U.S. Marines in the Pacific captured island after island chain-hopping toward Japan, as the Allied armies in Europe made assault landings on North Africa, Sicily, Salerno, and then Normandy two months ago. They hadn't even been bridesmaids at the wedding; they were more like distant cousins relegated to the far backseats. Neither man thought their black troops would ever be considered good enough, or *white* enough, to fight the global threat of fascism.

Escorted by destroyers and a cruiser, the transports and tankers of the convoy strung out in combat formation across the Atlantic's unsettled summer face. It was an awesome spectacle. Ships plowing through the seas, the sun hot and sparkling on their frothy wakes.

German submarine wolfpack attacks on American convoys had peaked the previous year, then abated after the New Year when Germany all but lost any command it exerted over the Atlantic Ocean. Still, the navy took no chances; Hitler retained control of seaports in the captive nations of Northern Europe and therefore remained dangerous at sea. Ever wary, white hospital ships with huge red crosses painted on their hulls traveled fully lighted returning from England with American wounded to let German submarines know they were under the protection of the Geneva Conventions. Sometimes, enemy subs trailed the hospital ships so their propellers could not be distinguished from the ships' propellers. Allied navies countered by randomly dropping depth charges behind any hospital vessels they ran across on the high seas.

Captain Williams drew in a deep sighing breath of salty air.

"This," he said, gazing out to sea, "is a historic occasion. It will be written about."

Captain McHenry, whose men of Charlie called him "The Burner" because of his predilection for hard training, was less idealistic. "Perhaps it would be," he responded, "if we weren't Negro troops."

Although the journey from New York to England seemed to take forever, its transitory nature was made clear by the way the men lived aboard ship. McHenry was assigned to a cabin with five other black officers. The cabin was about ten feet square and contained two stacks of three bunks each and a small adjoining toilet with a saltwater shower.

Cramped as it might be, it was absolutely luxurious compared to conditions endured by enlisted men who slept in "racks" and hammocks stacked five high in the holds. Each enlisted man claimed a space approximately two feet wide, two feet high, and six feet long. McConnell had to climb a pegged pole to reach his top swinging hammock on the starboard side next to a blacked-out porthole. Ruben Rivers's feet hung over the end of his bunk, since the sleeping space also had to accommodate the soldier's barracks bag.

That bag, about eighteen inches in diameter and three feet long, contained its owner's personal gear and had to be carried with the soldier wherever he went. Since there weren't enough bunks to accommodate everyone at the same time, some of the men had to sleep in shifts. They might not return to the same bunk for their next turn at sleeping.

George Blake thought the chow served in port as the ship prepared to sail was surprisingly good. He complained that it turned to garbage once they were out of sight of land. Many of the men, however, could not have cared less about chow. At least half the troops at any given time were seasick and busy throwing up over the gunnels into the sea—if they could make it topside in time.

Suffocating heat belowdecks magnified the stench of vomit. The decks and gangways were slippery and foul.

For those recovering from seasickness or who had not succumbed to begin with, there was always a crap shoot or a poker game under way somewhere on a spread blanket. MPs patrolled the decks to maintain order and break up the occasional fight.

H.M.S. *Esperance Bay* ported in England on September 8. The battalion would spend the next month up-training and being issued new Sherman tanks with 76mm guns before crossing the English Channel to France.

13

Armored monster, tank of steel,
Humble is my plea.
Shield my love in thyself,
And return him safe to me.

—TAFFY BATES

The hospital ship transporting the 14th Field Hospital to war arrived at Southampton, England, a week after the H.M.S. *Esperance Bay* docked there. As medical person nel carrying their gear prepared to disembark, a dock worker rushed aboard calling out Taffy's name, as though he were a messenger paging a tourist on a luxury cruise liner.

"Oh, my God!" Taffy's friend Melaney exclaimed with delight. "He's found her already."

Colonel Paul Bates had sent a message.

*I was here yesterday to wait for you, but you didn't make it.
Here's the number to call me.*

14

------

*Each, in his appropriate sphere, will lead in person.
Any commander who fails to obtain his objective, and
who is not dead or seriously wounded, has not done
his full duty.*

—GENERAL GEORGE S. PATTON, JR.

At 1200 hours on August 1, 1944, fifty-six days following
the Allied landings at Normandy, the Third Army became operational in southern France under the command of General George S. Patton, Jr. Never an officer to tarry,
Patton unleashed an American blitzkrieg that raced westward
two hundred miles through the gap at Avranches to reach the
port of Brest in six days. His armored spearheads bypassed centers of resistance and pushed up to seventy miles a day. He
hoped to reach the Rhine River in Germany by the first week in
September, before German forces could recover and regroup.
From there, he would charge to Berlin ahead of Russians probing in from the east.

"Continue until gasoline is exhausted," he ordered his elements, "then proceed on foot."

By the end of August, the Third Army had liberated more
than fifty thousand square miles of territory as it swept four

hundred miles to Verdun and the Meuse River, only sixty miles from Germany. Paris was liberated on August 25, and General de Gaulle walked in triumph down the Champs Élysées on August 28.

On that same day, Allied forces in southern France entered Toulon and Marseilles and took 47,000 German prisoners. Two days later, British forces crossed the border into Belgium.

"The whole Western Front has been ripped open," German Field Marshal Gunther von Kluge frantically radioed Hitler.

Caught between opposing armies, hundreds of thousands of dazed French men, women, and children took to the road as refugees. Relentless air and artillery bombardments were destroying their towns and villages. Homes and shops went up in flames. Livestock was slaughtered, wheat fields ground to dust, loved ones buried alive underneath mountains of rubble. Stunned survivors picked up what few possessions they could carry and set off on bicycles, mules, horse-drawn carts, carrying packs or pushing wheelbarrows.

Few knew where they were going, where they would sleep at nightfall, or where the next meal was coming from. They fled to neighboring towns, villages, or farms, only to pick up and flee again when the war caught up with them. Many set up temporary squatter homes in abandoned trenches, tunnels, caves, quarries, cemetery vaults, padded cells at otherwise unoccupied insane asylums, or within medieval cathedrals. They prayed the war would end soon.

George Patton, who intended to end it soon, was consuming more than five hundred thousand gallons of gasoline every fifty miles. His supply lines, stretched to the breaking point, reached some 350 miles back to the Normandy beaches and Cherbourg. Even the heroic efforts of the "Red Ball Express," the Negro-run motor transport system, could not keep up with his demand for fuel and supplies.

On August 31, the Third Army's advance ground to a halt.

Patton ran out of gasoline. He angrily pointed out that the delay gave the enemy time to reorganize and gather his forces.

Realizing that the Allies would soon be on German soil at their present rate of advance, Adolf Hitler ordered an editorial published in the Nazi party newspaper.

"Not a German stalk of wheat is to feed the enemy," it raved, "not a German mouth to give him information, not a German hand to give him help. He is to find every footbridge destroyed, every road blocked—nothing but death, annihilation and hatred will meet him."

15

Many of the black soldiers had English girlfriends, some of them got married.

—CORPORAL FRANKLIN GARRIDO

Bombed-out streets in England, orphaned children, barrage balloons filling the dirty skies, and nightly blackouts against German bombers brought the war suddenly very close, continued reminders of wartime suffering and sacrifice. The men of the Black Panther Battalion were ready to go to war, but of course they really didn't know what war was.

The outfit had jelled during the past two years into a first-class fighting force, molded into a fist as big and black and hard as that of the battalion's best slugger, Chico Holland, who stood straight up in the ring and hit like lightning, and Sergeant George Riley, who was fast and clever and had been a hard-hitting former middleweight contender from Detroit before the war.

When Specialist Kenneth Hamm from New York first came to the 761st, he thought he was smarter and more sophisticated than all the country bumpkins, sharecroppers, and sons of Old South slavery who made up a hefty portion of the battalion. Few of them enjoyed as good an education as he and the other northern boys. Some of them couldn't much more than read or write their own names.

Turned out, however, that it was *they* who expanded *his* education. Although they might not have much book learning, they compensated by being practical and commonsense. Hamm had a tough time taking a gun apart at first; the country boys had no trouble at all. He learned to respect them.

The Mississippi, Oklahoma, and Louisiana contingent also made excellent tank drivers. "That's from driving mules in the fields," James Peoples explained. "If you can drive a mule, stubborn as he is, you can drive a tank."

In addition to being a good driver, Peoples knew how to maintain a tank. His engine compartment was so clean it almost shone. Colonel Bates always complimented him on it.

Major Russell C. Geist, battalion S-3 for operations, was another man who came to the 761st with ingrained prejudices and hung around to change his opinions. A white man from a working-class family in Germantown, Pennsylvania, Geist initially resented being assigned to a colored outfit. When he reported to the 761st in October 1943, the colonel briefed him and concluded by asking if he had any questions.

"Just one," Geist said. "How do I get out of this chickenshit outfit? I don't want to serve with Negroes."

Colonel Bates slowly unfolded his lean form from behind his desk. Even though his voice remained soft, a core of steel threaded through the velvet.

"Go down to Headquarters Company," he said. "You are company commander. You will serve here. Is that clear, mister?"

Geist continued to so resent his assignment that he refused to be included when a company photograph was taken. Lieutenant Ivan Harrison stood in as company commander for the picture.

Geist's transformation did not occur overnight. A few men in the company, like PFC Thomas Ashly from Washington, were brilliant with radios and the new gyro-stabilizer that kept the big tanks on target even as they rumbled at full speed across the countryside. Intrigued by electronics, Geist stood around and watched as men worked on the radios and gyros, a look of amazement on his face that coloreds could be so adroit. He asked questions, and gradually questions and answers evolved into conversations. Soon, Lieutenant Harrison and Geist were friends. Harrison assured the other black officers that Geist was okay. All he needed was to rub up against a few black men personally to see that they were human.

When Colonel Bates moved Geist up to S-3, Geist recommended that Lieutenant Harrison replace him as CO of Headquarters Company. The tall, light-skinned Harrison became only the second Negro after Lieutenant Irvin McHenry to command a company in the battalion.

The Negro soldier got along very well in Britain. E. G. McConnell thought the Brits a very cheerful and open people with no color hate in them. Hostility came from white soldiers who resented Negro soldiers going after the white English girls. British citizens were amazed when mobs of white soldiers closed down dance halls where black soldiers danced with local white girls. Rumors were spread about the inferiority of black people.

"They're ignorant, lazy, and dirty, and they have tails that are cut off at birth," went the stories. "The only reason they have tanks is because they're taking them up to the front for the white boys."

The rumors largely failed to find much of an audience among the British. In his private diary, political editor Cecil King of the *British Daily Mirror* noted: "The feeling is fairly common that

Negroes are nicer and better behaved than the ordinary Yank. So there is some indignation when Negro soldiers are condemned to death for raping English girls. In the most recent case the evidence would surely have resulted in acquittal in an English court. In the far more numerous cases of rape or murder by white American soldiers, the punishment, if any, is of a wholly different order of severity."

Although the Brits had a less-than-complimentary saying about the GI—"He's overpaid, oversexed, and over here"—they proved surprisingly tolerant, knowing as they did that but for the United States they would all have been speaking German by now.

There was a farm next to the staging area. One night, Ruben Rivers, fatalistic Willie Devore, E. G. McConnell, and a couple of others got on their bellies and crawled over to do a little after-hours harvesting. They gathered some corn and were starting on the greens when Sergeant Rivers suddenly hissed, "Somebody's coming!"

The marauders ducked into the corn with their booty and flattened themselves in one of the rows, hoping not to be discovered. There was a full moon that lit up the field almost as bright as daylight. A voice with an English accent rang out.

"Hey, Yanks?"

There stood the farmer and his two healthy and robust sons.

"What're you Yanks doing on the ground?"

E.G. looked up at their challengers. Moms always scolded him about lying.

"We was stealing some greens and corn," he sheepishly admitted.

"What on earth for?" the farmer asked.

Chagrined, Rivers stood up. "We was hongra."

To the astonishment of the abashed Black Panthers, the farmer and his sons burst into peals of laughter. When the farmer finally caught his breath, he explained that the British didn't eat their corn. They fed it to livestock.

"You Yanks come over and get some corn any time you feel the urge to feed your *livestock*," he invited. "Next time, though, you blokes don't have to crawl on your bellies."

Friendly as the natives were, however, the men of the 761st had had about all the waiting they could stand. For more than two years they had waited Stateside, and now the weeks passed while they trained, made last-minute adjustments to equipment, trained some more—and waited. Endlessly, it seemed. Most could empathize with a sign some evangelist had erected on the highway: *Where Will You Spend Eternity?* Underneath it some wiseacre had scrawled: *In England.*

The 761st was a self-sustaining "bastard" battalion, which meant it was up for grabs to support any outfit in the army to which it was assigned. Companies, platoons, even individual tanks could be commandeered and shifted about as needed. Initially assigned to the Ninth Army, it was relieved on October 2, 1944, and reassigned to General George Patton's Third Army.

Colonel Bates said Patton himself personally asked for the Black Panthers; Patton took only the finest. He had sent a message to the War Department requesting more tanks, the best available. The only tank unit left was Negro.

"Who the fuck asked for color?" Patton shot back. "I asked for tankers."

The 761st Tank Battalion. Patton's Panthers.

16

We landed at Omaha Beach . . . and from what we saw we knew we were going into combat.

—SERGEANT JOHNNIE STEVENS

A healthy chop roughed the surface of the English Channel the night of October 9, 1944, when the Black Panther Battalion, now consisting of 760 black men and white officers, crossed from Britain to the Normandy beachhead of France. Colonel Bates had vowed even when they were cooling their heels at Camp Claiborne a lifetime ago that they would see battle. The time was rapidly approaching when his faith in them would be either vindicated or discredited.

The LSD (landing ship, dock) on which the battalion sailed was the largest of the Allied landing craft, necessary to transport armor. Specialist Kenneth Hamm nonetheless found the boat scary. It might be big, but the channel was bigger, and boats turned over all the time. He spent the night voyage topside near one of the lifeboats. His stomach felt a bit queasy from wave action, and on top of that he had butterflies of anticipation and anxiety.

Patton's Panthers were going to war. At last.

The general feeling aboard ship was that something momentous was happening, not only to the battalion but also to each man individually and personally, an event even more epochal than when the battalion had watched the Statue of Liberty recede into the morning haze in August.

Men clumped together in tight little groups on the decks for comfort and support, talking quietly among themselves. They balanced themselves at the railings and stared out at the flotilla of similar landing craft spread out across the rough water.

Everything bound for France to deliver supplies and increments of more than two million Americans who would eventually be ground into the war on the European mainland. A partial moon, bright at sea in spite of being less than complete, played hide and seek with scuttling rain clouds. Shadows chased back and forth across the Channel in a war of their own.

PFC Willie Devore hadn't budged from the fantail since the LSD broke port at Weymouth. He wore the same forlorn expression as when New York had disappeared on the horizon. E. G. McConnell walked up beside him and leaned against the railing. Together, without speaking for a long time, they watched stars playing peekaboo with the clouds, and the bright white wake the ship inscribed across the water.

Willie stood like that most of the night, looking glumly back as though he yearned to reach out with an amazingly long arm like the Plastic Man and pull the ship back to England. Everyone in the battalion knew about his premonition. He was convinced he would never see home again.

"Willie, you oughta get some sleep, man," E.G. said, trying to be helpful.

"Soon enough I'll be getting all the sleep I need," Willie sadly replied.

"Awww, man. Don't you be talking that stuff. The war's almost over. We'll all be back chasing them skirts faster than you can say Connecticut."

"Connecticut," Willie said, not moving, still gazing out to sea.

As dawn slowly broke after an endless night, Major Russell Geist and Lieutenant Ivan Harrison stood shoulder to shoulder, squinting as the sun rose to bring out the glare in the slate-blue sea. The coastline of France appeared on the horizon like a smudged pencil line in the yellow morning light.

"How do you reckon they'll do?" Harrison asked, as though seeking reassurance. "The men, I mean."

Major Geist responded without hesitation. "They're good soldiers," he said. "Damned good soldiers."

Ships and other watercraft bunched up offshore as far as the eye could see. Some circled in slow, lazy patterns as they waited for the beach master's signal. Others streamed toward the sand, trimming aft and dropping stern anchors about two hundred yards out in order to arrest forward movement when they rammed the beach.

Landing doors dropped to disgorge soldiers, vehicles, and armor of all types, pallets of supplies, truckloads of food and ammo. The beach resembled a working anthill even though four months had passed since D-Day. An average of thirty thousand troops a day were still pouring in, along with their food and tanks, armored cars, guns, vehicles, and ammunition—a greater tonnage of cargo than that handled by the port of New York.

All fighting had long since moved from the beach to the interior of France, leaving behind rear echelons to handle more incoming troops, and leaving behind the wreckage of the landing. Debris littered the sand for what seemed like miles in either direction. Sunken landing craft in the surf, remnants of German obstructions next to shore, burned-out hulks of tanks and half-tracks. It was as if some giant brat had thrown a temper tantrum, broken all his toys, and cast them aside.

E. G. McConnell wondered how there could be so much destruction and the Allies still have enough stuff to continue to wage war.

The 761st landed at Omaha Beach on October 10, 1944, creating a good deal of attention. There had been black soldiers in France during World War I, but this was the first time armored black soldiers had been on foreign soil in their tanks. "Eleanor's Niggers" came fully equipped with new tank models—the latest M4 Shermans with 76mm guns—and even with combat boots while many other troops continued to wear low quarter shoes and leggings. All the confusion and excitement and strangeness, plus being the center of attention, unnerved Private George Blake. He didn't know what to make of it. He resolved simply to follow the crowd and do what he was told.

Sergeant Johnnie Stevens realized with a final jolt that he really *was* going into combat. It excited him, but he still wondered what it was going to be like.

Everyone watched the black guys with the big tanks and the best equipment, curious. As the battalion consolidated and headed off the beach toward its assembly point, a couple of white soldiers stood alongside the ribbon-marked exit lane, their jaws hanging.

"Hey, what the fuck you guys doing with them tanks?" one of them called out.

Able Company's clerk, Specialist Kenneth Hamm, laughed. "We're just delivering them for you white boys to use," he shouted back.

That they would believe.

17

I called Paul the last knight in armor—out to right a wrong.

—TAFFY BATES

During the Normandy landing in June, thousands of Allied soldiers had clung desperately to the sand literally with their fingers while the Third Reich tried to shake them back into the sea. Nearly five months later, in October, Normandy was 350 miles to the rear of the fighting, the front lines having marched relentlessly most of the way across France. A receiving and processing center for supplies and men pouring across the channel from England, a tent city of OD-green, had sprung up on high ground once occupied by Germans.

One week after the 761st Tank Battalion came ashore, a tiny slip of a nurse with bobbed blond hair made her way through the debris and wreckage that littered Omaha Beach. Even garbed in drab OD uniform and without makeup, the nurse produced quite a stir during her brisk walk from the beach where the 36th Engineers that included her 14th Field Hospital had just landed.

She pushed aside the flap of a tent that housed personnel affairs. A young lieutenant behind a field desk glanced up and immediately sprang to his feet, surprised by his visitor's extraordinary beauty and unexpected appearance. She smiled sweetly, knowing that a feminine smile produced results in an atmosphere composed mostly of women-starved males.

"Lieutenant," she said, "has a black tank battalion come through here within the past week?"

"You wouldn't be Taffy, would you, ma'am?"

Taffy laughed. A woman's laughter was a delightful thing in the middle of a war.

"My God!" she exclaimed, delighted. "Has Paul told everyone about me?"

"Pardon my saying so, ma'am, but I would tell the *whole world* if I had someone like you."

He was younger than Taffy and he blushed soundly, covering it up by quickly adding, "The 761st is staging further inland. I'll show you on the map. They're fixing to move out to the front. Their colonel has been down here every day asking about the 14th Field Hospital."

The 36th Engineer Division was also attached to General Patton's Third Army. It would soon move toward the front with its engineers, maintenance, ordnance, and EOD companies and its medical, ground, and air ambulance services and hospital detachments. Service units like the engineers, hospitals, quartermasters, ordnance, and all the others required to support the insatiable appetites of armies on the move usually tagged along twenty to thirty miles in the rear of combat troops.

Barely had the 14th Field bivouacked in a field near Sainte-Mère-Église than Colonel Bates drove up in a Jeep. Taffy spotted him and threw herself into his arms with a little cry of happiness. They had seen each other regularly in England, but had been separated now for more than two weeks. By this time, their romance had spanned two years and two continents. Both knew this was more than another wartime fling. In the uncertainty of war, they vowed to spend the rest of their lives together, however long or short that might be.

They strolled hand in hand, pausing frequently to kiss in the light French rain, their happy faces wet, and the war was far away for a short time. When they finally spoke of the war, it was about Paul's black troops.

"I'll lose some of them," he said. "I have to accept it. It's part of fighting a war. Yet I dread more than I've dreaded anything in my life having to write those letters to next of kin. Taffy, I've come to love those men. Do you understand that?"

She did. Through Paul she had also grown to know and love them. Lieutenant Pop Gates and Johnny Long, First Sergeant Sam Turley, the kid E. G. McConnell, Sergeant Johnnie Stevens, Willie Devore . . .

"Promise me," she requested, looking deep into his eyes, "that you'll write me every day? Just write 'I'm alive' if nothing else, so I'll know you're okay."

18

Now we began to roll—long marches and shorter bivouacs.

—AL HEINTZLEMAN, MEMOIRS

Although the entire Western Front had gradually stabilized during September and early October, the Allies were starting to squeeze an iron ring in on Germany from every direction. In the north, British Field Marshal Bernard Montgomery's Twenty-first Army Group was attempting to circle Germany's defensive West Wall and attack the vital industrial Ruhr. U.S. General Jacob L. Devers's Sixth Army Group was approaching from the south end of the West Wall. General Omar Bradley's Twelfth Army Group held down two hundred miles of front between the French town of Épinal and Maastricht in Holland. General George Patton's Third Army, which had been stalled ever since it ran out of fuel in September, now protected Bradley's southern flank and prepared to attack the fortifications around Metz.

Surrounded by twenty-two forts, Metz had not been taken by force in more than a thousand years. Germans were building even more concrete fortifications and digging in on all sides. Four Third Army infantry divisions—the 5th, 26th, 90th, and 95th—were already hammering at the city and its satellite ring of key towns and cities along escape and supply routes.

As a "bastard separate battalion," meaning not attached to any particular division or army, the 761st was detailed to link with Major General Willard S. Paul's 26th Infantry Division, the command post of which was located several miles northeast of Nancy in the Moselle Valley forty-three miles south of embattled Metz. Fifteen such separate bastard battalions had been planned initially. However, the number rose to 26 by late 1942, to 41 by 1943, and now the 761st was one of 65 such units—and the only all-Negro battalion—now fighting in the ETO. The number of separate tank battalions outnumbered the 54 actually incorporated into armored divisions.

That was the war's "Big Picture" on October 22 when the 761st and its tanks moved out of the bivouac area at La Prix and headed toward the front. Of course, few Black Panthers outside Colonel Bates and his staff saw or understood the Big Picture. Like common dogface soldiers everywhere, the men of the 761st saw and were concerned with only what immediately surrounded and threatened them. It was a "good war" as long as they had something to eat and a dry place inside the tanks and vehicles where they could curl up at night, a "bad war" when they were being shot at.

During the next six days, the battalion would move four hundred miles through the Gauntlet, that area between the rear at Normandy and the front at Metz. Although the Allied breakout at Normandy and the balls-to-the-wall advance toward Germany were almost as disorderly as the German retreat, traffic control had been well planned and established. Dozens of roads had been bulldozed through sand dunes off the beaches to link to paved roads inland. Yellow tape marked the roads that led east toward the front. Road signs gave further directions, while other signs warned of *Mines to the Hedgerows*. None of the fields adjoining the road, not even the shoulder of the road itself in many places, could be guaranteed mine free. Evidence of that lay in the numerous Jeeps and other vehicles that had hit mines and now lay alongside the highway in scorched and broken ruins.

"We ain't all coming back," Willie Devore gloomily predicted.

The bocage country, ancestral home of the Normans who invaded England in the eleventh century, extended inland from Omaha Beach throughout the Normandy area. In time of peace, it was a storybook land of small, quaint villages seeded into gently rolling hills, each settlement and most of the little farms enclosed in picturesque hedgerows that had mired the American army in death traps after the breakout from the beachhead.

Gradually, the country became more forested and mountainous, patched in between rivers such as the Loire and the Seine, whose bridges had been repeatedly blown and rebuilt by both sides. Most villages through which the 761st convoy passed had seen so many American troops by this time that weary French citizens could barely muster a few curious stares at the black troops and an occasional desultory *"Vive le Liberation."*

The weather had closed in over France at the beginning of October with a kind of wet, depressed resignation, the overcast skies warning of winter's approaching storms. Rain fell nearly every day, a slow, cold drizzle that crept down the back of the neck like melting icicles and turned parking fields into bogs of slimy mud in which tanks slipped and skidded and occasionally got stuck.

"I should have listened to Moms and stayed home," E. G. McConnell fussed. "Nobody told me war was going to be so *miserable.*"

Depression seemed to settle over the drenched countryside. It was as if the country and its people were waiting for something to finally end and something else to begin. Things got worse the nearer the battalion came to the front. Huge iron teeth appeared to have mangled the land. Burst sewers, broken gas mains, and dead people and animals left overpowering stenches cloying in the damp air. Shattered glass paved the streets. Electrical and telephone lines dangled broken and netted together. Women and little children sorted through the rubble of collapsed buildings looking for lost treasures and memories of lost lives.

Wrecked cars, trucks, trolleys, buses, tanks, half-tracks, self-propelled guns, and dead horses littered the sides of the highway, pushed out of the way by tank dozers. Overlapping bomb craters made some places resemble the moon's surface. Everywhere lay spent tank shells, paper melting into the ground in the rain, shot-up German vehicles, broken and burnt horse caissons with dead animals still attached—a vast, sad wasteland.

"We are sure enough on the right road to get to the war," decided Chico Holland. "All you have to do is close your eyes and follow your nose."

At first, men were awed and somewhat shocked by the destruction left in the wake of armies marching back and forth, trampling the world underneath their boots. But they soon became accustomed to it. Mankind had an unflagging ability to adjust to almost anything.

"I got a feeling that we are gonna see more shit than most of us can even imagine," remarked Sergeant Harding Crecy, adjusting his glasses to somberly survey an old battlefield upon which two tanks had been destroyed and left overturned.

As darkness fell each night, the Panther tanks pulled off the road into fields marked by yellow tape to signify they were mine-free bivouac areas. Men erected shelter halves off the back ends of tanks in order to repair engines in the dark and prevent even the slightest glimmer of light from attracting low-flying enemy aircraft dropping butterfly bombs.

Private Ivory Hilliard, overcome by curiosity, ventured out of the bivouac at dusk one evening and came hurrying back wide-eyed a short time later. He collected Ruben Rivers, E. G. McConnell, Sergeant George Shivers, and a couple of other men. Thus reinforced, he showed them a Mark V Panther German tank in the woods that had been knocked onto its side by a demolition bomb. A foul odor oozed from the sprung hatch.

Hidden behind faces of disgust, the stalwart little band cautiously approached the Panther and peeked in through the open hatch. The stench was overpowering. Nonetheless, they were determined to take a first look inside an enemy tank. Rivers struck a match and thrust it inside. The others closed in to shield the light. They looked over his shoulders.

McConnell jumped back, startled, and collided with Hilliard, who had also seen enough. Revealed in the dim flickering light provided by the match, grinning up at the tankers from the depths of the dead machine, loomed the yellowed skull of a human being, skin and hair still clinging to its scalp, eye sockets empty, teeth shining in a frozen rictus. It wore a ragged and dirty gray-green uniform with lightning bolt insignia on the collar.

Rivers and Shivers stared until the match burned out and plunged the skull back into eternal darkness.

"Reckon who he was?" E.G. whispered.

"A dead Kraut," Shivers said.

"God Almighty, this is awful."

Ruben Rivers turned and walked off. "He's dead, ain't he? Ain't that what we come here to do—kill Germans?"

19

They gave a very good impression, but I have no faith in the inherent fighting ability of the race.

—GENERAL GEORGE S. PATTON, JR.

The battalion reached Saint Nicolas de Port east of Nancy on October 28, arriving with no losses of vehicles other than one tank that arrived a day late because of mechanical failure. Battle, as one of the tankmen casually mentioned, was imminent. The battalion paused for a breather, final checkups, and repairs. Anxious troops greased and serviced their machines, made sure the swinging gun traverses were in good working order, checked and cleaned breeches, stored ammo underneath the turret floors of the tanks ready for instant use, and took care of their personal weapons and gear. In addition to the tank's guns, each crewman carried a .45 pistol and a second weapon of his choice—usually a grease gun, carbine, or Thompson submachine gun.

The front lines lay only a few miles ahead. Sometimes the thunder of exploding shells and the deep-throated rumble of dueling artillery awoke the tankers. Twice a German fighter plane flew over but remained high, its destination elsewhere.

"It's not much longer now," said Lieutenant Pop Gates, commander of the Assault Guns Platoon. Six Shermans carrying 105mm howitzers constituted his platoon.

PFC Willie Devore listened to the distant sound of guns, the drizzle of rain cold and brittle against his skin. None of his buddies could talk him out of the conviction that he was going to die. It was simply a matter of time. After all, the Krauts had dropped a bomb on General Leslie McNair, chief of the army ground forces and an early champion of black soldier equality, while he was observing operations after the Normandy landing. If a *general* could get killed, how much easier must it be for a lowly black enlisted man to get it.

"Snap out of it, Willie," Daniel "Club Foot" Cardell admonished.

"I be doing my job—until it happens."

On Halloween, General Willard S. Paul, commander of the 26th Infantry Division to which the 761st would be attached, welcomed the battalion.

"I am damned glad to have you with us," he said to the formation. "We have been expecting you for a long time, and I am sure that you are going to give a good account of yourselves. I've got a big hill up there, and I want you to take it, and I believe you are going to do a great job at it."

"Does he mean trick or treat?" someone murmured.

Two days later, Colonel Bates called another battalion formation. Company first sergeants and the battalion command sergeant major made sure the troops were looking their best. The formation assembled on a low hill in front of the tanker bivouac area. The front had been quiet most of the morning, and the rain had sucked back into a swollen, bruised overcast.

Suddenly, a bunch of quarter-ton Jeeps loaded with MPs and .50-caliber machine guns rolled in and took up strategic defensive positions. A few minutes later, as the men stood at attention, a single Jeep and an armored scout car dashed to the head of the formation and stopped next to Colonel Bates.

A three-star general jumped out of the Jeep, received Colonel Bates's salute, then vaulted to the hood of the armored car. He stood there with his feet spread apart, fists on his hips, and his eyes sharply surveying the ranks. Lieutenant Johnny Long knew from the two ivory-handled pistols holstered at the man's belt that he was looking at the legendary General George S. Patton, Jr.

Sergeant Johnny Holmes thought him the most dashing figure he had ever seen, standing up there with his stars and two pistols. Corporal George Blake, driver for Dog Company's CO, was awed by the occasion. He stood in ranks at attention, but his widened eyes followed Patton's every move.

In addition to the pearl-handled pistols, Patton wore an Eisenhower jacket, brightly polished riding boots, fawn-colored riding britches, and a brass buckle to hold up his gun belt. He was said to display more stars than any other general officer in the army—three on his helmet, three on each side of his collar, three on each epaulet of his jacket. It was all part of his mystique.

His bearing, his rugged features and piercing eyes, his very presence froze the tankers immobile. Sergeant Johnnie Stevens noticed that no one so much as batted an eye.

When he began to speak, the Panthers were shocked to discover that he had a very high-pitched voice and sounded almost like a woman with a bad cold. Colonel Bates suspected he used profanity in order to be taken seriously.

"Men, you are the first Negro tankers to ever fight in the American army," he began in that high, almost-squeaky voice. "I have nothing but the best in my army. I don't care what color you are, so long as you go up there and kill the Kraut sonsofbitches. Everyone has their eyes on you, and is expecting great things of you. Most of all, your race is looking forward to your success. Don't let them down, and, damn you, don't let me down. They say it is patriotic to die for your country. Well, let's see how many patriots we can make out of those German sonsofbitches."

He paused. No one blinked. High-pitched voice or not, General Patton was a man to be taken seriously.

"There is one thing you men will be able to say when you go home," he concluded. "You may all thank God that thirty years from now when you are sitting with your grandson on your knee and he asks, 'Grandfather, what did you do in World War II?' you won't have to say, 'I shoveled shit in Mississippi.'"

Afterward, during his formal inspection of the battalion's tanks and crews, he climbed on top of one of the tanks and looked down the open hatch. He climbed down again. E. G. McConnell snapped to greater attention. General Patton looked him straight in the eye.

"Listen, boy," he said, "I want you to shoot every gawd damn thing you see—church steeples, water towers, houses, old ladies, children, haystacks. Every gawd damn thing you see. This is war. You hear me, boy?"

E.G. trembled in his combat boots. "Y-yes, sir, General."

Just as swiftly and dramatically as he had arrived, General Patton left again in a chase of Jeeps and MPs. Corporal Howard "Big Tit" Richardson turned to his company commander, Captain David Williams, for whom he was a personal driver.

"Sir, that old man is crazy as hell. Did you see the way his eyes roll around when he talk? That's no bullshit about him being a hornet. That is for damn sure. I'm more afraid of him than I be of them Krauts. That boy in Sicily was lucky he just got slapped. The old man could have had him shot."

20

You're the best thing that ever happened to me in my whole life.

—Lieutenant Colonel Paul Bates to Taffy

The 761st, having staged for action at Saint Nicolas de Port, was on heightened alert, preparing for action within the next day or so. The commander of the 26th Infantry had given his pep talk, General Patton gave his, even more spectacular, and Colonel Bates delivered his short and low-key. Now the Black Panthers waited. Waiting was sometimes the hardest part of going to war.

In preparation for the fighting to come, the 14th Field Hospital had moved up and erected hospital facilities some twenty miles behind the front lines. Ironically, some of its first patients would inevitably be tankers from Colonel Bates's battalion. Taffy dreaded it. From here on, Paul's men and tanks would be in constant combat. He might not be able to see her again until the war ended, or until . . .

She preferred not to think about *or.*

Colonel Bates sent a staff car for Taffy when he knew the battalion might be kicking off and he would not be able to see her again for a while. Shortly after dark, the command car, with its canvas sides buttoned down against a driving cold rain, growled through the ankle-deep mud that surrounded the tents of the field hospital. A slight figure dressed in fatigues, poncho slicker, and steel helmet ran out and jumped into the car. The driver, a corporal named Forbes, turned the vehicle around and headed back to the front, following tank tracks chewed through dark, dangerous countryside patrolled by both

Germans and Allies. Tiny slitted blackout lights provided his only illumination.

The unnerving journey ended when a figure suddenly stepped out of the darkness and blocked the road.

"Who dat?" it challenged, M1 rifle at the ready.

The driver unzipped his side window and stuck his head out in the rain so he could be seen.

"Dat me. Forbes."

"I knows you, Forbes. Who dat with you? Stand out and be recognized."

The rifle clicked off *Safe*. Taffy struggled to open her door, no easy task in a command car. Forbes got out and walked toward the sentry. Taffy finally escaped the car and stood in the pouring rain, a skinny little thing in a too-big helmet and a poncho that went slickety-slick in the breeze. The sentry looked her over suspiciously, but couldn't see much because of the dark and the rain.

"Dat's the colonel's lady," Forbes hissed.

The sentry didn't understand. "If the colonel want a lady," he stubbornly insisted, "let him go and get one hisself."

"Man, it's Lieutenant *Taffy*."

Colonel Bates had been waiting. He ran down from the bivouac area.

"I just be doing my job, Colonel. Them Germans is sneaky."

"You did exactly right, Corporal," the colonel commended him.

The commander of the 761st, by right of his rank and position, occupied a pup tent all to himself. He shared it on that rainy night before the battalion launched itself into the war.

21

*Kill! Kill! None of the Germans are innocent, neither
the living nor those yet unborn . . .*

—POET ILYA EHRENBERG

On November 8, 1944, the rumored "Big Offensive"
against entrenched German defenses on the way to
Metz kicked off at dawn. It had been delayed, then delayed again for a week before everything finally came together.
Black American armored units would be used in battle for the
first time ever. Most of the Black Panthers thought the actual
fighting couldn't be any worse than waiting around in the rain
for something to happen. Green as they were to combat, they
still believed they were fighting, as General Patton put it, in
order not to let him and the black race down. That illusion
would not last long after the first shots were fired.

The 26th Division, with Patton's Panthers attached, would be
fighting in the same sector where it had fought in 1918. Its section
of the front began on high ground south of Château-Salins and ran
through Moncourt Woods to a hill northwest of Bezange-la-Petite.
First Sergeant Sam Turley, Charlie Company, observed how blood
fertilized the grass and made it grow taller over the depressions left
by the old trenches of World War I—and how that same grass was
likely to be fertilized again before the day was done.

Opposing the 26th Division on the other side were the German 11th and 13th Panzer divisions. The 11th had been rebuilt
since its August encounters and infused with twelve thousand
fresh troops, thirty big guns, and many additional tanks.

Repeated Allied Air Corps bombings had cracked the Dieuze
Dam, flooding the Seille River and low-lying valleys. Bogs of

mud and standing ponds made the terrain treacherous, deceit-
ful, and a thoroughly miserable place to fight. Continuing rain
merely added to the dreariness and the foreboding that hung in
the French air.

Assault elements composed of two task forces moved up to the
line of departure (LD) near the town of Athainville under cover
of darkness, cloudy skies, and a slowly falling rain. The task forces
were to separate at the LD and swing out in opposite directions to
form an attack front twelve kilometers wide. They would then
sweep forward, driving the enemy before them, until converging
again to funnel into the heart of the Germans' stoutest defenses
near the town of Rodalbe. Rodalbe was a railroad center and important junction point for roads and communications.

Captain David Williams's Able Company was assigned to the
first task force, made up of the 101st and 104th infantry regiments
of the 26th. Two platoons under his command would fight with
the 101st. Able's Third Platoon, led by Lieutenant Charles Barbour, would go with the 104th to spearhead its lead rifle platoons.

The other two Sherman companies and Dog's "Mosquito
Fleet," all under the direct command of Colonel Bates, would
kick off with the second task force, made up of the 602nd Tank
Destroyer Battalion, one engineer company, and the 328th Infantry Regiment of the 26th.

The mission of a separate tank battalion, as outlined in FM-
17-33, was:

Lead the attack;
Support by direct fire the advance of light tanks, other
     medium tanks, and ground troops;
Feel out the enemy and develop weak spots;
Serve as a reserve for exploiting a success or breaking up a
     counterattack;
Accompany the infantry and assist the advance by destroy-
     ing or neutralizing automatic weapons and pillboxes
     holding up the advance;

Fight enemy tanks when necessary;
Destroy dug-in pillboxes;
Reinforce artillery fires;
Assist the infantry in mop-up.

While the heavy armor divisions waited in reserve for the fast, major slugfests, infantry and the separate tank battalions remained in the thick of the fighting on the line, always under fire, always fighting and getting hurt at the front of the supported division's sector.

Air remained on call to support the task forces. The 26th Division's heavy artillery and Pop Gates's assault guns lined up on the hills and high places overlooking the intended battlefield as dawn unavoidably replaced the almost-total blackness of the darkest night in PFC Willie Devore's memory.

22

We must not allow mobile warfare to develop, because the enemy surpasses us by far in mobility. . . . Therefore, everything depends on fighting a war of attrition to wear him down and force him back.

—ADOLF HITLER

Battalion Command Sergeant Major Bob Jenkins got the company first sergeants up in a drizzling dark rain long before dawn. The first sergeants—Sam Turley, Fred Cornelius, Hubert House, Purvis Easley, McClinton Kelly, Bob

Linzy—made sure the men rolled out of their sleeping bags and pup tents.

"Drop your cocks and grab your socks. They's a war on—and ya'all are invited."

The obligatory bitching and the drizzle would soon stop. Most of the tankers had gotten little sleep anyhow. E. G. Mc-Connell had read his prayer book until dark, then closed it and prayed. Willie Devore had little to say. He stood in the night staring toward enemy lines as though listening for sounds of his own funeral. Chico Holland in Supply worked with Captain Phil Latimer in preparing to feed bullets, beans, and gasoline to the battalion during the expected heavy fighting ahead. Senior staff members, company commanders, platoon leaders, and first sergeants met with Colonel Bates until late as they tweaked finishing touches on the battle plan and tomorrow's movements. Colonel Bates appeared confident and relaxed. His executive officer, Major Charles Wingo, on the other hand, was so tense he jumped at every unexpected sound.

In exchange for rank, privilege, and control, officers were entrusted with the responsibility to look after their men and do everything they could to help them survive once they were committed to combat. The men of the 761st trusted Colonel Bates to look after them as he had looked after Jackie Robinson when they were at Camp Hood. Black Lieutenant John D. Long, Baker Company, always said only two white combat officers in the outfit were worth a God damn—Colonel Bates and Captain Dave Williams. The rest, he said, weren't worth a shit, and at the very bottom of the shit pile was Major Wingo.

It was an opinion shared virtually by the entire battalion. Captain Williams never forgot Wingo's remark about needing "a mean coon to keep these boys in line" when he reported to the 761st at Camp Claiborne. Wingo's attitude toward Negroes had not changed. When around white officers he derisively referred to black men as "coons" and "niggers," a contempt the tankers returned tenfold.

It was in combat that a man's true colors came out. The Panthers adopted a wait-and-see attitude about their white leadership.

"Keep your heads down, don't do nothing stupid," they cautioned each other.

They shook hands with one another, punched each other lightly on the shoulder, and tried a feeble joke now and then— "The ol' lady will have a helluva time on my insurance check"— as they lined up tanks and vehicles in the dark for movement to the line of departure. They had received their mission to spearhead the two task forces with mixed pride and apprehension. They were all scared, scared as hell, and they expected to get even more scared when the battle actually started. Yet, scared as they were, they had all gotten out of their holes and pup tents and got ready to go.

The morning was strangely quiet as if there were no war at all. Company commanders held final meetings and inspections with their officers and sergeants, sort of pep talks. Over in Able Company, which would lead assaults on the towns of Vic-sur-Seille and Mozenvic, black men gathered around the white commander's tank. A few sipped from canteen cups full of coffee, others cupped cigarettes in their hands to keep enemy surveillance aircraft from seeing the glowing tips.

Captain Williams had attended Officers Candidate School with Pop Gates at Fort Knox, Kentucky. He had heard about segregation and the treatment of Negroes but had not witnessed it for himself until he left Pennsylvania and went south for training. He had been appalled. He got on a bus and saw Negroes sitting and standing crowded behind a white line at the back of the bus while there was still available seating up front. He looked out the window and saw the little ramshackle black towns along the way. The results and effects and tragedies of segregation hit him over the head. He had volunteered for leadership in a black tank battalion after he learned most white officers wanted nothing to do with Negro outfits. He had vowed that the men he commanded, that he led into battle, would be treated the way United States soldiers deserved to be treated.

Williams's driver, Corporal Howard "Big Tit" Richardson, eased the tension of Able Company's last meeting when he produced some black grease paint.

"We hear they shoots officers and you stick out among us," he said.

He painted his boss's face while the others looked on approvingly.

"Hey, you look as good as any nigger," declared Sergeant Johnnie Stevens. "Now let's go shoot some Krauts."

Johnnie Stevens was a tough, nasty maverick who would cut a man's throat in a heartbeat. He might get his chance at it today.

H-Hour rapidly approached. Company meetings broke up and platoon leaders and platoon sergeants took over. Five-man crews loaded into their war wagons. There were no ladders down from the top hatches. Crewmembers merely dropped down from the top hatch and crammed themselves into position among the equipment and ammunition. Everything had its place—fire extinguishers, repair tools, a tarp, ax and pick, radios, blackout lamps, water cans, food, gun-cleaning materials, first aid kits, extra periscopes, searchlights. Compartments in the side walls contained machine gun ammo while high-explosive (HE) and armor-piercing (AP) shells for the 76mm main guns were stored underneath the turret floor.

Once a tank buttoned up, its vision of the outside world became severely restricted. Periscopes provided most views. A hand-held periscope allowed the crew to open a hatch and look around without exposing themselves.

Every tanker was all too mindful of the Sherman's nickname—the *Ronson,* "lights every time." Even if the Ronson was hit and *didn't* light up, white-hot shell fragments ricocheting around inside a tank could tear the guts out of a crew, spilling them all over the clean white walls and glistening floors. There was not a damned thing a man could do about it either if his tank got hit, except get the hell out through the hatch if he were able and run like hell. His personal weapons, a Thompson, carbine, or grease gun, allowed him to fight his way back to the rear if necessary.

Daylight would soon break. Enemy fortifications, machine guns, mortars, artillery, *Panzerfausts,* and tanks lay directly ahead. Germany, the Siegfried Line, and the Rhine River were only fifty miles away. The world remained little more than watery gray shadows in the morning light. An eerie silence seemed to hang over all of France.

Even as Colonel Bates's battalion moved out to the line of departure, a patrol returned with the intel that much of the ground out front looked impassable due to incessant rainfall and the bursting of the Dieuze Dam. Orders went out over radios to change the direction of the attack by thirty degrees to take advantage of more favorable terrain. Colonel Bates, whose call sign was "Hard Tack," jumped into his Jeep and drove up to the line of departure to watch the kickoff and make sure the assault elements were in order and heading in the right direction.

The low ground that stretched out ahead, spotted here and there by darkened French towns in the distance, remained full of spilled ink. Trees, the river, meadows, the spires and roofs of Vic-sur-Seille, and other features slowly began to emerge. The colonel noted that there would be no sun until perhaps later in the day, but at least the rain had sucked back to releasing only an occasional spitfall from lowering clouds. His breath made balloons in the cold air. He felt snow coming.

The artillery duel that always preceded an attack had not begun. Either the Jerries were being caught by surprise or they were biding their time, waiting for targets to get well within range. It was such a quiet, peaceful morning that Colonel Bates found it difficult to believe that this entire valley all along the front would soon erupt into chaos, destruction, and death. Some of his men, these black men he had known and led for the past two years, whom he had promised would go into combat on an equal basis with white soldiers, would not be returning.

He mustn't think of that. A commander had to look at the "Big Picture." His Negro tankers were just as good as any white soldiers. Today, they would prove it.

He stood on the hood of his Jeep, a tall, imposing figure in helmet and combat gear, out front and visible, firing up his troops by his mere presence. His tanks growled past in a long green line, crawling beyond the LD before they spread into attack formation. TCs with their heads stuck up out of open turrets waved at him and flashed V signs and thumbs-up and grins.

Nervousness and anxiety increased chatter over the radios as men reached out to touch each other by voice and be reassured.

Are you moving out?

Roger. Out.

We are moving on down to help Charlie Company. They are at Phase Line Red.

There is a mistake in their location. They are down between Blue and Red. There's somebody else at Red . . .

Baker Actual wants to know where you are . . .

See that crossroads straight ahead? We're slightly to the right of that . . .

The other unit went to the left instead of the right . . .

Major Wingo rode one of the three tanks assigned to Headquarters Company. His high, shrill voice broke into air space to warn the tankers against unnecessary radio traffic.

"I want absolute silence. Is that understood? You boys keep quiet on those radios."

A radio crackled. "Yo' mama."

The tanks crept on by, buttoning up for combat, rolling into attack formations. White doughboys of the 26th Infantry splayed out behind the tanks. Some of them hopped on and rode.

Captain Williams's cheery voice broke into his company's radio band, speaking in Harlemese: "Now, looky here, ya cats. We gotta hit it down the main drag and hep some of them unhepped cats on the other side. So let's roll on down ole Seventh Avenue and knock 'em, Jack."

Suddenly, the ear-piercing shriek of a German 88 clove through the air and exploded off to the right in a cloud of gray smoke spiraling against the low-hanging clouds. The quiet terror of prebattle was shattered.

Captain Williams's voice again cut through the air with the Black Panther motto: *"Come Out Fighting!"*

Colonel Bates wondered with pride if this might not be the first time Negroes had led white Americans into battle.

23

I had never been in combat before, and there was something exciting about going in. You can do the job, but you're just wondering what it's going to be like.

—SERGEANT JOHNNIE STEVENS

The artillery duel began. The detonation of the first 88 triggered an immediate following salvo of artillery explosions that filled the valley and lowlands with walking mushrooms of smoke as Germans attempted by sheer volume and ferocity to knock off the attacking American infantry and supporting tanks. American howitzers and heavy mortars from the opposing highlands answered the challenge as they strove to overwhelm and destroy the enemy's artillery and soften up the resistance. Heavy shells of HE and AP freight-trained overhead, crisscrossing.

The din of the battle was one hellish racket the likes of which no one could imagine beforehand and which one never forgot thereafter—eruptions and the thundering, cracking roll of artillery; heavy machine guns thumping; bullets clanking against armor; exposed infantry doughboys shouting and shrieking, giving encouragements and orders, sometimes screaming as they died. Rather than the steel walls of the tanks buffering the noise, they seemed to magnify it, something like riding in a giant metal trash can pulled down a rocky road at top speed.

Smoke, burned powder and propellants, and mud pulverized into dust would have blotted out the sun had not the sun already been hiding behind cloud cover. The small towns lying directly ahead, the declared objectives of the attack, flashed in and out of sight through the swirling smoke and dust. They were only a mile or so away, but it seemed an impossible journey of immense distance.

They're throwing artillery at us . . .

What was that coming in . . . ?

Sounded like HE. Must be 20mm . . .

Confusion reigned. The fight broke into individual skirmishes, little dramas in the giant scope of the battle.

Sergeant Harding Crecy's tank driver, Corporal Harry Tyree, gunned his Sherman across a short stone bridge spanning a stream and made an immediate left turn. Doughs mixed in with the darting tanks and artillery explosions, dodging and yelling and scampering about like terrified insects. There would be a white-hot core of banging light where a soldier had been—and he simply melted into the light and vanished.

"Gone!" Tyree muttered, horrified. *"OhGodOhGodOhGod . . . Gone!"*

By the farmhouse! See 'em? See 'em? Get the bastards . . .

TC Sergeant Ruben Rivers encountered a roadblock of dragon's teeth (wedge-shaped concrete antitank barriers) at a narrows in the road. Heavy forest on either side prevented tanks' going around the obstruction. Wide fields directly ahead funneled devastating fire down the road and into the column of advancing tanks. Stalled, Sergeant Rivers in the lead tank flung back his hatch and vaulted to the road carrying nothing but a roll of cable.

While small arms and machine gun muzzles flickered at him from the woodline beyond the fields, sounding like powerful strings of detonating fireworks, Rivers rapidly but calmly attached one end of the cable to the concrete section of dragon's teeth and the other end to his tank.

"Pull her!" he shouted.

Bullets chewed the air and terrain all around him, popping and snapping past his head. Once he cleared the roadblock, he retrieved the roll of cable for future use and leaped back into his tank. Vic-sur-Seille lay ahead. He led the charge as tanks poured through the opening, scattered off the road, and got on-line across the crop-stubble fields, their long-barreled 76s booming and their machine guns ripping into German lines.

At the far end of the line, TC Sergeant Johnny Holmes spotted Kraut snipers running and burrowing into a haystack, from which they began picking off infantry with accurate rifle fire. He reached with his foot and tapped his driver's helmet.

"The haystack," he said.

He expected the driver, Corporal Coleman Simmons, to maneuver the machine into a position advantageous to the tank's on-board machine guns. Instead of reacting, however, Simmons's eyes bulged white against his dark skin. He froze.

"Don't do dat, Sergeant!" he protested. "Dat's *murder!*"

Inhibitions against killing other human beings, ingrained in young men since birth, surfaced under stressful conditions.

"*What?*" Holmes roared. "Get your black ass in gear, man, and do what I tell you."

"But, Sarge . . ."

Doughs out in the open, vulnerable to fire coming from the haystack, were falling like ducks in a row. There was no time to argue. Holmes whipped out his .45 pistol and thrust the muzzle against his driver's temple. Sergeant Stevens wasn't the only tough, nasty maverick in Able Company.

"I'll blow your gawd damned brains out," Holmes snarled. "When I tell you to kill somebody, you kill him. Turn this gawd damned tank around and keep the main gun on the haystack. God damn you, *go!*"

That settled the issue. Simmons charged the tank at the haystack like a monstrous knight. Sergeant Holmes took over the bow machine gun and chattered deadly streams of tracers into the hay.

Two unnerved Jerries in gray-green battle dress flew out of the hay with their arms stretched above their heads, shouting frantically in German and broken English.

"Kameraden! Kameraden! No shoot! No shoot!"

Simmons stopped the tank directly in front of them. The steel monster crouched there rumbling in a deep growl with its main gun pointed directly at the Krauts' chests. Holmes cracked the turret hatch. These guys didn't look so fucking bad; one of them was no more than a kid.

"Kameraden! Kameraden!"

"Yeah, great," Holmes said. "Okay, you Kraut bastards, drop your gear. Understand? Drop everything."

While these skirmishes were under way, the spearhead of Able Company moved unknowingly into a minefield. Germans made extensive use of mines as a defensive weapon. The most frightening thing about mines was that they could strike any time, anywhere, without warning, and in an instant a tank was knocked out or a foot soldier killed or maimed for life. The first indication Captain Williams received of his company's predicament came when the lead tank suddenly leaped into the air on top of an eruption of smoke, dust, and flame.

Crewmembers whose tank was disabled by a mine were trained to evacuate immediately and scurry to the rear using the vehicle's own tracks as a pathway. They lost no time in abandoning the area, either. Jerries habitually targeted a disabled tank with artillery to make sure to destroy it and prevent its repair. The five men from the smoldering Sherman tore toward the rear like the Devil himself was hot on their asses poking them with a fiery pitchfork.

True to habit, enemy mortars homed in on the checked tanks. Instant mushrooms sprouted in the field. The soft, calm tone of Captain Williams's voice over the radio prevented panic, cool as could be.

"Everybody hold what you got and keep your heads. We're gonna back out of this fucker and go around. Follow your own tracks out. Okay, you badasss cats, let's shuck this joint."

Smoke and dust helped conceal movements of the tanks navigating off the killing field. Able Company lost two more tanks in the process, hit by mortars, but no crews were wounded. The abandoned crews hotfooted it back toward Headquarters to bum a ride with other tank crews or scrounge a replacement vehicle from HQ.

"Okay, Panthers," Captain Williams radioed. "We're clear. See that town up ahead? It's ours. Let's go."

24

Ahead was some of the bitterest fighting of the war.
—WAYNE ROBINSON, AUTHOR OF *MOVE OUT, VERIFY*

The casualties that Colonel Bates dreaded, that gave all the men nightmares, began to arrive in the rear, carried back by litter bearers and three-quarter-ton trucks converted into ambulances by painting large red crosses on their sides. Sometimes the "rear" could be just as hazardous as the front lines. Captain Garland Adamson, one of the battalion's black surgeons, was kept busy dodging shells while he performed life-saving surgery on wounded troops, clipping off bleeders, opening airways, pressure bandaging, splinting, treating for shock. Germans targeted rear areas in an effort to destroy supply trains and command structures and to sow chaos and break down morale.

As soon as Doc Adamson stabilized a patient, an ambulance made a broken-field run through exploding shells and skidded to a halt in the mud next to him. Two aidmen jumped out of the truck and helped the doctor stretcher the patients into the back of the ambulance. The ambulance then cut a mud-slinging doughnut and raced toward the field hospital farther back. The doctor looked around for his next BAS (battalion aid station) patient, lugging his heavy canvas medical bag over one shoulder.

An artillery shell blossomed in the exact spot he, the wounded trooper, and the ambulance had just vacated.

Some of the first casualties came from Captain Irvin McHenry's Charlie Company, which had been tapped as part of the provisional task force assigned to penetrate enemy lines to Rodalbe. Jerries in the sector had dug in deep and prepared to offer some of the fiercest resistance of the American offensive.

"The Burner" made his initial move against Hill 253 and the town of Bezange-la-Petite. A muscular man with light brown skin and an inner quiet that refused to be rattled, a good combat leader, McHenry placed ten tanks belonging to platoon leader Lieutenant Jay Johnson and Sergeant Moses Dade on point while he located his own machine farther back in the center of the company for better command and control.

As the column, with attached infantry, approached the town and the hill on its outskirts, a barrage of enemy fire roared out of the defensive line, snapping and flashing and cracking like a thunderstorm. Lieutenant Johnson had his turret hatch open, exposing himself to constant danger in the storm of splattering slugs and shrieking shell fragments. If he ducked down and buttoned up, however, which severely limited visibility, he would have to depend upon radio contact with infantry to guide him, and he would have to slow the armored column to a crawl, presenting the enemy with even easier targets.

Heedless of his own welfare, Johnson was coolly directing Able's point element when a shell air-burst directly above him in a brilliant white-hot flash, searing the young lieutenant's eyes. Shrapnel slammed ricocheting through the open hatch and wounded Sergeant Sam Saunders and Corporal James Edwards, neither critically.

Because of the tactical situation, the wounded men could not be immediately evacuated. Although in severe pain and unable to see, Lieutenant Johnson became one of the first Black Panthers to win a medal for heroism. He remained with his platoon, blind though he was, and fought with it as the attack surged forward against the Germans.

Brutal as the fighting was on the front lines with Able and Charlie companies, however, it was an aidman with the medical detachment and not a tanker who became the battalion's first man killed in action. Private Clifford Adams, a lanky Texan, and Corporal Floyd Humphrey were rendering aid to a wounded doughboy next to Doc Adamson's BAS when a shell landed nearby. Shrapnel shredded Private Adams and splattered Humphrey with his friend's blood.

The Black Panther Battalion had suffered its first dead. No one expected Private Adams to be the last.

KIA (Killed in Action)
Private Clifford C. Adams

25

I began to realize what a big job it was to supply ammunition, gasoline, and rations to a battalion.

—CAPTAIN PHIL LATIMER

Captain Phil Latimer, the white S-4 in Supply, had been teaching at a little high school in Texas when he was drafted into the army as a private in 1941. He completed OCS, Officers Candidate School, in October 1942 and began serving as commander of an 81mm mortar platoon in the 12th Armored Division. In January 1943, requests went out to the 12th for lieutenants willing to serve with Negro tankers. Latimer volunteered and was finally transferred to the 761st Tank Battalion in July 1943, shortly before it moved to Camp Hood.

Once the 761st went into combat, Latimer and his staff of seven, along with transportation support from Lieutenant Horace Jones, who commanded Service Company, were charged with supplying the needs of more than seven hundred men, fifty-four medium tanks, and seventeen lighter tanks. It turned into a daunting and sometimes hazardous task.

Since fuel points and supply depots, terminal points for the Red Ball Express, lay miles back from the front lines, the various combat units were required to ferry their own replenishments forward for distribution. Latimer's small staff used deuce-and-a-half trucks to haul goods to within five or six miles of the lines, at which point Captain Latimer sometimes commandeered men from the companies to help complete the transfer.

During the Panthers' first full day of battle, gofers were kept busy relaying gasoline and ammo to the companies. Each of the Shermans held more than two hundred gallons of gasoline, and its miles per gallon made even the largest, most gas-guzzling Cadillac seem downright thrifty. Gunners were also burning up a lot of ammo, as could be attested to by the constant roar and rumble of the battle echoing up and down the valley.

Early in the day, Captain Richard English's Mosquito Fleet of light Stuart tanks, patrolling and reconning just back of the battle lines, pulled out of the action because of fuel shortages. English's driver, Corporal George Blake, waited with the Jeep back at battalion HQ. English radioed a request for gasoline. He and his tanks would be waiting at a designated road intersection.

Blake loaded the Jeep with all the four-gallon cans of gasoline it could carry and set out at high speed, not stopping for anything. Cans were stashed in every available space. Being short and skinny, Blake took up little room, leaving that much more space for fuel. He even shared his driver's seat with a can. He dared not even contemplate the fireball he would become if he ran into Germans.

Sounds of fierce fighting came to him from the vicinity of Vic-sur-Seille. Walking wounded were starting to dribble back along the road, many of them wearing that proverbial thousand-yard stare of shock and disbelief. They didn't even see the Jeep as it dodged them to get by. Buddies accompanied the worst of them to make sure they didn't wander off.

Occasionally, a few German POWs with their hands clasped on their heads were being escorted into captivity, the first actual enemy Blake had seen. He glanced at them, curious, but then switched his eyes back to business and kept his foot rammed hard against metal.

Captain English's tanks were splayed out in a defensive posture around the crossroads. Everything in the immediate vicinity appeared peaceful. Blake waited and caught up on the situation along the front while the tanks refueled. Only one tank had been lost, he learned, when an 88 AP clipped the turret off Sergeant Floyd Dade's machine. No one in Dog Company had been killed or injured, although there were some reports of casualties in the other companies. Everyone appeared in good spirits, almost excited.

Blake gathered up his empty cans and headed back through the French countryside to refill them. A mile or so back, he found himself in lovely country that the war seemed to have skipped over. The day was still cloudy, but the rain had stopped. Livestock grazed contentedly in pastures surrounding little farm cottages. Even the fences were still up and there were no tank tracks or shell craters in the meadows.

The picture changed completely, however, in the short time it took him to reach HQ, load up more gasoline, and retrace his route to Dog Company. No longer did he travel through an idyllic pastoral scene. The Pale Rider leading the other Horsemen of the Apocalypse had ridden through while he was gone. Jerries had shelled all along the road between the division trains in the rear and the front lines, apparently hoping to catch resupply and reinforcement convoys.

Dead cows and horses now lay in cratered fields. One horse with both front legs broken screamed in pain and fright while it flopped about in vain trying to get up and run. Blake covered that side of his face with his hand to keep from seeing and hearing the terrified animal. He kept going as fast as the Jeep would run, gluing his eyes to the road to keep from looking at the carnage on either side.

Colonel Bates had moved his CP (command post) to high ground overlooking the valley battlefield. A soldier stopped Blake from going any farther. He got out of his Jeep and watched mortar explosions stomping around the crossroads where he had rendezvoused with Dog Company not an hour ago. How quickly everything seemed to change.

26

It can't be true. He ain't dead. He can't be.

—CORPORAL MILTON DORSEY

Events were unfolding in the rear that would affect the Black Panther Battalion as profoundly as anything the Germans threw at it on the assault line.

Although Colonel Bates was as green to combat as his men, he retained control of the situation under difficult circumstances and fought his battalion like a complete professional. He exuded confidence and reassurance, an air that his subordinate commanders and junior officers passed on down to noncoms and men. Radio mike clenched in his fist, eyes pressed to binoculars, he supervised the unfolding battle, coming up on the air again and again as "Hard Tack" to offer a word of encouragement, advice, orders, or to make some correction of movement. It seemed to the Panthers that nothing could deter them or prevent their attaining their objectives as long as that tall, stern man stood on the hill watching over them.

Earlier, as the fight began and the tank and infantry companies moved forward, a French drover with a herd of cows temporarily blocked the road. A collaborator, perhaps, sent out by the Germans. Colonel Bates dashed down in his Jeep and personally arrested the man.

Now, the fury of the battle as it began to develop rolled like thunder all along the length of the attack line. The various channels of his Jeep radio gabbled in the hyperactive staccato of men talking, questioning, passing orders, shouting, cursing, even inserting a few words of prayer, all at the same time. The colonel's rugged face, always impassive and under control, turned into a mask of determination. He let no emotion show even when Able Company ran into a minefield, and reports of casualties and tank losses filtered back.

The lowlands below literally crawled with the antlike figures of rushing, maneuvering infantry darting and dashing about among the larger beetle carapaces of the tanks. Even in the misting rain, smoke and dust brooded over the battlefield, shot through repeatedly by the constant lightninglike flicker of explosions and the stabbing flames of the tanks' main guns.

Much of the ground, though boggy, was open and provided reasonably good armor country. Little farms were scattered all over the valley, their individual boundaries secured by rows of trees or hedges. Forest also lined the main road that dropped off the highlands where commanders of armor and infantry established their battle CPs and led toward Vic-sur-Seille, whose church spires in the distance stuck up white above a brown winter's forest relieved here and there by the green of conifers.

As the colonel viewed the fight, inwardly agonizing over the sight of disabled tanks and the possibility of dead or wounded gladiators, but not letting his agony show, a small German recon/combat patrol worked its way toward him through the woodland thickets alongside the road. High-ranking officers at the CPs had no idea of the nearness of enemy presence until the patrol opened up at close range with an explosive rattle of small arms fire. Rifles and burp guns.

Colonel Bates was standing on the hood of his Jeep to get a better look at his tankers' action below. Submachine gun bullets splattered into the side of the Jeep. He sprang for the driver's seat. A slug caught him in midflight, knocking him out of the air like a bird winged on takeoff.

Word that Hard Tack had gone down spread through the battalion with alarming rapidity. No one knew if he were KIA or wounded, only that he was evacuated. The commander they trusted and depended on had fallen on the very first day of battle, the man who had developed the Black Panthers' pride as an outfit and forced them to believe in themselves, who had kept them focused amidst the bigotry at Camp Claiborne and Camp Hood. Gone. The ship felt rudderless, not a good omen.

"My God!" groaned Lieutenant Charles Barbour. "Do you know what this means? We are in deep shit. Major Wingo is the new CO."

Dread tainted by dust and burned powder spread throughout the battalion. Colonel Bates's fate had barely sunk in, however, before news about Major Wingo's more dubious fate reached the companies.

The three tanks assigned to Battalion HQ guarded the supply trains, all of which had come to a halt on high ground behind the front, waiting for a lull before continuing. The kid of the outfit, PFC E. G. McConnell, got out of one of the tanks and stood on the hill looking off into the distance a couple of miles where his friends of the 761st were engaged in bitter battle. He was so scared his tongue stuck to the roof of his mouth and threatened to stop up his airway. Several tanks were burning, emitting columns of black smoke. The infantry seemed pinned down by heavy German resistance.

E.G. had his two dog tags and a lucky half-dollar piece on a chain around his neck. He had the little pocket prayer book Moms had given him. Nonetheless, in spite of this protection, Colonel Bates's getting shot seemed to have left the battalion and E.G. personally vulnerable. If it hadn't been for the colonel, E.G. would likely have gone home in irons and disgrace, considering all the misdemeanors and violations of Army Regs he had committed in attempting to get himself kicked out of the army.

"I'm not sending you home, Private," the colonel had said. "You're going to stay with the 761st and become a soldier and a man. You may as well accept it. Some day you'll thank me."

E.G. wasn't sure that day had come yet. All he knew was that he missed Colonel Bates already.

Smitty got out of his tank, walked over, and stood next to E.G. He had transported Major Wingo up from the rear to take the colonel's place at the CP, since the major was now acting battalion commander. E.G. looked around.

"Where's Major Wingo?"

"He went nuts."

"Huh? What's he doing, hiding in the tank?"

"Naw, man. I done told you. He might not be plumb chicken-shit, but he sure got henhouse ways. He went plumb-dee crazy. That cowardly motherfucker get out and looks down there and starts shaking all over like a stray dog shitting razor blades in the rain. Crying and going on. Saying he gonna get kilt and he can't do this. He took off in a Jeep and went to the rear like his ass is on fire."

First the colonel got shot. Now the executive officer, despised though he might be, had deserted, leaving the battalion without leadership at the top when the men needed it most. Major Wingo was never to be seen again. He was later reported to be suffering "battle fatigue" in a cushy office job back in the States.

Smitty gave E.G. the major's trench coat, which Wingo had left in the tank, and he kept the officer's binoculars. E.G. took the insignia off the coat's epaulets and tried it on. The rain had stopped completely and it looked as though the sun might shine later. The air remained chilly. E.G. stuck his hands into his new coat pockets and gazed morosely out over the fighting. Smitty offered a strange, humorless laugh.

"Motherfucker," he said. "He's always saying niggers ain't gonna fight. Now who is it done turned yellow and run off when he hears the first shot—and it ain't even aimed at him."

"Dis-gusting," E.G. said.

The two men stood side by side, shoulders hunched. Things looked bleak for Patton's Panthers on their first day of battle.

27

Now I realized this was war—total war.

—PFC E. G. McConnell

The sun played peek-a-boo with the scattering clouds of approaching winter as the first shocking day of the Black Panthers' baptism of fire drew to a close. The wind had a real bite to it. Someone said it might snow. E. G. McConnell shivered and thrust his fists deep into the trench coat previously worn by the battalion's executive officer. Having no access to the "Big Picture," E.G. knew little of what was going on ahead of him on the front lines; it seemed only that hell had opened up a big gap to let mortal man catch a glimpse of what awaited him if he didn't shape up and walk the straight and narrow.

The two task forces had taken Hill 253. E.G. knew that much. They seized the towns of Bezange-la-Petite and Bezange-la-Grande before threatening darkness turned the tide and the Germans pushed the Americans back from their main objectives. There was still fighting. E.G. heard it banging and crashing away beneath a darkening sky that looked bruised and wounded. He learned that units were digging in for the night to repel possible counterattacks.

All day long, HQ elements and supply trains had moved forward as the FEBA (forward edge of the battle area) moved forward, advancing onto contested ground where men and machines had battled throughout that terrible day, following to keep within command distance of the units in contact. *Whoever* was in command at this point in time. Someone said the infantry commander had taken charge and would be the boss until Third Army dispatched someone to take over.

American soldiers and German soldiers lay scattered all over the landscape, their bodies broken and grotesquely twisted in the fields, lying out there in the mud among all the busted war equipment, like so much busted equipment themselves. Some of the corpses had been marked out of respect with a rifle stuck bayonet first into the ground and the casualty's helmet placed on top. The doughs were paying a heavy price for a relatively small piece of real estate.

The grinder was still grinding. Streams of ambulances poured back from the front—Jeeps, trucks, half-tracks, anything that could roll. Bloodied and torn bodies of the seriously wounded lay on top of the vehicles, on the hoods, fenders, in the back, anywhere there was available space. The vehicles left blood trails in the mud and on the roads. A spoor of cries, moans, and screaming followed.

Walking wounded also issued from the battle, like pus from an infection, arms and legs and heads and torsos wrapped in muddy, bloody bandages, walking like zombie mummies, leaning on each other, helping each other, eyes sharp and staring and filled with pain and horror.

This was only the *first day*.

E.G. expected even more terrible times ahead, knew that he would be frightened again and again until, perhaps, it became a constant state, like a toothache. Knew that he would be further exposed to a great deal of suffering and devastation. Tears filled his eyes and he felt himself succumbing to a wave of self-pity.

He had never even had a girlfriend before Moms helped him lie about his age so he could get into the army. Didn't know what it was like to kiss a girl except for an embarrassed and self-conscious peck at a spin-the-bottle party. At sixteen when he enlisted, he hadn't even started to *live*—and now he feared he was going to die before the living had hardly begun.

He took out the prayer book Moms had given him. He read a passage, then clenched the little book hard in his hands, dropped his chin to his chest, and unabashedly prayed.

"My dear God, I'm too young to die like this. Please, dear God, don't let me die."

"Amen," said a voice, and a hand dropped onto his shoulder.

Trezzvant Anderson seemed much older, but was probably no older than thirty or so at the outside. He was a black correspondent from the Negro press who had attached himself to the 761st and would remain for the duration of the war, however long that might be. The Panthers considered him a little mad to *volunteer* like that when he wasn't even in the army.

The black man and the black youth in uniform stood in the gathering darkness looking out over all that carnage. Movement from the other side of the road attracted their attention. They had thought the German soldier dead, one of many corpses, until a hand feebly lifted and he made a strange mewling in his throat. They cautiously approached to where he lay on his belly in the shallow drainage ditch.

The guy was in bad condition, a pitiful-looking specimen of the Super Race. His bottom jaw had been shot off, leaving nothing but exposed, shattered bone, upper teeth, and a pulpy mass of hanging flesh. He lifted himself partially off the ground on weak arms and looked at the black Americans with pleading eyes. Gurgles of blood erupted from the mangled opening to his fully exposed throat. E.G. had never seen anything quite so hideous. Even his worst nightmares could not have conjured up something like this.

E.G. had been a Boy Scout and knew some rudimentary first aid on top of what he had learned in basic training. He ran back and got an aid kit from the tank. Then he didn't know what to do with it. How did you bandage a wound like that without suffocating the guy? Since he had no mouth other than a few top teeth, he couldn't even swallow an aspirin to help ease the pain.

Anderson produced a flask filled with brandy. E.G. dipped battle gauze in the brandy and dabbed at the wound. Although the German couldn't speak, E.G. saw the gratefulness in his eyes.

"Oh, my God. What are we gonna do?" he wondered aloud.

What *could* they do? All the ambulances and medics were either down in the fields with the fighting or delivering wounded back to the aid stations and field hospitals. Besides, ambulances weren't going to transport wounded Germans when Americans were hurt and needing help.

Mortar rounds suddenly impacted nearby, shaking the ground and blasting shock waves through the air. E.G. and the reporter abandoned the German, not knowing what else to do, and sought cover underneath the tank. There wasn't anything else they could do for him anyhow.

The wounded German lifted himself on his arms and tried to crawl deeper into the ditch. An infantry scout car, a half-track, came tearing up the road through the mortar detonations, as though chased by them. The driver spotted the wounded enemy soldier and deliberately swerved off the road to hit him. The body underneath the tracks thumped and split open like a melon.

The guy couldn't even scream.

E.G. reached for his prayer book. *Oh, dear God, my dear God . . . !*

28

The enemy is at present fighting a defensive campaign on all fronts.

—BRITISH TWENTY-FIRST ARMY GROUP REPORT

Lieutenant Colonel Hollis E. Hunt of Yuma, Arizona, assumed command of the 761st Tank Battalion on November 9, the day after Colonel Paul Bates was hit. He brought word with him that Colonel Bates's leg was shattered but that he would live. Whether he would return to combat was a question still unanswered.

Although shaken by the loss of their commander, the men of the 761st rallied to continue the fight against entrenched Krauts on the route to Rodalbe. Word of Major Wingo's cowardice, on the other hand, was greeted with much mirth and with an even greater amount of relief. Someone even coined a new term—"Don't go Wingo-ing." It was the general consensus that he would have gotten the battalion wiped out and all its men killed had he remained in charge.

"He just plain chickened out," Lieutenant Johnny Long opined, showing no mercy. "That sonofabitch was evacuated for combat fatigue. Combat fatigue? Hell, that cracker hadn't even seen combat."

Lieutenant Long, Baker Company CO, had come an impressive distance since starting out in the army at Fort Knox as a cook, one of the few positions open for Negroes. He was still an excellent gourmet cook. After graduating from OCS, he and Lieutenant Ivan Harrison became the first two black officers in the U.S. tank corps.

"Not for my God and my country, but for me and my people,

that's why I fight," he told reporter Trezzvant Anderson, who was always interviewing men in the battalion. "I swore to myself when I entered the army that there would never be a headline saying my men and I chickened. A soldier in time of war is supposed to accept the idea of dying. That's what he's there for; live with it and forget it. I expect to get killed, but whatever happens I am determined to die an officer and a gentleman."

Not run, not "Wingo," and live the rest of his life knowing he was a coward.

The town of Morville-les-Vic, located only four miles from Vic-sur-Seille, which had been captured the previous day, promised to offer the most stubborn resistance as the two task forces consolidated to continue the drive on the morning of November 9.

It was snowing lightly, getting heavier, when Captain David Williams's Able Company, spearheading the task force on the left end of the line, punched through the forest of Bezange-la-Grande and attacked Château-Salins. Able and the 104th Infantry Regiment occupied the city after four hours of fighting house-to-house. It was the first major town east of Nancy taken by the 26th Division and its attached separate tank battalion. The city would subsequently be used by the XII Corps as its headquarters for the rest of the offensive in the area.

Able then headed toward Morville. The Germans had constructed a two-mile-long antitank ditch to block the most likely avenues of enemy approach. The ditch was festooned with dragon's teeth, barbed wire, log obstacles, and reinforced concrete pillboxes expertly concealed with dirt. Machine guns, mortars, rocket launchers, and *Panzerfausts*—antitank shoulder-fired weapons equivalent to American bazookas—were planted all along the ditch in double strength.

A German artillery officer candidate school on the outskirts of nearby Marsal threw everything it had at the advancing Americans. Captain Williams drew his tanks into position and began shelling the town.

At the same time, Lieutenant Johnny Long's Baker Company found itself blocked by heavy resistance. That left Captain Irvin McHenry's Charlie Company exposed to concentrated fire from pillboxes and heavy artillery concealed in woods behind the ditch. Able and Baker companies continued to pound Morville with their big guns while Charlie suffered losses.

Elsewhere in the area of operations, Dog Company, led by Captain Richard English, a former schoolteacher from New Orleans, moved out of Vic-sur-Seille to shell Salival before infantry entered the town against light remaining resistance. The company's lighter, swifter Stuart tanks then took up screening for the rest of the advance.

Six Sherman tanks in each armored battalion were equipped with heavy 105mm howitzers instead of normal 76mm cannon. These made up the Assault Guns Platoon attached to Battalion Headquarters and commanded by Lieutenant Pop Gates. Gates's assault guns and the 81mm Mortar Platoon led by Lieutenant James Lightfoot supported the advance on Morville by pounding German targets of opportunity.

When two liaison airplanes surprised a column of German reinforcements attempting to reach Morville via Ham Pont, Gates's howitzers trapped and destroyed the entire company, consisting of some thirty motor vehicles and two hundred Germans.

Snow fell in greater quantities as the day wore on. It covered the ground in a white mantle and threw a protective cover over well-camouflaged German positions. American tanks stood out dark on the snow like warts or, when they moved, like cockroaches or beetles.

Excellent targets.

29

You learn one basic axiom, and that is kill or be killed.

—Irwin Shapiro, armored infantryman

Morville-les-Vic was a rather small town of spires on churches and thatched roofs on little stone cottages. It lay in a bend of the Seille River that twisted on around the town to gorges in the high country. In the predawn of the second day of the offensive, the tanks of Captain Irvin "The Burner" McHenry's Charlie Company tactically crossed the bridge over the Seille River that engineers were still repairing. They pulled out and away from the river, doughboys following, and stretched into a combat line, rumbling and growling like great steeds pawing the dirt in their eagerness.

It was daylight now and beginning to snow more heavily, the first snowfall of the approaching winter. A frost of snow growing deeper by the minute already covered a wide stretch of open grazing land lying between the river and the town. Sullen skies, a biting wind, fog, and snowfall made life miserable and restricted vision to the point that the forested hills to the right were barely discernible. Tree trunks stood out through the swirling snow like etched ink marks as the timber thinned out beyond the field and encircled the town like a narrow fringe collar around the neck of a fat man.

Charlie Company had to cross the open ground in order to reach the town; there was no way to go around. The ideal use of armor was to break through the main line of resistance, bypassing pockets of enemy intransigence, to reach the enemy's rear where it could maneuver and use its speed. The danger for armor lay in getting bogged down where it had to move slowly.

McHenry scanned the proposed route of attack through binoculars. Nothing seemed to be moving in the timber beyond the field. Even had he known about the two-mile-wide antitank ditch that stretched all the way across, he might not have seen it, camouflaged as it was and now covered in snow.

Heavy artillery explosions began to rumble from the direction of Baker Company's sector, like a distant thunderstorm. Captain McHenry got on the radio with First Sergeant Sam Turley, who drove the company's lead tank. The regular driver of that tank had come down with a severe case of jitters, trembling and vomiting and barely able to control his bodily functions. Turley took over for him.

"Whatta you think, Top?" McHenry asked his first sergeant.

"They are over there, Captain. We can't see 'em, but I can feel 'em."

McHenry, a regular army man from Leavenworth, Kansas, took a deep breath, pulled his head back in, battened the hatch, and issued the order.

"Move 'em out. Come Out Fighting."

In the timber twenty-five to fifty yards behind the nearly invisible ditch, Germans waited patiently in their hidden pillboxes and cleverly concealed defensive positions for the unwary tanks and accompanying doughboys to venture within hard-to-miss range. The fifteen or so tanks crawled out over the open snow. Infantry straggled along behind, either using the tanks for cover or spread out on-line, weapons at the ready.

First Sergeant Turley reached the antitank emplacement first and spotted the trap, a formidable ditch fifteen feet wide and four feet deep, studded in the bottom with steel spikes. He radioed an alarm.

Too late. His tank was already hit.

Devastating fire poured down onto the exposed assault force. Mortars, artillery, and buried mines erupted in a broad, deep swath among the American war wagons and foot soldiers. Few things were as terrifying as being caught in the target area of an artillery barrage where an ambush had been carefully laid and executed.

The whirring noise of German artillery shells landing— *Wrack! Wrack! Wrack!*—made every sinew and synapse scream for a man to run. *Run!* Tracers crackled and wove designs across the white field, lashing about like electric snakes, throwing infantry in every direction. Wehrmacht MG-42 machine guns sounded like giant pieces of canvas being ripped close to the ear. *Panzerfaust* rockets contrailed into the melee. Bitter-tasting cordite fumes, rattling concussions, smoke, and confusion immediately shrouded the field.

A number of tanks got hit in the initial volley. Several blazed brightly—the Ronson effect—and with such heat that the snow for yards around instantly melted down to brown grass and mud, and then the grass caught fire. When a tank was penetrated, severed electrical cables often shorted out and sparked a fire, even if the gasoline failed to explode. The crew had to evacuate quickly or be burned alive. The tank might be saved if someone thought to pull the fire extinguisher switch on the way out. Otherwise, the tremendous heat softened the armor and destroyed the machine.

Tankers were abandoning their broken mounts all over that snowy field of death, helping each other, carrying or dragging the wounded, fleeing toward the rear. Others removed heavy machine guns if their tanks were only disabled and not burning and crawled underneath them to lay down fire against enemy positions. Those cast out near the tank ditch and the German lines scrambled into the freezing, muddy water at the bottom of the ditch while hot shell fragments fell all around.

Surviving tanks pounded enemy lines with their machine guns and 76mm cannon. Doughs ran in short spurts across the snow, firing and yelling and flopping to the ground, then rising again for another short charge. The sound of firing rolled back and forth across the field.

Corporal Autry Fletcher got entangled in a .50-caliber ammunition belt when a shell set his tank blazing. Flames licked all around him. Desperate, screaming for help, he thought he was a goner until Private Dennis Osly appeared to pull him out.

Osly dragged the injured gunner to the temporary shelter of the antitank ditch where both men, breathless, flung themselves into the slush at the bottom. The relativity of the refuge became immediately apparent when an exploding shell overhead peppered them with shrapnel. Both men were wounded.

Staff Sergeant Frank Cochrane rescued Corporal Earnest Chatmon and Tech Five George Collier from their disabled tank. They headed for the rear, bent over and running hard.

Tech Four Horatio Scott sustained an abdominal wound from ricocheting shrapnel when a shell penetrated his tank. Corporal Dwight Simpson carried him across his shoulder through a hail of enemy fire. They stopped once to rest behind an immobile tank that sat on the battlefield, its hatches still closed and apparently undamaged. Simpson banged on it. No one answered. He hadn't time to speculate about why it was sitting there like that, not moving, not firing, as useless as a boulder.

"You doing all right, Scotty?"

"If it's all the same to you, Dwight, I feel much better if we be someplace else."

Simpson chuckled in spite of himself. He picked Scotty up and continued running toward the rear.

An 88 smashed head-on into Sergeant Johnny Holmes's tank. An M4 Sherman was equipped with two and a half inches of armor laid at a forty-five-degree angle on the front glaxis plate to deflect incoming rounds. Yet the Ripsaw AP pierced the front and went all the way through the crew compartment, through the engine, and out the back. The concussion was like nothing Holmes had ever experienced. It deafened him. His ears and nose bled. Stunned, he looked around as fumes and smoke fogged inside the death trap.

The urgency of the situation struck him with a jolt.

"Damn! We're hit. Get the hell out!"

Flames licked out of the engine compartment as men scrambled through the top hatches and the escape hatch in the floor. As TC, Holmes lagged behind to make sure everyone got out.

PFC Alexander Anderson, the assistant driver, remained in his right seat, unmoving, helmeted head lolled back and eyes wide open and fixed. Blood seeped from his eyes like scarlet tears. Holmes shook him and shouted his name.

The man was dead, killed by the terrific concussion of the shell freight-training through the tank. Holmes paused a last moment.

"Alex . . . Alex . . . damn it all."

He pulled himself out through the top hatch and flew over the back end of the pile of useless junk as bullets spanged, rattled, and splattered all around him. He looked back once, saw that his tank was engulfed in flames with Anderson's body still inside, cremating, and kept running all the way to the rear.

Platoon leader Lieutenant Kenneth Coleman ended up in a similar situation and had to abandon ship. Lieutenant Ivan Harrison, whose Headquarters Company sat tight among a scattering of buildings on the far side of the Seille River at the bridge, watched Coleman through his tank periscope.

The fleeing lieutenant looked disgusted and winded but otherwise uninjured. For some inconceivable reason, he suddenly sat down on the bridge with his legs dangling over the edge, like a country boy getting ready to go fishing. He glanced nonchalantly back toward the field roiling with smoke and thunder. White engineers laboring frantically to complete repairs on the bridge cast curious looks his way but kept silent and continued to work. Only a few minutes before, a barrage of artillery had landed around the bridge, shook slates loose from the roofs of buildings, and scattered them on the road and on the tops of Lieutenant Harrison's tanks.

Harrison started to shout a warning to his friend when Coleman unexpectedly vanished in the white-hot detonation of an 88 shell. Blood, bone, flesh, and pieces of the bridge flew in all directions. Engineers vacated the bridge and scattered as several more shells landed. Jerry was trying to prevent any more Americans crossing it.

A white engineer lieutenant charged out of the smoke and fire, his face blackened, eyes crazy, and pieces of Coleman all over him. He dropped to his knees next to Harrison's tank and burst into fervent and heartfelt prayer. It shook Harrison all the way to the soles of his feet. His body trembled and shook with horror. He wanted to run, run for his life. But of course he couldn't.

"This has got to be hell," he decided. "It has got to be."

He felt like praying himself.

On the other side of the field, the antitank ditch was starting to fill up with marooned and wounded tankers and doughs. Fragmentation shells were exploding everywhere, stomping up and down and around the ditch, slinging wicked little shards of shrapnel into flesh, searing, burning, tearing up innards. Private William Kiser buried his grease gun in the mud because it was no longer useful. He wanted out of there in the worst way possible, but all he could do was crawl on his belly in the slush while he felt himself slowly freezing to death. To lift one's head a single inch above the top of the ditch invited instant and certain death. The cries of the wounded made Kiser think of the wailing of the condemned in the depths of hell.

First Sergeant Turley, his tank having been the first struck, had commandeered the .50-caliber from its turret. He realized GIs in the ditch were doomed unless they escaped right away. With a belt of ammo slung over his shoulder, the gun held firmly in his big hands, oblivious of danger, he ran up and down the ditch shouting at soldiers to head uphill in the ditch toward the highland timber where they might find cover to make a break for it.

"Clear out!" he yelled. "Get the lead out of your asses and keep 'em down if you value 'em."

He punctuated his orders with short bursts from the machine gun.

When Private Kiser looked back, he saw to his astonishment that Turley had jumped out of the ditch to provide better cover and diversion for the other soldiers. He stood straight and tall behind the ditch, snow swirling around him, the belt of ammo wrapped around his neck and the spitting .50-cal held close to his hip to absorb the recoil. He raked the muzzle back and forth, spitting a constant flame of death at German positions in the woods.

Kiser thought it the bravest act he had ever witnessed or was likely ever to witness again.

Turley fired the machine gun until he drew his last breath. German machine gun bullets ripped into him. As he crumpled to earth, his finger frozen to the trigger and the gun continuing to bang, an 88 HE landed almost directly on top of him, as though the Krauts knew bullets alone could never bring down such a man. The explosion shredded the earth, leaving only a crater and a mangle of bloody flesh in the snow and mud where big Sam Turley had been.

Tears filled Kiser's eyes.

Black Panthers were dying that bloody day. Back at 26th Division HQ, the brass were asking each other: *Can the Negroes take it?*

KIA (Killed in Action)

Lieutenant Kenneth W. Coleman
First Sergeant Samuel J. Turley
Private Alexander S. Anderson

30

*During combat, segregation did not exist. We fought
side by side with the white infantry divisions.*

—Lieutenant Ivan Harrison

Artillery, machine gun fire, *Panzerfausts* that could penetrate a tank with impunity, and road blocks held up Lieutenant Johnny Long's Baker Company for several hours
while Charlie Company fought for its life at the antitank ditch.
Orders came from Colonel Hunt's HQ that Baker would spearhead a slash right through the center of Morville, blast away,
and break out the other side. Tanks at close range gave Jerry a
large enough target, but at least they provided steel walls to hide
behind. The doughs had nothing to protect them except their
woolen uniforms and a prayer.

Long called a meeting of his platoon leaders and NCOs before
the attack launched. He had come up on the streets of Detroit and
was known as something of a hard ass, earning him the nickname
"The Black Patton." As those under Patton's command would follow him anywhere, so it was with the men of Baker Company. Long
kept them informed, considered their opinions, and never asked
them to do anything without his being up front to show them the
way. They knew he would never pull a Wingo on them.

The meeting gathered behind Lieutenant Long's tank in the
cold falling mixture of sleet, rain, and snow.

"There's a little town over the hill they want us to take," he
said. "We're going to spearhead. Ride through it, shoot up the
town, throw some hand grenades, and wipe out the town."

"Sort of like Detroit on a Saturday night?" Corporal Raleigh
Hill asked, eliciting a few nervous chuckles.

Long remained somber. He assigned his platoons their orders of march, orders of battle, and control sectors.

"Ole Johnny Long is long-faced," Horace Jones noticed. "So we are to go in there and soften up the Krauts, huh? It seems to me more like they want the black boys to get kilt first."

Baker Company raced into battle out of the highlands to Charlie Company's flank, through an artillery bombardment on the edge of town, into the outskirts where they flushed enemy soldiers and opened up on them with machine guns.

"Mo' than two, use the big gun," the canoneers chanted. "Mo' than two, use the big gun."

TC Eddie Donald's gunner, Sergeant Horace Evans, had drunk water from the hydrant of a Frenchman's house the day before. The water, coupled with Evans's own nervous stomach, gave him diarrhea. More than diarrhea, he had a full-blown case of dysentery, a mean condition in combat.

"It ain't the trots," he said. "It's the *runs.*"

The inside of a tank was cramped and smelly enough to begin with, what with the pungent odors of cordite from the weapons and the stench of five men who hadn't bathed or shaved regularly. Stir in the revolting stench of a man with dysentery he couldn't control, and the resulting effluvium was almost unbearable.

"It's an emergency!" Evans cried, his face contorted in pain.

"Oh, God, not *now!*" Sergeant Donald groaned.

The gunner wriggled out of his pants, a major feat in itself inside a tank traveling at better than twenty miles per hour across rough terrain, placed his upturned helmet in the seat underneath his bare butt, and a gaseous *Whoosh* promptly filled the helmet and fouled the air for his mates, who coughed and cursed and gagged and fought on anyhow.

Humor had a way of injecting itself even, or perhaps especially, in moments of dire danger. Between giving orders and cursing the contaminated air, Sergeant Donald lost his patience and snapped with a sour laugh, "Criminy! Somebody stuff Evans into that gun. He's our secret weapon that'll wipe out everything from here to Berlin."

Evans balanced on his helmet and kept firing away on the big gun. "When you got to go, you got to go," he said. He always thanked God for giving black men a sense of humor.

The tankers roared into Morville ahead of the infantry. Jerry was waiting to throw the proverbial kitchen sink at the invaders. The town literally blew apart in vicious house-to-house, building-to-building fighting that soon reduced it to smoldering ruins collapsing into the narrow streets.

Snipers in upper-floor windows and on rooftops made the doughboys pay at every crossroads, for every street, for every house. Machine gun fire tapped from cellar windows and from piles of rubble. Every inch of urban terrain was fraught with the possibility of mines that could blow holes in the bottoms of tanks. Tank-killing *Panzerfausts* always posed a threat.

Infantry were mowed down in wholesale lots. There was nothing clean, dignified, or glorious about dying in battle. Men seldom crumpled and neatly fell as they did in Hollywood movies. They were flung into the air, whipped about, dismembered, torn apart, knocked hard to the ground. Blood and flesh splattered on their friends. Their bodies lay cast aside in the intersections while Germans in hiding continued to fire into them out of hatred or sport, perhaps both. Doughboys climbed through the smoldering ruins like rats to force German machine guns to retreat so the wounded could be carried back to safety.

Even snow in the streets was dirty and ugly.

The doughs are pinned down by an MG. Want us to do something . . . ?

Where is the MG?

Somewhere up the street to the right . . .

Can you pull up and see it?

Fuck! Cover me . . .

Pull your section around the corner. It's better than sitting here . . .

The doughs are up ahead. They want us to fire into the hard-ware store or whatever . . .

Let me pull up to help you . . .

I can see the machine gun that's firing at us now. I'll take care of it if the doughs will get down . . .

Be careful of our doughs . . .

It seemed every small French village had a town square—a little park at the main intersection downtown where workers came to eat their lunches on better days. Two of Baker Company's lead tanks made a wrong turn and ventured out ahead into the park. *Panzerfaust* rockets trailing contrails of smoke hissed out of a nearby alley and detonated the first tank like a giant match being struck.

Sergeant Roy "Love" King was the second TC. His tank was still inside the mouth of the alley that emptied traffic around the square. Through his periscope he watched, stunned, as Corporal Raleigh Hill scrambled from the burning tank. Machine guns gnawed concrete and asphalt all around him as he made a broken-field run through the rubble and around the fallen bodies of doughs who had died there in the fighting. He passed King's tank at a dead run and, though wounded, quickly disappeared down the street.

King dueled it out with a machine gun. He knocked it out with a 76mm HE, collapsing the top floor of a building into the street. Earlier he had spotted a Ripsaw 88 concealed farther down. It let off a round now and then that was undoubtedly doing damage to some poor GI or tanker outfit. He decided to sneak up on it.

Barely had the war wagon crawled out of hiding before a *Panzerfaust* banged through the tank's side armor with a teeth-jarring jolt and exploded in the crew compartment. Flying shrapnel wounded every man, Corporal Herbert Porter the most critically. Tech Five James Whitby and Private John Mc-Neil slithered out the escape hatch in the floor, dragging Porter with them. Gunner Nathanial Ross and Sergeant King, already in the turret, went out through the top hatch.

Machine gun fire sparked and clanged off the steel hull as the disabled tank came under fierce crossfire from a number of upstairs positions. A slug caught Ross in midair as he jumped off the tank. It slammed him against the street, where he lay writhing in agony.

Another round snatched King's leg out from underneath him and dumped him next to Ross. There was no pain. His leg simply went numb. It seemed paralyzed.

The first tank still burned in the street. Black smoke boiled and eddied in the square and among the surrounding buildings as muzzles flickered and flashed. The Krauts intended to finish what they had started. To King, everything seemed to have gone into slow motion. Even the banging and rattling of weapons came from a great distance away. Lying in the snow and slush, he felt a sudden sense of warmth and well-being.

"Sergeant King! Sergeant King!"

Awareness gradually returned. He lay with his cheek against wet street brick, a position that gave him a clear view of his tank's underside. Porter seemed to be unconscious. McNeil and Whitby fired their grease guns at several Germans attempting to dart across a side street. McNeil moved closer to the inside track and shifted his fire to an upstairs window, suppressing fire coming from it to allow King and Ross to crawl underneath the tank with the rest of the crew.

"How bad they got you, Sarge?" McNeil asked.

"I can still kick ass."

"Sarge, them Krauts is all around us," Whitby pointed out unnecessarily.

"I think we can hold 'em off if this mother don't catch fire on us."

Five of them between the treads made it crowded. Lying on his back, King tied off his leg wound with a bandage. He crawled to the front and peeped out. The other tank was only a few yards away, engulfed in flames. He felt the heat on his face. All the snow around it had melted into a hissing steam. Fresh snow continued to fall. Flames scorched the nearest storefronts.

Machine gun bullets skipped off the pavement. The sonof-abitch was attempting to bounce slugs under the tank. King ducked back. As he did so, he thought he saw movement from one of the white doughs lying in the street.

He crawled to the back of the tank to check for an escape route. Nothing there. They would be chopped to pieces before they made it halfway to other cover.

They were stuck where they were for the time being, pinned down. From the sound of things, the rest of Baker Company and doughs had enough fighting of their own to go around. Lord only knew how long they were going to have to hold out.

McNeil popped away with his grease gun, pinging at muzzle flashes in the smoke.

"Save your ammo," King advised. "We might be here a spell."

He took inventory of their defenses. Three grease guns and two .45 Colt pistols. He didn't think the Germans were foolish enough to rush them. They would probably hold what they had and attempt to ricochet rounds underneath the tank and get them that way. He didn't want to think about what might happen if they fired up the tank with another *Panzerfaust*.

Porter lapsed in and out of consciousness, shivering occasionally. The rest of them were in pain from their own wounds and also shivering from lying in the snow. They listened to the sounds of fighting coming from other sectors of the town. They craved water, but the jugs were inside the tank.

Time passed, truncated and in slow motion. The situation remained unchanged. Jerries held the town square.

A low, agonizing groan caught their attention. Falling snow covered the dead doughboys in the street. One of the mounds moved. A hand reached out.

"Damn it," King said. "Damn it! We can't just leave him to die."

"Don't do it, Love," Whitby argued. "We can't go out there, Love. Somebody'll come."

"Would you want to be left out there?"

"Do you think a white guy would do it for a nigger?"

King looked at him. "Yeah, I do," he said.

"Damn it then," Whitby said. He reentered the tank through the open floor hatch to provide cover for the rescue attempt.

He checked the radio, intending to call for help. It was dead. He then loaded the 76mm and tried to fire it three separate times before he gave up. The breech had been damaged. He moved to the bow machine gun. It seemed to be in operating condition.

"All right, Sarge," he called down. "Let's do it."

He lay on the trigger, hammering an enemy position in a window on the other side of the square, screaming at the Germans even though they couldn't hear him, venting his rage and frustration and fear.

Sergeant King rolled out from underneath the tank and sprang to his feet. His leg gave out and he tumbled in the snow. He gained his feet again and sprinted toward the wounded GI.

The dough lifted his head from the snow. Gratitude in his eyes, *love* in them. Then, horror.

The Germans had gotten Love King's range. A swath of bullets geysered toward him, *through* him. Slammed him backward. Hands reached back toward the tank.

"I told him! I told him! Gawd damn, I told him!" Whitby screeched, firing the machine gun until he smelled it almost burning.

McNeil crawled out and dragged King back. He had only made it a few steps.

The Germans rekilled the corpses. The standoff continued.

It continued for three long, painful hours while the crew fought to keep the Germans at bay. *Panzerfaust* rockets struck the tank twice more, but they failed to penetrate. Whitby remained inside and on the machine gun. Underneath, lying in the snow and the cold, Sergeant Roy "Love" King bled to death. Died trying to save a white man.

His body was already stiffening by the time Baker Company's main element fought its way to the square and secured it. Lieutenant Johnny Long got off his tank and stared down at the body for a long time. Sergeant Horace Evans wiped his eyes, then rustled off to a nearby standing wall behind which he could hide to answer another urgent call of nature.

KIA (Killed in Action)
Sergeant Roy King

31

I never saw him in action, but everyone who did gave enthusiastic support to the idea that he was a great fighter.

—CAPTAIN PHIL LATIMER

Sergeant Warren G. H. Crecy always wanted to do things better than anyone else. Although a meek-looking, small, dark-brown man with horn-rimmed glasses and fuzz that never seemed to grow into whiskers on his baby-skinned cheeks, quite the opposite of what a battle hero was supposed to look like, he turned into a true warrior on the battlefield.

"Crecy, man, you are one gung-ho little dude," Sergeant Johnnie Stevens admonished.

During the fighting around Morville, Crecy's tank driver, Corporal Harry Tyree, got so scared because of his TC's daring that his feet shook on the pedals. Crecy rarely buttoned up. He stood in the turret with his head out the open hatch so he could

man the .50-caliber machine gun mounted on his light Dog
Company Stuart. He looked down into the tank.

"Damn it, Ty," he said through the intercom. "Steady on the
gas, man. You're about to whip my head off."

"Shi-it, Harding. I am scared."

"Don't tell anybody. Maybe they won't notice."

As Dog Company conducted screening operations, an infantry lieutenant from the 26th Division flagged Crecy down.
He wanted a lift to the other side of some woods so he could
take a look at a hill. He thought the mission would be safer and
faster in rolling steel rather than humping it.

"Get in, sir," Crecy said, adding, "and hold on."

The lieutenant crammed himself into the assistant driver's
seat, displacing that crewman. The tank kept bogging down in
the woods, slipping and sliding in the snow. American Shermans
and Stuarts had narrower tread than any of the German tanks,
which made them prone to get stuck.

"Take it easy, Ty."

The grade past the woodlot turned steep and more slippery.
The tank barely crept up the hill. Tyree couldn't see shit
through his periscope for the thickly falling snow. Crecy directed him from the turret, communicating through the head-
sets and throat mikes.

"Take it to the right . . . okay, now hard left."

They had almost reached the summit, coming out of the
white-cloaked stunted shrubbery that the tank rolled right over,
when Tyree heard a sudden *Whing! Whing! Whing!* Machine
gun bullets bouncing off armor.

"Back it up, Ty! Back up!"

Tyree kicked the machine into reverse and in his haste and
blindness backed into a shallow antitank ditch concealed by snow.
The tank stood at an awkward angle with its rear down and its vulnerable underbelly partially exposed. Tyree gunned the engine,
rocking the tank back and forth. The hidden machine gunner
walked rounds toward them, trying to reacquire the range.

"Can't you get us out?" Sergeant Crecy sounded anxious but still quite calm.

"Damnit, Sarge. I'm trying."

He rocked the tank some more, winding the engine tight and loud.

"I'll get one of the other tanks to pull us out," Crecy offered, radioing for help.

By the time help arrived a few minutes later, the Kraut gunner was peppering the iron wagon, hoping to get lucky and disable it. Crecy ducked down and peered through the periscope. If he could locate the bastard, he'd give him a dose of his own medicine. He looked down into the compartment. The crew and the lieutenant hitchhiker looked back at him, their eyes as wide as rats caught in a trap.

"I'm going out to hook us up," Crecy said.

"Kee-rist, Sarge."

"Keep that thought."

Crecy adjusted his horn rims in that scholarly way he had, as if he were about to read complicated instructions on how to get out of a tank ditch. Then he disappeared out through the turret. He emptied a magazine from his Thompson .45, shooting in the direction of the enemy fire, then attached a cable between the two tanks, stood up, still under fire, and waved the other tank to pull, all this as calmly as though he was stuck in his Ford coupe on a lazy country road on a Sunday afternoon and a friendly farmer on a tractor had showed up to drag him out.

When the tank lurched free of the ditch, Crecy unhooked and climbed back inside, first pausing an instant to adjust his glasses and scan the woods for the annoying Kraut gunner. Lead whinged off the tank and chewed to shreds the new pair of boots Tyree had bought in England and inadvertently left hanging outside on the turret. Crecy climbed back inside with a look of disgust on his face.

"That boy can't shoot shit," he said. "His sergeant ought to ship him back for retraining."

"The motherfucker got my boots," Tyree groused.

By this time the dough lieutenant was about to soil his pants. In a tank, there was no place to *hide*. His adventure wasn't over yet. The Kraut machine gunner must have called in a big brother.

As the two Stuarts scurried away, an AP shell bounced off the ground and struck the tank a jarring, glancing blow on its right side. The tank jolted to a halt once more. The lieutenant was ready to start praying. There wasn't an ounce of blood in his face and his lips trembled.

"I think it's the suspension," Tyree called out. "We've lost a tread."

"Abandon ship? Or can you get us out?" Crecy asked.

"I still got one track working."

By skillfully coordinating brakes and throttle, himself fueled by adrenaline, Tyree limped the big target out of the area and back to a safe place. Crecy remained stuck on the machine gun, pounding away with it, muttering to himself and every so often readjusting his glasses.

The infantry lieutenant had to be helped out of the tank, he was so weak and exhausted from the frightening experience. With his new respect for tankers, he vowed never to hitch another ride on one of the monsters.

"Just another day on the Western Front," Crecy quipped, unsmiling.

The tank on its single track limped back to the rear for repairs. There Crecy found out his best friend Horatio Scott had been wounded and evacuated to a field hospital. Scotty and he, along with Aaron Jordan and Crecy's wife, Margaret, had hung out together on Wall Street at Camp Hood. They had been inseparable. Scotty had sent back a message because he knew Crecy would fret.

"I'm okay, man. I'll be back soon."

32

You don't never know how the game is going to come out.

—SERGEANT JOHNNY HOLMES

All positions were finally secured around Morville late in the afternoon, not long before dark. Death and destruction appeared random and impersonal. Dead Americans were hauled to the rear by the truckload, white soldiers and black soldiers indiscriminately thrown in together, lying face down on top of one another, as many as a truck would hold. Many of the bodies were burned and scorched, with the glistening white of an arm or leg bone protruding from charred flesh. Lips burned away to leave rictus grins that seemed to hint at horrible and grisly jokes shared only among the dead. The stench of burned flesh and death followed them down the road.

The debris of combat littered the terrain: tanks, half-tracks, self-propelled guns. Snow continued falling in the first and heaviest snowfall of the year, the beginning of what would prove to be the worst winter on record, blanketing corpses and waste as though God intended to mask the ugliness from view.

Clean-up units moved in while the well-blooded combat outfits set up defenses and installed green identification panels so they wouldn't be mistakenly bombed by friendly aircraft. Engineers began clearing minefields. Graves Registration searched out dead GIs and quickly trucked them away for burial on foreign soil. Dead Germans were often left where they fell, to the mercy of the elements. Some wouldn't be found until after the winter snows melted; some bones wouldn't be recovered until many years later.

Maintenance groups went forward to locate damaged rolling stock, bringing with them T2 recovery vehicles to evacuate the shot-up equipment. Any vehicles that could not be repaired on-site due to lack of spare parts were left in place for later evacuation to army base ordnance companies. The fate of one 761st tank left the Black Panthers stunned and speculative. It became the subject of hushed midnight conversations, of stirrings deep in the soul over the meaning of divine destiny.

"When it be your time to go," Willie Devore darkly declared, "God's gonna get you one way or t'other."

The Charlie Company tank TC'd by Sergeant Harvey Woodward sat stalled on the open field in front of the dreadful anti-tank ditch where Sergeant Turley had made his last stand. The hatches were all buttoned and it appeared undamaged. There wasn't a mark on it. Snow fell and mounded up on the closed turret and on top of the big gun, still pointed toward where the enemy had been dug in that morning.

However, an eerie and unearthly picture presented itself when the tank was uncorked. All five crewmen were still inside—Sergeant Woodward, Tech Four Claude Mann, Corporal Carlton Chapman, Private L. C. Byrd, Private Nathaniel Simmons. Each still sat at his station. Mann's hands still gripped the control levers. All seemed frozen in a moment of time from which they would momentarily awake and go on about their business. They sat there with eyes staring, pupils dilated, no terror on their faces. No marks or wounds of any sort on their bodies. Each wore only a faint look of surprise.

And they were all, inexplicably, mysteriously, dead.

The army ultimately wrote off the casualties as "a concussion from an HE landing over the turret top, which set the waves to whirling inside the tank."

Willie Devore wasn't buying that. To him, it was additional proof that death was sneaking around waiting to pick him off. It was just a matter of time.

When the 761st first reached the front mere days ago, infantry veterans confided that there was no way of knowing how men would behave under fire as individuals. Panthers worried about whether they would find the courage to fight and kill.

"They think we can't fight and that we'll run because we're just niggers," Lieutenant Johnny Long said with a tinge of resentment.

In its first major battle of the war, the green and untested Black Panther Battalion had proved to be a tough outfit in Patton's army. The "niggers" didn't run, contrary to most white expectations. The only example of cowardice in the outfit turned out to be Major Wingo, and he was white. The battalion had given a good account of itself.

Naïveté could be a sort of advantage in the beginning, before men tasted battle and knew what it was. It didn't take long, however, to lose that naïveté. In the first day of combat, the Panthers began to learn things about themselves and about each other. First of all, they learned that to be afraid did not mean you were a coward. Bravery meant you went on, did your job, even when you were terrified. During moments of fear and weakness, they could always look around and see somebody else who had conquered his terror and continued to function—like Lieutenants David Williams and Johnny Long, brave Sergeants Sam Turley and Harding Crecy, Captain Irvin McHenry, and Sergeant Ruben Rivers. Even little Willie Devore, convinced that he was going to die, went out there and fought.

Few men could be stalwart and brave all the time. One would shoulder the burden of personal example and leadership one day, someone else the next. Today's coward might be tomorrow's hero, and vice versa. All began to live with the creed, with the *hope*, that if they were fortunate enough to get through the first thirty days of combat when they were green and learning how to fight, their chances of seeing the end of the war were greatly enhanced.

The men had trained together, ate and slept together, had become brothers in every sense of the word during more than two years at Fort Knox, Camp Claiborne, Camp Hood, in England, and now in France. They had battled prejudice and bigotry and discrimination and ridicule, had been told that as "niggers" they weren't as good as white men and that they would run when the time came to fight. Well, now they had fought, and they had fought well. They had paid a dreadful price.

The list of those Panthers who died in battle, and the even longer list of wounded, was tacked onto the outer flap of the HQ tent for all to see—a total of fifteen men KIA in two days. Lost friends. An air of mourning lay over the battalion during the lull after the fight. The survivors took their losses hard; they were not yet accustomed to it.

"If it goes on like this," declared Willie Devore, looking depressed and sounding more fatalistic than ever, "ain't none of us going back home."

Captain David Williams, Able Company, stood in the darkness outside a building he had commandeered as a CP and bivouac for his men in the wrecked town of Morville. There were no lights on the war front with the exception of an occasional smoldering building glowing like a pinprick of light through a black velvet cloth. Even the men who smoked—and that included most, since cigarettes came free in their rations— lit up underneath their jackets or ponchos so that even the flame from a match could not be seen. They cupped their hands around the cigarettes' burning tips, having discovered that even the glow of a cigarette might draw enemy fire.

Tech Five Chico Holland and First Sergeant Sam Turley were the first two black tankers Captain Williams met when he arrived at Camp Claiborne as an idealistic new lieutenant in 1942. He and Turley ended up getting booted out of the 758th and into the 761st at its formation stage, apparently because they had insulted the commanding officer of the 758th by a white man and a black man shaking hands. Now, Turley was dead. Captain Williams was glad to have shaken the hand of one of the bravest men he had ever known.

With Dog Company, Sergeant Harding Crecy thought his buddy Horatio Scott was safely back in the rear at a field hospital being cared for and that he was all right. He found out differently the next day. Scotty had died in surgery during the night.

In a state of shock, Crecy sat down on a tree stump and thought about everything that had happened, about Scotty and the good days. He stared off into the distance, his eyes as cold as the layer of snow that blanketed the land. His mouth tightened. It was almost as if the men of Dog Company watched him transforming from mild Dr. Jekyll to raging Mr. Hyde right before their eyes.

Captain English came around later with a bottle of brandy he had liberated from somewhere. His men had gone long-faced from their losses.

"There's not much of it," he said, "but I think if we all take a nip everybody will get some."

The bottle made its round in the silent approach of nightfall.

KIA (Killed in Action)

Sergeant James W. Harrison
Staff Sergeant Harvey Woodward
Corporal Carlton Chapman
Tech Four Horatio Scott
Tech Four Claude Mann
Private Robert W. Briscoe
Private L. C. Byrd
Private Emile I. Armstrong
Private Nathaniel Simmons
Private Willie C. Lofton
Private Theodore R. Cooper

33

He couldn't wait to get back to his men.

—Taffy Bates

The army had a clearly defined and efficient process for taking care of wounded. They were removed from the battlefield to aid stations and collecting companies by ambulances or Jeeps. From there they went farther back to a BAS (battalion aid station), the medical facility nearest to the front, where they were triaged into three groups: the lightly wounded who were in no serious immediate danger; the more critically wounded who required more immediate attention; and those who had little or no chance of recovery, who were in fact dying barring divine intervention. These were administered only pain relief.

The second group was the largest, most of whom required early evacuation. These were treated and then moved up the chain to regimental, division, and field hospitals in the rear where they could be evacuated by ship or plane to England. Some of them would return to duty; most would not. It was in this group that Colonel Paul Bates fell after being ambushed by the enemy patrol during the first hours of his battalion's maiden engagement. A bullet had smashed into his ankle and shattered his leg. He was flown from regiment directly to Great Britain, bypassing the 14th Field Hospital.

"You've a million-dollar wound, sir," he was told. "You won't be back."

"You're wrong, Doc. I'm coming back to my men."

Mail moved slowly in the European Theater of Operations. Even though Taffy requested Paul write her every day, if only to say "I'm alive," sometimes days passed before she received let-

ters, usually collected in a bundle. Therefore, rather than by letter, she learned of Paul's wounding when a medical aide in England got through to her on a field phone. The news threw her
into a frenzy. In her mind he could have lost a leg, he could be
in severe permanent pain, paralyzed, even . . . dying.

Willing to take any risk to reach Paul's bedside, she ran out of
the hospital, intent on hitching a ride to the nearest airfield to
beg some pilot to take her to him. She was hurriedly stuffing a
few possessions into an AWOL bag when the hospital commandant rushed over.

"Taffy, don't do it. Nobody can do it. We're at war. You'll be
court-martialed."

"I have to go to him. Don't you understand?"

"It's not worth it, Taffy. Not for a boyfriend."

Her jaw tightened. She defiantly tossed her bobbed blond
hair. "He's *not* just a boyfriend," she corrected him.

The commandant changed tack. "Taffy, from what I know of Paul
Bates, he wouldn't think highly of any soldier who deserted his post,
no matter the reason. That's what you'd be doing. You're needed
right here, nurse. There are wounded and sick boys coming
through, hundreds of them. The Negro boys ask about you every
time. It seems they've even named one of their tanks after you."

Taffy was a strong-willed young woman, but the sense of what
he said took the wind out of her. She sat down heavily on her
bunk, tears easing down her pretty cheeks. It was just that she
was so terribly in love with Paul, had been virtually from the
first time they met at the Camp Claiborne theater. She intended
to spend the rest of her life with this man—and nothing, *nothing,* was going to take him from her.

She thought about him lying alone in a hospital bed. While
she knew he loved her, Paul Bates *needed* no one, not even her.
That was part of what attracted her to him. His strength. His in-
dependence. He was the only man she had ever known who was
totally complete within himself. At least one man in the world
could be an island. Paul Bates walked tall on his own road.

The first present she ever gave him was an identification bracelet with an expansion band. Her love for him, she acknowledged, had to be flexible enough to give and yield like that band. She had written a poem to go with it.

Like this little present,
So must my true love be.
He must have last to come and go,
For I would have him free.

Taffy truly believed Paul was one of those rare persons born and sent to earth with a purpose larger than himself.

Her commander placed a kindly hand on her shoulder. "Taffy, I know he'll come back. I promise you when he does, he'll find you wherever you are. You can take off then as long as you need to."

Taffy knew it too. Paul Bates would return to her—and to his men.

34

It is always in the last lap that races are either gained or lost.

—WINSTON CHURCHILL

The war was not going well for the Führer on all fronts. On the Eastern Front, the Russians had crushed twenty-five German divisions and inflicted upon the Reich its worst defeat ever. They were now overrunning Poland on their way to the border of East Prussia.

In the south, the Italians had surrendered. The Allies had captured Rome and were attacking the German lines more than 150 miles north of the capital.

On the Western Front, French, American, and British forces had burst out of Normandy and its beachheads to virtually annihilate two enemy armies. They were now driving northeast through Belgium and northern France toward the German border. A second invasion of Americans and Free French raced up from the Riviera to entrap elements of a third German army.

On all fronts, German units were scrambling in disarray back toward the Deutschland. The fighting continued, fiercer than ever, as Hitler dug in to defend the homeland.

Allied Supreme Commander Dwight Eisenhower, who had assumed control of Allied land forces from British General Bernard Montgomery on September 1, 1944, favored a "broad front" strategy of advancing on Germany from all sides. In keeping with this strategy, General Omar Bradley, commander of Twelfth Army Group, was given as his objective the taking and clearing of areas around the ancient city of Aachen. General George Patton's Third Army would maintain its drive through the French Lorraine to the River Saar and Saarbrucken and the industrial region of the Saarland, then on from the Maginot Line to the Siegfried Line and the Rhine River.

The primary objective of Eisenhower's strategy was to defeat the enemy west of the Rhine, seize a foothold on the east bank, and then march across Germany.

Although many had predicted during the summer that the war would be over by Christmas, Hitler's fanaticism, German tenacity, and the early approach of winter ensured the war would continue into a new year. Patton champed at the bit. Given the chance, he declared, "I will go through the Germans like shit through a goose."

The Germans remained a formidable fighting force even as

they withdrew all along the Third Army's front lines, exacting a heavy toll with delaying tactics, counterattacks, minefields, road-blocks, obstacles, and increased artillery fire.

"I hope that in the final settlement of the war you insist that the Germans retain Lorraine," General Patton wrote in a letter to the U.S. secretary of state, "because I can imagine no greater burden than to be the owner of this nasty country where it rains every day and where the whole wealth of the people consists in assorted manure piles."

After Third Army units, including the 761st Tank Battalion, cleared the area around Morville, they formed a single spear-head thrusting through the densely wooded area of the Forest de Koecking toward Benestroff and Metz, vital towns for the enemy because of rail, road, and communications services. Three Third Army divisions of XX Corps slowly closed in from all sides in a pincer, wresting town after town from German con-trol—Nomény, Rouves, Vigny, Foville, Viviers, Obreck, Moyen-vic, Guebling, Dedeline, Chateau-Voue, Wuisse . . .

35

These men were such terrific fighters. They would do unusual things.

—LIEUTENANT COLONEL PAUL BATES

As the men of the 761st pushed forward, operating with the 26th Infantry and the 4th Armored Division, rough going against rain, mud, cold, snow, driving sleet, and an enemy who bitterly contested every inch of ground, they learned to live with war and its constant stench, taste, sight, and threat. It was more terrible than they could have imagined when they arrived in England only weeks earlier. It was more terrible than the mind could comprehend, so sometimes the mind tried to shut down the worst of it.

The earliest and most impressive sounds were the distant thumping and rumble of artillery, the distinctive ripping of German machine pistols and the rapid rattle-clatter of burp guns, the deadly high whing of German 88s passing over or air bursting ahead in puffs of gray-white smoke, and, most terrifying of all, the warble-screech of the "Moaning Minnie" shells that the Krauts rigged to sound like banshees from hell.

These sounds always seemed to generate corpses, living beings only minutes ago, breathing, talking, laughing, suddenly reduced to ruined bloody slabs of meat strewn on the ground. And there were the wounded, some of whom would soon become corpses. Groans and screams, prayers and primordial shrieks as they glimpsed the Great Beyond, cries of "Mommy!" and "No! No!" and "Help me!" Missing arms or legs, hands and fingers, pieces of face and other parts of the body lost and the wounded staggering around out there looking for their missing pieces. Primitive expressions of animal fear on faces. Sounds of new soldiers crying and praying before battle, and the louder silence after the battle.

No wonder the mind sometimes tried to shut down.

War was being filthy and hungry and itching, fatigue and numbness, the endless bodily discomfort of being cold and wet and miserable. It was eating out of dirty fire-blackened canteen cups, sleeping in the mud and snow or, if you were lucky, inside some bombed-out house or curled up inside the refrigeratorlike interior of a tank. Mud in food, clothing, weapons, gritty between the teeth, clogging the nostrils. Eating in mud, sleeping in mud, digging foxholes in mud, repairing machines in the mud, hating the mud, cursing the mud, and sometimes dying in the mud.

Waking in the mud and ordered to be ready to go. Standing in the sleet and snow and ubiquitous mud waiting. Hurry up and wait. Finally, crawling back into holes to sleep some more in mud and muddy water three inches deep at the bottom.

Little ailments. Sometimes lice. Ringworm. Crotch itch. Sores that never healed. And trench foot due to the cold wet weather and boots and feet constantly soaked. General Patton gave orders that each commander down to platoon and squad level was to personally ensure that his soldiers had fresh, clean socks and that they changed daily.

"It is more important in war to keep your feet in good condition than it is to brush your teeth," he said.

"Right!" Private Everett Robinson growled sarcastically. "I'll go down to the laundry first thing in the morning."

Dysentery, that constant companion, made its regular rounds. Sergeant Horace Evans wasn't the battalion's only "secret weapon." Men ran for the woods on urgent business to drop their drawers, and then of course they always got snow in their drawers. Sometimes they went in their helmets and set the helmets on the outside of their holes until morning. They went in empty K-ration boxes and tossed the boxes out. Things smelled raunchy, but it beat getting shot.

Strangely, living under these conditions with the sights of mutilation and death, men not only learned to live with it, they learned to accept it, as one accepted the white noise of a freeway behind the house.

Black Panthers for the most part had similar backgrounds. They hailed primarily from two distinct sources—either they came from the Negro ghettos of the big northern cities like Detroit, Chicago, and New York, or they were farm boys from the rural South. They were untraveled, unsophisticated, and certainly unprepared emotionally and psychologically for the hell of war. All were as afraid of not being equal to facing death as they were of death itself, of letting down their buddies or pulling a Wingo and appearing cowardly.

The tough guys in the battalion, like Sergeants Johnnie Stevens and Johnny Holmes and Floyd Dade, were a bit more boisterous than the quiet ones like Warren G. H. Crecy, E. G. McConnell, and Ruben Rivers. They would laugh and joke and grabass and talk trash before an action. Putting on a front even though everybody, including themselves, was scared spitless. Wishing each other good luck and trying to bolster the courage of the quiet, introspective, less-aggressive men who suddenly looked terrified.

A few of the men were like Tech Five Willie Devore, who confronted death every second of every minute of every hour of every day, considering it, mulling over it, obsessed with it, *waiting* for it. One afternoon, Devore's tank came upon an elderly Frenchman walking barefooted and coatless on the road in the snow and slush.

"I'm holding up a minute," Devore said. He was the driver.

He got out and gave the old man his extra pair of boots. The ancient gent seemed so touched that he broke into tears and hugged Devore soundly. Willie looked embarrassed as he climbed back into the tank. He shrugged.

"Hell fire," he murmured. "I ain't gonna be needing 'em. I ain't gonna be around long enough to wear out the pair I'm already wearing."

There was one thing they all had in common, however. Young E. G. McConnell's lips weren't the only ones moving in prayer whenever they moved into battle lines. The tough ones, the weak ones, the frightened ones, all asking God to let them live through just one more fight.

36

*To look at Warren G. H. Crecy, you'd never think
that here was a killer.*

—TREZZVANT ANDERSON

During the assault on Hill 309 and the town of Wuisse,
Sergeant Harding Crecy lost his ride to antitank fire.
He scrambled out of the light Stuart and commandeered a Sherman that had also been hit but was still mobile. Its
cannon was gone, the breech frozen, but the .50-caliber machine gun remained functional. Under heavy enemy fire, urging
his new crew to gallantry bordering on recklessness, he charged
the tank at the enemy position that had destroyed his first machine and wiped out a German antitank squad.

Still under fire, he eliminated enemy forward observers directing artillery and mortars on Able Company, then turned his
attention to machine guns targeting advancing infantry. It
seemed the little man with the horn-rimmed glasses was all over
the battlefield, like an avenging angel calling down the wrath of
God upon anyone or anything that stood in his way. Scotty's
death had created a berserk hellcat, a savage whose only
thought was to kill. He rained down destruction with such desperation and abandon that his comrades thought he must have a
charmed life and that, most likely, he was living on borrowed
time.

His second tank bogged down in mud. The enemy mounted a
counterattack and began moving forward, catching doughboys
in open terrain and pinning them down. Instead of abandoning
his stuck tank, Sergeant Crecy adjusted his glasses in that scholarly manner of his, squinted, and lay down such a heavy fusillade

of fire with the .50-cal, knocking off Krauts in rows, that the German foot soldiers retreated in panicked disarray. The tank crew had to pry him away from the gun to stop the shooting. He shook his head as though coming out of a trance and readjusted glasses that had jarred down on his nose.

"Let's go find some more of the bastards," he said.

37

I would have court-martialed Johnnie Stevens, except he was too good a fighter.

—CAPTAIN DAVID WILLIAMS

Sergeant Johnnie Stevens always bragged that he had the best tank crew in the battalion. He depended upon their well-oiled teamwork for his survival, and they depended upon his brash guidance for theirs. His gunner, Corporal Joe Kiah, once knocked out an enemy Mark IV panzer at a range of more than five hundred yards. He missed the first shot. The shell exploded a small shed short of and to the right of the Kraut beast. The monster continued to fight back.

"Come on, come on, *come on!*" Stevens urged through the intercom. "Give him another."

A flicker and a flash from the German war wagon. The shell whickered past like a Jeep hurled through the air.

Kiah's second shot caught the panzer below the turret and splashed fire. Its crew abandoned ship and ran for their lives. Kiah grinned, swelling with pride in his deadly skills.

"Sarge, how'd I do?" Fishing for praise.

"You stink."

"How come?"

"Because you should have got him on the first shot."

That had since become a little joke between the two of them.

Before the assault on Wuisse, a 26th Division patrol ran a recon on Hill 309 and reported the hill abandoned. There was nothing up there. Able Company's Third Platoon rumbled up the hill expecting little more than a Sunday drive. Suddenly, the whole world seemed to explode. Accompanying doughs began vanishing in banging flashes of light or being mowed down by grazing machine gun fire. The recon had fucked up big-time.

Almost immediately, two tanks burst into fireballs near Stevens's vehicle. Surviving crewmembers scrambled out of the crippled machine and flopped down in the grass, snow, and mud to hide from machine guns burrowed in on top of the hill and in a woodline to the right. Two of them didn't make it—Walt Campbell and George Shivers.

Before Stevens could even get into the firefight, an AP round slammed into his Sherman, knocking out the engine. Smoke poured from it. Tongues of flame leaped along the drive shaft below.

The first thing Stevens felt was—nothing. He couldn't move his legs. He was paralyzed from the waist down. He struggled to open the top hatch and pull himself out, using only his arms. The other four crew escaped through the lower hatches. Instead of hugging the ground or running to the rear, Kiah and driver James Peoples leaped back onto the tank and pulled Stevens from under the master gun and out the top.

They all flopped in the grass alongside. Kiah and Peoples wriggled to a nearby ditch to escape the mortar rounds thumping all over the open side of the hill, overlooking in the confusion the fact that Stevens was incapacitated and couldn't walk or run. He lay in the open, burying his face in the mud and snow and wet grass, his combat suit covered with blood.

One of those odd thoughts that occur at such moments passed through his head. He and his best friend, Sergeant Paul "Corky" Murphy, had made a pact whereby the last of the two of them to get married became godfather to the other's first child.

"If we make it back home to get married," Murphy had said.

It didn't look as if Stevens was going to make it. Germans feared and despised American tankers and tried to kill as many of them as they could, any way they could. Exposed as he was to the enemy, Stevens's best bet was to play dead. More often than not, however, that didn't work. Germans liked to make sure the dead were *really* dead.

A tall white sergeant from the 26th Infantry lay nearby in a ditch. He lifted his head.

"Hey, Sarge," he called out to Stevens. "You hit?"

"I'm hit hard as hell."

Although the white dough was relatively safe in his ditch, he jumped out without a second thought, putting himself in danger to run to a black tanker's aid. He grabbed Stevens by the back of his jumpsuit and shoved him over the embankment and into the ditch. Then, before he could duck down himself, some German in the woodline cut him across the middle with a burp gun. The white sergeant's warm body fell on top of Stevens.

Not so long before, Sergeant Roy King had tried to save a white dough in Morville's town square and was killed in the attempt. Now a white dough had died saving a black man. It profoundly touched Johnnie Stevens. He didn't even know the white sergeant's name.

KIA (Killed in Action)
Tech Four Walter J. Campbell
Private George Shivers

38

Ruben Rivers was good, and he probably would have been an officer. No, he probably would have been company commander.

—CAPTAIN DAVID WILLIAMS

Sergeant Ruben Rivers was a rather awkward young man socially, an Oklahoma red dirt kid who expressed himself in a few carefully chosen words and was then content to step back and listen. He was rather tall and lean with high cheekbones that spoke of possible Cherokee ancestry mixed in with the blood of slaves and slave owners. He had warm eyes and lips that always seemed ready for a self-deprecating smile. It was in combat that he released his fiercer nature.

After Sergeant Johnnie Stevens went to the rear after being wounded on Hill 309, Sergeant Rivers took his place in the vanguard of Captain David Williams's Able Company. It became a byword that Rivers would lead the way whenever it was time for the 761st to "Come Out Fighting."

Air reconnaissance advised that the Germans were going to stage a big fight and defend Guebling. All the roads behind the enemy's main line of resistance at the town were clogged with vehicles and infantry being sent up to relieve and reinforce panzer troops. Rivers's tank ran over a Teller antitank mine on the road to Guebling. The explosion hurled the tank sideways and blew off the right track and the volute springs and damaged the undercarriage. Able Company's trailing elements found Rivers and his crew—Corporal Otis Johnson, Tech Four Ivory Fox, PFC Louis Gains, Private Homer Neely—crouching behind the disabled tank for cover. They had knocked out two

Kraut tanks at an incredible range of more than five hundred yards, firing only one round at each of them, before the mine put *them* out of commission.

The blast shredded the flesh on Rivers's leg. Most of his knee was gone. Shank bone gleamed startling white. Medics cleaned and dressed the wound, then attempted to administer morphine for pain. Rivers pushed them away.

"I ain't needing that stuff," he protested. "I gotta be alert. We got a job to do."

"The only place you're going with that leg, Sergeant, is back to the BAS."

"That's what you think."

The medics advised Captain Williams that his sergeant refused to be evacuated. Williams took a morphine syringe and, accompanied by his driver, Corporal Big Tit Richardson, approached where Rivers sat in the snow and muck with his back against his ruined tank, smoking a cigarette. The captain knelt without a word and quickly started to insert the needle. The needle was about a half-inch away from flesh when Rivers noticed. He snatched Williams's wrist.

"Sir, please, no."

"Ruben, you're going back. You've got a million-dollar wound. You're getting out of this war and going home to Tecumseh. You've already got a Silver Star and a Purple Heart."

"Captain, you're going to need me."

"I'm giving you a direct order. You're going back. Medics, bring up a stretcher."

Rivers pushed the needle away again. He lurched to his feet.

"Sir, this is one order I'm gonna have to disobey."

Captain Williams could have ordered Big Tit to hold him down. He hesitated in giving the order, taken aback by the TC's courage and resolve.

"Listen to me, Ruben. There's no turning back once we cross that bridge up there. The Jerries are over on our right flank. The 4th Armored is getting murdered."

"Who said anything about turning back, sir?"

The Germans chose that exact moment to lob in smoke to mark a target for their artillery. Plumes puffed from behind a stone barn about a hundred yards away. HE was sure to follow. Rivers hobbled over to the tank commanded by Corporal Henry Conway, whom he outranked, and took over it and its crew. He turned back toward Captain Williams.

"Sir, what are you waiting for? We'd better haul ass out of here. The Krauts is about to throw us a party."

Just as cool as could be, in spite of the pain. He mounted the open turret and stood with his head and shoulders out as the tank rumbled off. Captain Williams looked after him, then shook his head in admiration. He ordered Rivers's old crew to return to the VCP to see if they could scrounge up another war wagon.

"Medics, you might as well go back too," he said. "I'll check on Sergeant Rivers tonight."

The town of Guebling, a Kraut stronghold, lay on the other side of a narrow river whose only bridge in the vicinity had been blown by the retreating enemy. Engineers would have to erect a portable Bailey across in order for tanks and troops to cross and engage the Germans. A small village, a mere scattering of houses, lay on the near side. No one could be sure of its defenses, but whether strong or weak, they would have to be crushed before engineers could begin work.

Led by Sergeant Rivers, the lead echelon of tanks blazed its way toward the village. Lieutenant Bob Hammond, Rivers's platoon leader, radioed a command to his willful sergeant. "Don't go into that town, Sergeant. It's too hot in there."

Resistance had been stiff but comparatively light. Rivers's tank and two others already occupied the bank of the river.

"Sorry, sir," Rivers's response came, quick as a flash, "I'm already through that town."

The Krauts made a desperate attempt to stop the bridge construction, raining down explosive death in barrages. Using whatever cover they could find, tanks of the 761st lined up all along the river to provide protection for the engineers. The rattle and roar of their 76s reverberated against the lowering sky as they banged away at anything that moved on the other side, gradually establishing fire superiority. Clouds and smoke merged to turn a gray snowy day even drearier.

Sergeant Johnny Holmes's element of Charlie Company plugged in on the line to the left of Able Company. He pulled his tank in behind some bombed-out buildings to concentrate on a snowy knoll on the other side of the river where some thirty or forty Jerries had dug a Texas prairie dog town, out of which holes they popped to lob mortar and machine gun rounds across at the American engineers.

Holmes and his crew raked the knoll with machine guns, chewing at it until it resembled a pile of black mud. Then they threw in HE, further pulverizing the knoll until the surviving rodents jumped out of their burrows and ran toward Guebling. The withdrawal helped relieve pressure on the engineers.

At one point during a lull, Holmes saw Ruben Rivers standing outside his own tank. He had concealed it behind some damaged houses near the bridgehead. He was obviously hurt and in pain. He dragged one leg in a hobble to the corner of the house and looked around it to study the battlefield. Satisfied after locating a source of enemy fire, he labored slowly back to his machine. Someone appeared in the turret to give him a hand back inside. The tank maneuvered to a more advantageous location and leveled down on more targets, pounding away.

That Rivers. That crazy bastard.

Construction of the bridge sped up under the screen of darkness. It was a night so cold that moisture in the air froze and sparkled and snow crunched underfoot. There was a break in the dueling of big guns, as though both sides paused to gird themselves for the main event tomorrow. Captain Williams, as was his custom, paid a visit to each tank in his company. He wanted his men to see him. General Patton always taught that a leader never *pushed* his outfit, he stayed up front and *pulled* it. It would never do for the black men to even *think* any of the remaining white officers would pull a Wingo on them when the going got tough.

Accompanied by two medics, the captain and his driver slipped from building to building, all now abandoned and many irreparably damaged. They found Rivers's tank parked behind a house where it had been all afternoon. Taking advantage of the quiet time, Rivers had pillaged a wicker chair from somewhere and was sitting in it in the snow with his bad leg propped up on the side of his tank to relieve the pain, nibbling half-heartedly on a K-ration.

The medics checked him over. His temperature was spiking at over one hundred degrees.

"His leg's infected," they informed Captain Williams. "He needs to go back to a field hospital."

Williams issued Rivers another direct order. Again, Rivers disobeyed, saying, "Captain, you're going to need me."

39

Staff Sergeant Ruben Rivers found himself . . . with a proud unit in which wounded soldiers would sometimes avoid hospitalization for fear that when healed they would be reassigned to another unit.

—S. H. KELLY, U.S. ARMY PUBLIC AFFAIRS

Braving sporadic enemy fire, engineers completed the Bailey bridge early the next afternoon. Rivers's was one of the first tanks across, leading an onslaught of armor and infantry toward Guebling. The Germans threw everything they had at the attack in a desperate effort to stop it. The whirring and *Wrack! Wrack! Wrack!* of Kraut artillery merged into one continuous roar. The sudden *Hoosh!* of a *Panzerfaust* echoed forever afterward in the sleep of many tank crews. The most heart-stopping sound of all was the wail of the "Moaning Minnie" rocket bombs fired almost simultaneously in clusters from *Nebelwerfers*. These shells were equipped with little sirens that made them scream through the air like Stukas, terrifying enough to drive GIs insane.

A battlefield was a horror-filled, violent, and insane caldron of evil sights, sounds, and odors. Sergeant Rivers, on point, led Able Company and accompanying doughs right down the road toward the town as bogy wheels, tank tracks, helmets, backpacks, rifles, arms, legs, and blood flew in all directions and screams came from everywhere, his engine wound tight and his guns hammering, leaving wispy trails of gunsmoke hanging in the cold air of his passage.

Tanks were not supposed to fight other tanks. They were supposed to bypass any armor, if possible, and attack enemy objectives in the rear. Able Company with Rivers up ahead had no choice, however, but to engage anything that got in the way. A pair of German panzers scuttled out of hiding at the edge of town and commenced firing on Rivers at near-point-blank range. His land battleship hurled back AP and HE and charged directly at the enemy wagon.

"Damn you, don't slow down!" Rivers challenged his driver.

Both sides continued to fire as fast as they could reload. The distance between the stationary panzers and the single charging American Sherman narrowed rapidly. One of the German machines exploded during the exchange. The other stopped firing. Shadowy figures bailed out of it and hightailed it toward their rear.

Able Company's mission was to secure a crossroads on the outskirts and hold it until dawn tomorrow when it could be used as a staging area to resume the attack on the rest of Guebling and the nearby town of Bougeltroff. Rivers reached the cross-roads first and took on a second pair of panzers. They withdrew before either side inflicted damage. However, Rivers's tank struck a mine and became the second knocked out from under him during the current drive.

At 5:00 P.M., he commandeered a Sherman driven by Tech Four Jonathan Hall. His new crew consisted of Hall, PFC Frank Jowers, bow gunner PFC Ivory Hilliard, and Private Everett Robinson, cannoneer.

Fighting continued at a fierce and savage pace in all quadrants of the town. Much of the town was burning. Black smoke sifted soot and ashes on the countryside for miles around. The Germans were indeed putting up a real fight. It looked as though it would last throughout the night as more and more doughboys were fed into the grinder.

At the crossroads, Able Company set up defenses in anticipation of a counterattack. As in most European towns, buildings in city centers lined narrow cobblestone streets like walls. Here on the outskirts residences stood shoulder to shoulder, mostly of stone and plaster with red tile roofs. Nearly every house had a basement or root cellar. Tanks pulled down each street, forming a ring with horns thrust outward like threatened African Cape buffalo.

Sounds of heavy fighting came from the south and from the downtown area. A few mangled corpses, mostly Germans, littered the intersection. The Americans had already removed their losses. There were no lights coming from the houses, no movement; most civilians had evacuated the city ahead of the battle. Those who remained huddled in their cellars and waited for it to be over, praying for the salvation of their homes, possessions, and loved ones. The town was falling to the attackers, but at a terrible cost, and the fees had not yet all been collected. Doughs were taking a terrible beating, and darkness was coming on.

Sleet mixed with snow hissed in the darkening air. A runner

appeared, yelling for Captain Williams. A tanker directed him to the CP.

"Captain Williams? Colonel Lyons from the infantry just lost an eye and a leg. You're in charge."

A captain of armor, a company commander, was the only one left to assume command of an infantry battalion! The doughs must have taken more of a thrashing than anyone expected. Where was Colonel Hunt? Where was *anybody?* It was only a temporary command, a necessity of the moment in the fog of warfare, soon to be rectified, but something had to be done immediately. Battle indeed created strange circumstances.

"All right," Captain Williams said to the runner. "The Krauts are too much for us. Find all the officers and sergeants you can and have them bring their grunts back to the intersection."

The runner was a real bundle of joy. "The Krauts are trying to come around behind us," he said.

"Let them come once we're in the houses and cellars. We can hold them off. Now hurry, man. Get those doughboys back here."

Night slowly settled over the burning city as the infantry, battered and bloody, withdrew out of the town proper and established a defensive position with the tankers around the crossroads. Williams was informed by radio that a major would be dispatched to take command of the doughs but that he wouldn't be available until morning. A tense silence settled around the crossroads as both sides settled down to catch their breath.

Captain Williams and Big Tit Richardson made their customary rounds, taking along medics to treat casualties. Tank wounds, being vehicular, were particularly nasty, even relatively minor ones.

They found Sergeant Rivers in greater pain than ever.

"He's got gangrene," a medic said, changing dressings. "He'll be lucky if he only loses his leg."

"Ruben, I'm giving you another order," Captain Williams said. It was the third time. "Richardson will take you back tonight."

"Captain, you know better than that," Rivers said in that quiet way of his. "Tomorrow's gonna be tough, sir. Another day won't make any difference."

"Ruben . . . damnit!"

Artillery walking down the street, erupting buildings, setting some afire, cratering the street, interrupted further conversation. The breather was over. Jerry was coming and, boy, was he pissed off.

"Sir, I'll be all right. Give me one more day and I'll be going back. I promise."

Who the hell ever thought these black men would not fight?

40

He was fighting mad. He went out there, and it was the last I saw of him.

—CORPORAL KENNETH HAMM

Fighting in Guebling continued throughout the night as both sides held and defended positions. Battle shifted from place to place like a wave, kicking up first in one sector, then dying down only to spring up elsewhere. Parachute flares lit up the dreary urban terrain, exposing awesome and terrible doomsday panoramas.

Colonel Hunt paid Able Company a visit to see how Captain Williams was doing in his temporary command of infantry. Although Hunt was a capable commander, he had failed to establish the same rapport with and win the same loyalty from the

Black Panthers that Colonel Bates enjoyed. He arrived standing up in a half-track, wearing an immaculate woolen uniform.

"Williams, you've had quite a battle here," he commented, looking around.

"Yes, sir."

"Sir, his company really stayed in there," an infantry captain offered.

Able Company had lost a number of tanks and suffered quite a few WIA (wounded in action). The doughs had bled even more.

"Colonel, I want to put Sergeant Rivers in for the Congressional Medal of Honor," Williams said.

"What did he do? He's got the Silver Star already."

"Sir, that was for November 8."

Colonel Hunt expressed little interest in the conversation going further. It was generally acknowledged among white officers that black soldiers were not to be recommended for awards higher than the Silver Star, commonly called the "Battalion Commander's Good Conduct Medal." The reasoning went that any outfit with an "N" for "Negro" in its designation didn't deserve anything higher.

"Sir, he destroyed at least two enemy tanks and his crew has killed over three hundred Germans. He's wounded but won't leave his men."

Colonel Hunt lifted an eyebrow. "Well, put it in writing," he relented, although it was clear he still had little interest.

Captain Williams went to see Rivers once more as tension built in anticipation of the renewed attack at dawn. Rivers still refused to abandon the field.

Daylight slowly arrived, cold and frosty with thin crusts of sleet over snow in those few places that hadn't been trampled or shelled. Reinforcements of infantry, artillery, and tanks from 4th Armor filtered in from the fog to the staging area. Sergeant Rivers's platoon leader, Lieutenant Bob Hammond, awoke from a brief catnap and looked out the turret of his tank to where fog eddied and oozed in a vacant field of hedgerows in the direction of surrounding farmland. Things had been comparatively quiet for the past hour.

As he looked, he became aware of something moving in the fog, something large and indistinct but whose rumbling sound signature he recognized immediately. His spine seemed to turn to ice.

"Tigers!" he cried.

The *Jagdtiger* was the heaviest of Hitler's armor, a monster armed with the fearsome 128mm SPA gun and two MG-34 machine guns. As Hammond and his gunner, Tech Five Roderick Ewing, attempted to unlimber their 76mm, the Tigers belched flame that seemed to scorch light out of the morning.

Hammond's wagon detonated like a match as the round impacted the gun sight and twisted the turret nearly off its mount. Hammond and Ewing died instantly, their bodies burned and torn.

Staff Sergeant Teddy Weston raced forward to counterfire, but his tank likewise took a disabling blow. His crew dismounted and ran toward the crossroads and out of range.

German antitank positions concealed on the far side of a slope beyond the hedgerows lit up the gray morning sky. Barrages of explosions stomped all over and around the intersection. German Mark IV panzers and *Panzerjaegers* rumbled out of the fog to join the attack initiated by the Tigers, an awesome sight that seemed to be generated by something evil in the mist. The German juggernaut caught a number of tanks and doughboys in the open.

"Pull back, pull back, Panthers!" Williams radioed, seeing what was left of his company about to be dismantled.

"I see them. We'll fight them!" Rivers responded.

His tank darted from cover, side by side with the Sherman commanded by Sergeant Walter James. Outnumbered and outgunned, the two iron steeds charged, diverting the German onslaught long enough for the Americans caught in the open to withdraw and regroup.

Captain Williams shouted into his radio, trying to turn the tanks back before it was too late. "Move back, Rivers!"

Rivers and James smashed through the hedgerows and up the slope toward the enemy, all guns blazing, like jousters on steel mounts. For a few moments, the American Shermans held their own. They seemed to exist in a charmed atmosphere as they tore furiously through fiery blasts of light and smoke and as brilliant tracers of green light bounced off their thick hides.

Then a shell caught Rivers's tank and cracked it like an eggshell.

"Pull up, driver! Pull back, driver! Oh, Lord!"

Those were Rivers's last words. A second AP shell finished the job. It struck the turret, almost ripping Rivers's body into two parts. Blood gushed into the crew compartment as the survivors quit the vehicle. Gunner Ivory Hilliard, who also occupied the turret as gunner, was so disoriented from the concussion and his own injuries that when he hit the ground he took off running in the wrong direction, toward Kraut lines. That was the last anyone saw of him alive.

Seeing his mate tank destroyed and therefore coming to his senses, Sergeant James scurried his tank back to the crossroads, whose defenders were already laying down a field of fire and calling in artillery support. Rivers's tank continued to smoke and smolder out there on the field of battle for the rest of the day as American forces rallied, repelled the attack, and secured Guebling.

The Black Panther who would not quit was now dead.

KIA (Killed in Action)
Lieutenant Robert C. Hammond, Jr.
Staff Sergeant Ruben Rivers
Tech Five Roderick Ewing
Private Ivory V. Hilliard

41

Ruben Rivers did not have to die on that cold, dreary
November morning in France.

—JOE WILSON, JR.

Telegrams bearing bitter news about sons and fathers often arrived at a home about the time a family gathered in a warm, bright kitchen for supper. There would be the older generation, perhaps, grandfather and grandma, and the wives, the sisters, the younger boys eager to grow up and go to war, too. Maybe they would be reading out loud a letter received only that day from the front. And then, a knock on the door. The telegrams always sounded impersonal and to the point. *The secretary of war desires me to express his deep regret . . .*

Colonel Hollis Hunt wrote a personal letter to Ruben Rivers's family, as commanders did to the families of all their men killed in action.

"I know only too well that words cannot bring comfort to your aching heart in these hours of loss. However, as your son's battalion commander, I want to tell you that all of us who remain in this battalion grieve with you in the loss of our comrade.

"Your son, Staff Sergeant Ruben Rivers, was killed in action on 19 November 1944 during our attack on Guebling, France. He was buried in the province of Lorraine, France, after an appropriate service at which a Protestant chaplain officiated. You may secure more detailed information concerning the location of the grave and the disposal of your son's remains and effects by communicating directly with the Quartermaster General, Army Service Forces, Washington 25, D.C.

"He did his duty splendidly and was loved and admired by all who knew him. We will not forget.

"He gave his life in the service of his country and these simple words cannot lighten your sorrow, but they bring great pride and inspiration to us all.—LTC Hollis Hunt, Commanding 761st Tank Battalion (N)."

42

We didn't destroy their stuff, although I can't swear
that troops didn't steal a few items.

—CAPTAIN PHIL LATIMER

Chow, as might be expected, was the highlight of a GI's day; a day offered few other highlights. Field kitchens were hauled around in the backs of deuce-and-a-half trucks traveling with HQ. The mess section tried to turn out at least one hot meal every day, providing conditions were favorable. Usually that meal was a breakfast consisting of powdered eggs the consistency of soft rubber, cold pancakes, or what the cooks called, with no irony intended, "French toast." E. G. McConnell, Big Tit Richardson, and Joe Kiah, or some other similar trio, would squint, examine a piece from all angles, and engage in a conversation of mocking solemnity. The black men of the 761st always tried to find humor in an otherwise dangerous and bleak environment.

"What do you suppose it is?" one would ask.

"It ain't alive. It sure looks like it be dead for a long time."

"I been missing the sole off my boot for damn near a week. I bet if you look, half the brothers ain't got no soles left. Them cooks been sneaking around stealing 'em for breakfast."

It was often difficult for the kitchens to serve everyone in the battalion because companies and platoons of the 761st were frequently farmed out separately to various infantry units. At those times when hot chow was served, however, the lucky tankers—or *unlucky*, according to how the fare was viewed—picked an area a few hundred yards back from the front lines and designated it as a chow site. The kitchen set up and began mixing, frying, and baking.

Groups of tankers would rush back with their canteen cups and tin mess kits, pilfered silverware stuck in the straps of their combat boots, and load up with food and a cup of black coffee heavy with the taste of chlorine. If the tankers couldn't make it back to the "messhall," carrying parties in Jeeps brought hot food forward in insulated Mermac containers.

Rain, sleet, and snow often made eating a challenge, as it did everything else. It made mud and slop and cold wet clothing. It disintegrated C-ration toilet paper in a GI's pocket when he needed it most. It was hard to eat in an icy drizzle.

"Shi-it!" exploded Sergeant George Riley in disgust, glaring at the watered-down mess on his tin plate. Powdered mashed potatoes going liquid, slab of Spam with the salt and glaze washed off, biscuits melting into everything else, all laced in a thin rind of sleet ice.

He dumped his mess kit in the mud and fished a "dog turd" from his field coveralls. Nothing, not winter rains or the fires of hell, could melt or alter the D-bar, a hard bitter-chocolate survival candy designed primarily for when there was no other food. The brothers claimed it went in one end and came out the other in the same shape—a dog turd.

Nonetheless, tankers were more fortunate than the grunt doughboys. They had the opportunity and the wheels to drive back to HQ where a real mess tent was set up, complete with

chow line, *tables,* and honest-to-God hot coffee. The only thing
to mar such an idyllic setting were the dirty Krauts, who, likely
as not, chose chow time to shell the area. The tankers were sure
it was deliberate.

One afternoon as some of the tankers sat down in the mess
tent for a rare meal of leisure, they heard the whirring clatter of
a shell coming through the air.

"Incoming mail!"

Diners broke for the door to seek cover. Battalion Sergeant
Major Bob Jenkins danced aside to let Major Russell Geist, the
white battalion executive officer, precede him.

"After you, sir," he cracked.

Lieutenant James Lightfoot of Mortars and Pop Gates of Assault Guns hit the mess tent door simultaneously. Pop Gates was
a former physical education instructor in Kansas City, Missouri,
and had been a most valuable player with the Hampton Insti-
tute football squad. Yet the much frailer Lightfoot bowled him
out of the way. Pop later commented that it was the most perfect block he had seen in all his years in football.

Usually, however, chow in the rear offered a respite, however
brief, from the horror and stress of combat. It gave men time to
chill out, to smoke and joke and try to forget, to sit around after
a meal with a cup of coffee and a cigarette. Almost everyone
smoked. Cigarettes came four to a pack in field rations. Willie
Devore burned up four packs a day.

"Hell's bells," he said darkly. "Maybe if I'm lucky I'll smoke
myself to death before the Krauts get me."

The men sat around and talked of what they would do when
they got back home, where the pretty girls were learning to jit-
terbug and sing songs like "Deep Purple," where families were
feasting on fresh buttermilk and cornbread, fried chicken, pinto
beans, and taters.

"Not *this* garbage," Corporal Kenneth Hamm moaned.

Henry Conway laughed. "Eat your garbage, Hamm. People
in China is starving."

"So am I."

One of the men scavenged up some alcohol. Canteen cups rattled as they mixed in a little corn syrup and water to dilute and stretch the amount so everyone could have some. They drank in hearty gulps. Faces flushed. Looking more alive than before. Kidding each other in the dark humor of combat soldiers.

Motel Johnson pursed his lips and went prissy as he mock-imitated Sergeant Crecy's wife, teasing Crecy by pretending to try on a fur coat.

"How does I look, honey buns?" he cooed in a falsetto voice, grabbing his "boyfriend" Milton Dorsey's arm. "Ain't I just so pretty? I been wanting me a mink fur coat for a long time. I knows how I gonna spend ole Harding's ten-thousand-dollar life insurance if he don't come home. Now, honey, where to you taking me out to dinner tonight?"

Crecy adjusted his glasses and chuckled along with everyone else.

Whenever they had an opportunity, they boiled water and washed the mud and filth out of their OD-issue, lighting up gasoline in fifty-gallon drums to get warm while they waited for their clothes to dry. Sergeant Floyd Dade and Steven Reed passed a football around. Dade got cold and stood next to the burning drum to warm up. Reed chunked the football at him. It landed square in the fuel, splashing flames on Dade and setting him ablaze.

He shouted in alarm but retained wit enough to throw himself to the ground to roll in the mud and snow. Someone ran to get a blanket with which to extinguish him. The others laughed when they saw he hadn't been seriously burned.

"Sergeant Dade, think you might want to fricassee yourself again?" E. G. McConnell asked. "I don't think everybody seen it the first time."

"Screw all'a you perverts."

Hot chow, hot coffee, a warm fire, and stimulating conversation were luxuries not always available. Most of the time the men had to make do with field rations. There were three types—C-rations, K-rations, and 10-N-1-rations.

A C-ration box contained two cans and an accessory pack. One can held the main course, such as frankfurters and beans ("fuckers and beans"), spaghetti and meatballs, macaroni and cheese, beef stew, pork slices and potatoes, corned beef hash, or ham and eggs. The other can contained either fruit or a cake. The accessory pack provided crackers, peanut butter or jelly, cheese, instant coffee, sugar, salt, toilet paper, candy, and four cigarettes—Chesterfields, Camels, *or* Lucky Strike Greens. Since the contents of each box were marked on the top, sergeants opened the cases upside down to give everyone an equal chance at getting the better meals. The hungrier the soldier, the better a C tasted, although it was a constant complaint that the chow would get him before the Germans did.

An empty C-can made an excellent little stove, too. The lid was peeled back and vents cut, after which the bottom was filled with pine needles and gasoline and set afire. A canteen cup with food to be heated fit nicely on top. The stove also provided enough warmth to take the chill off the faces and hands of the tankers who huddled around it.

K-rations weighed less and were easier to carry, since they came in a box like a small cigar box. They were marked as B, L, or D, for breakfast, lunch or dinner, and contained mixtures of foodstuffs that GIs insisted weren't always identifiable by either taste, sight, or smell. Like the Cs, they provided accessories of instant coffee or cocoa, toilet paper, four cigarettes, matches, sugar, and a dog turd. A hot meal of sorts could be had by heating the flat main menu can on the burning paraffin-coated box. GIs claimed Ks were edible if you were hungry enough. Like starving. "Here, now you hold the gun on me while I eat."

Corporal Milton Dorsey, driver for Supply's Captain Phil Latimer, broke open a K that contained cold, greasy potted meat. He hunched over the top of the can to shield it from sleet and rain. He heard tanks booming away out there on the forward line. Nearby lay a dead Jerry sprawled on the road. The guy's decaying face reminded Dorsey of the contents of his lunch. He looked at the greasy mess in his can, he looked at the Kraut. He gagged but dug in anyhow. He was hungry.

"Stay down, you greasy bastard," he murmured after each bite.

The 10-N-1-rations, a cardboard box containing meals for ten men—usually Spam or corned beef—were all but worthless for infantrymen, who often had to eat on the run. The 10-N-1s required a fire to make them remotely edible. They were also bulky and very difficult to carry. Tankers, therefore, and rear-echelon types who had room to carry them were usually the only ones to enjoy the treat. But since tankers often raced ahead of their supply lines, 10-N-1s were not exactly standard fare for them, either.

Soldiers throughout history have always been shameless scavengers, depending on the countryside and the local populations to supplement their normal spare diets. The American soldier was no different. The average dough or tanker saw indigents as fair game for anything edible, part of the rightful spoils of war. Even though the French also suffered—one day tankers saw a toddler trying to nurse from his dead mother—GIs were not above liberating some eggs, fresh meats, or vegetables as they passed through. They often left behind in more or less fair exchange their own unwanted rations. French civilians always seemed overjoyed with the bargain, or perhaps they were just grateful not to lose everything.

One day, Sergeant Isiah Parks, a TC in Charlie Company, liberated a nice fat hen while another Charlie TC, Sergeant Daniel "Club Foot" Cardell, took a young rooster so black its feathers shone. They tied the legs of the fowl together to keep them from flopping around inside the tanks and carried them until the company bivouacked that evening. Some of the men grabbed the hen and chopped off her head with a bayonet while they teased Parks about almost being caught by the farmer whose henhouse he and Cardell raided.

"I don't s'pect he was gonna be nearly as understanding about catching foxy ole Isiah and Dan in his chickens as the English farmer was when he caught Ruben and Willie and them in his cornfield," Johnny Holmes said, guffawing.

They settled down to fixing supper, fire crackling, kettle of water boiling, plucked, dismembered chicken in the kettle already on its way to making a delicious stew, everything quiet and appetite-expectant except for the muffled boom of distant artillery. They licked their lips and waited, canteen cups in hand. It wouldn't be long now.

A whine and a scream in the air announced the approach of an 88. Tankers scrambled and dove for cover. As bad luck would have it, the shell landed directly in the pot of chicken, blowing everything to Kingdom Come and leaving nothing but a smoldering crater in the ground.

Isiah walked up to the crater, stuffed his hands deep into his pockets, and regarded the scene of devastation with the utmost sadness. Sergeant Holmes cast a hungry eye toward Cardell's black rooster, for whom the TC was building a small coop out of some scrap net wire he had found.

"Don't cast them greedy eyes of yours in this direction," Cardell warned. "This fine black gentleman is our new mascot."

"A *chicken?*"

"Huh-uh. A *Cool Stud* chicken." The next day *Cool Stud* would appear painted on the side of Cardell's tank as its new name.

Isiah continued to stare at the crater.

"Shi-it. This war really sucks, you know that? I could almost taste that chicken—"

43

Beast that sleeps on the other side of the Rhine.

—FRENCH DESCRIPTION OF GERMANY

After World War I ended, France vowed never again to let Germany violate its territory. Toward this goal, the country began construction of the "Maginot Line" in 1930. This network of forts, blockhouses, pillboxes, and other defensive obstacles stretched 150 miles along the French-German border from Sedan in the west to beyond Wessembourg in the east.

It consisted of powerful artillery works built four miles apart. In the spaces between were smaller works, such as pillboxes designed for machine guns, mortars, and smaller artillery pieces, all of which were reinforced by a gridwork of trenches, shelters, and antitank and antitroop defenses. Barracks, headquarters, ammunition rooms, and other vital resources needed to support life were buried deeply in the ground, virtually impervious to enemy infiltration. Underground rail trolleys transported troops between their elaborate barracks and heavily fortified combat bunkers.

The strongest part of the line lay in Lorraine Province, with the walled region of Metz being the most formidable. Here, eleven artillery works and seven infantry works had been built along a twenty-seven-mile front.

The Maginot Line was still under construction in May 1940 when panzer and Wehrmacht forces under the command of General Gerd von Rundstedt attacked France. The German invasion simply went around the line and penetrated France through the Ardennes Forest. It then turned toward the North

Sea and charged Boulogne and Calais, encircling French and English forces and setting them to flight.

The French high command began evacuating the Maginot Line on June 15, 1940.

Now, four and a half years later, Germans occupied the Maginot Line to defend their Reichland from invasion. In November and December 1944, Patton's Third Army swept through Lorraine on its way toward Metz and the strongest point of German defenses along the Maginot Line.

44

Get me out of this and I will be a better, decent person.

—Sergeant Johnny Holmes, making deal with God

Captain David Williams's Able Company bivouacked in a picturesque French village. Its inhabitants had deserted it even though the village had seen relatively little fighting and remained largely intact. Footfalls echoed along the cobblestone streets, the way they did late at night when everyone had gone to bed and left the town empty.

Snow began falling at daybreak. The previous snow had melted during several past days of sunshine, so the new snow dusted everything lightly with fresh, clean cover. Corporal Walter Lewis, shoulders hunched into his field jacket against the subfreezing weather, pounded on the door of a dry goods store

Captain Williams had commandeered for his CP and attached sleeping quarters.

"What's happening, Walter?" Williams asked sleepily.

"Sir, it's Sunday. The men are having a memorial service at the church. We'd like you to come."

Sergeant Eddie Donald always said Captain Williams was the blackest white man he had ever known. Leadership had more to do with trust and respect than it did skin color. What the company had endured welded the men permanently together.

The church was ancient and constructed of gray stone worn smooth over the centuries. It had probably been ancient when Columbus set sail to find a faster route to India. Its weathered spire stuck up from a lot studded with rows of equally ancient tombstones.

Williams, Lewis, and Big Tit Richardson propped their weapons in the vestibule just inside the doorway, where they could reach them if necessary but where they would not intrude in the House of God. A number of other weapons had already established the site as a convenient armory. Tankers filled the little church's worn wooden bench rows. Every head was bowed, the only sound the murmuring of prayers and quiet weeping. Williams's was the only white face.

Williams's Negro soldiers, he had discovered, were deeply spiritual beings, as men must be to survive times terrible enough to wither the unprotected soul. Death feckless and indiscriminate became a constant companion to the living. The truth of that could be seen in German corpses lying where they had fallen, bloating up like blackened balloons before bursting and slowly drying out to skin stretched over broken bones. Men awoke from every catnap or few hours' sleep wondering if they would make it through the day or the rest of the night, or if they would join the world of the corpses. Prayer and the belief that a benevolent God listened and cared gave them a crutch to lean on in battle. It helped comfort them and preserve their collective sanity in a world where one rule prevailed: kill or be killed.

The men divided themselves roughly into three groups: those like Willie Devore who had decided they were going to die; those like E. G. McConnell who hoped to make it through; and the rest who didn't know one way or the other and were often so burned out they didn't care anymore. Whichever category they fell in, however, a common thought haunted them whenever they saw a comrade or one of the doughs struck down: *Thank God, better him than me.* The thought then made them feel guilty, and they carried that guilt around with them as an additional burden. *Why him and not me? Could I have done something to save him?*

God helped by sharing the burden.

There was no formal service, no minister or lay preacher leading the congregation. It was merely a quiet collection of black soldiers and one white soldier, all bedraggled and muddy and ripe with the odors of combat, confined together inside an old church, each communing with God in his own way.

Williams and Corporal Richardson sat next to Walter Lewis on the first row of benches. The captain bowed his head and felt a quiet sense of peace descend upon him. From his heart he thanked God for his Negro tankers, their loyalty and brotherhood, their deep humanity. He prayed for those in Able Company and in the battalion who had fallen in battle. He asked God to look out for them and not judge them by their skin color as they had been judged on earth.

He wondered if souls *had* color.

He thought of First Sergeant Sam Turley and how heroically Sam died holding out at the antitank ditch so his men could escape. How Turley had been kind to him when he arrived at Camp Claiborne as a fresh, green lieutenant—and how they both were transferred to the 761st partly because a white officer and a black noncom shook hands.

He thought about the gentle and sensitive Lieutenant Kenneth Coleman and of the stoic and fearless Ruben Rivers. Of Sergeant Roy "Love" King, who had died trying to save the life of a white infantryman. Of Clifford Adams, the first of them to die on the first day of combat. Of Sergeant Crecy's best friend Horatio Scott, whose death transformed Crecy into a cold killing machine. Of Roderick Ewing, who, like Rivers, was from Oklahoma and had been a wonderful baseball player. Of Ivory Hilliard running in pain and blind panic toward enemy lines the day his tank was hit in Guebling. What must have been his last thoughts as he died in an enemy's ditch?

He prayed for the souls of all the others, men he had known through Louisiana and Texas and England and France: L. C. Byrd, Harvey Woodward, Willie Lofton, Nathaniel Simmons, Alex Anderson, George Shivers . . .

Lord, there were so many of them. So many.

He prayed for the wounded who had lost arms, hands, legs, and feet, or pieces of their souls. Prayed that they would recover and be sent home rather than back to the front. The depleted ranks of the Black Panthers needed them, but their families needed them more. They had sacrificed their share of flesh and blood.

He wondered about Sergeant Johnnie Stevens and where he might now be plying his defiant, confident swagger. A white soldier died saving him when he was hit. Why weren't black men and white men able to get along like that off the battlefield?

He wondered how Lieutenant William Blake was doing. A building had fallen on him during the shelling and fighting at Morville. Although seriously wounded, the young lieutenant regained consciousness and crawled on his belly through the rubble of dangerous streets to reach the command post and deliver a vital message with which he had been entrusted.

He prayed for Colonel Bates. "Lord, we need him back with us, if you deem it fitting."

Then he prayed that the remaining black tankers would make it through the war, even though he realized God surely had His own plans and that there would be more to die before this thing ended.

He lifted his head and looked around at the reverent black

men with their heads bowed in the dim gray light of morning suffusing through the stained-glass windows. Tears of pride and humility and of sorrow filled his eyes. He no longer saw skin color; skin color didn't matter. Any barriers that might have existed between him and them had fallen when the first shots were fired. They were as one body.

This single small company of black soldiers was rising above the nightmare of segregation at home to prove themselves men among men in the deadliest manhood rite ever devised. As Captain Williams left the church, he knew deep inside his soul that among these black men he was also finding his own manhood. He hoped, he prayed, that his courage would equal theirs in the even more trying and difficult days ahead.

He remembered something Sam Turley once said. "Cap'n, courage ain't nothing more than being scared and saying your prayers."

Captain Williams had said his prayers.

45

I kill as many Germans as I can because I hate the whole Nazi system.

—SERGEANT WARREN G. H. CRECY

Life on the Western Front was often short, cheap, difficult, and brutal. Snow melted during the day to expose burned German corpses looking like twisted charcoal mannequins strewn about in grotesque positions, littering fields on both sides of the roads. Small personal items lay among the dead—photos, wedding rings, letters, coins, a broken pipe . . . pathetic reminders of better times. On warmer days, the awful sweet sickening stench of rotted flesh polluted the air.

"How many you kilt today, brother?" someone asked Sergeant Harding Crecy.

The mild-looking little sergeant didn't so much as blink. "Twenty-five. I made a promise to Scotty to kill as many as I can." Not boasting, simply stating facts. "When I kill the motherfuckers I like to look right in their eyes. I like to see them drop. When they drop I can almost see a picture of my dead brothers smiling at me."

Tanker combat meant constant movement, spearheading for the doughs and providing fire support. When tanks had to pull back out of the fray to get more fuel and ammo, crews learned of other tanks that had been hit and friends maimed. Then they rushed back and fought some more.

Men honored an unspoken contract to look out for one another, to die for one another if necessary, to adhere to Patton's admonishment not to let their race down. Black tankers would have said *Kiss my ass* if ordered to charge across a field to die for President Roosevelt or anyone else not a member of the battalion or the doughs they supported. But there were no limits to what they would do for each other.

First Sergeant Bob Linzy of Charlie Company refused to stay in the rear and handle paperwork and the details of running a company. An eighteen-year veteran of the Regular Army, he chose instead to go to the front as a tank crew member of Teddy Weston's platoon.

The sooner they got the job done—staying in one piece, they hoped—the sooner they could all go home.

Towns fell one by one to the ruthless advance of the Third Army. Patton's Panthers continued spearheading with the 4th Armored Division for the 26th Infantry. Demolished German tanks, half-tracks, vehicles, self-propelled guns, some of which still burned, littered the roadsides as Krauts either were smoked or fled.

The American juggernaut crushed through German defenses to take Saint Suzanne Farms, Marimont, Guenestroff, Guebestroff, Ergaville, so many that one soon lost track and the names ran together, heading for the Maginot Line.

Yank magazine reported that Command A of the 4th Armored Division seized the town of Dieuze. Trezzvant Anderson, the Panthers' own correspondent, contested the assertion. He reported to his Negro newspaper base that Lieutenant Pop Gates's Assault Guns Platoon of the 761st battered Dieuze into submission, after which the Panthers were told to stand down while the all-white 4th Armored "took" the objective.

"They just want to show the *white* boys in the news," Sergeant Johnny Holmes grumbled. "They don't want no niggers as heroes."

Lieutenant Irvin "The Burner" McHenry's Charlie Company entered Torcheville unopposed, then traversed more than twenty miles of Forest de Koecking to Benestroff, a railhead. The town collapsed after a terrific tank shelling. A French woman waving a white flag walked out to the edge of town, after which the Germans either withdrew or surrendered.

Beyond lay the towns of Munster and Honskirch, a junction point for highways going in all directions. Charlie Company moved in to occupy a portion of Munster. Tankers and infantry attacked and counterattacked for fifty-one hours in vicious house-to-house and room-to-room fighting. Artillery barrages falling on this important communications center, a natural gateway to the even more important center at Honskirch, reduced it to smoldering rubble.

By all indications, Honskirch promised to be another Morville or Guebling. Two small streams whose bridges had been blown separated Munster from Honskirch. To reach the town, American forces had to ford the streams on hastily erected Bailey bridges and travel through the right edge of the

Forest de Givrycourt. Enemy armor, artillery, and mortars occupied posts in strength in high ground timber on the left side of the road. The town itself was reported to be "teeming with enemy armor," beyond which lay more high ground to provide Krauts a commanding view and an open field of fire against all approach routes. The Germans apparently intended to fight with everything they had to hold the town.

Sergeant Horace Evans, TC Eddie Donald's gunner and "secret weapon," came down with a nervous stomach and diarrhea just thinking about Honskirch. Willie Devore seemed gloomier than ever.

46

You were just gun fodder, really.

—LIEUTENANT CHARLES "POP" GATES

The snow had melted, and now Lieutenant Pop Gates stood in a cold driving rain looking down the narrow gray road to Honskirch, shoulders hunched in that stubborn way he had whenever he disliked or disapproved of something. Colonel Hunt had turned command of Charlie Company over to Lieutenant Gates after Lieutenant McHenry broke his wrist at Munster from a cannon recoil.

North breezes tugged at the ends of Gates's wet-slick poncho, like a dog seeking attention. A white regimental commander, a full colonel from the 26th Division, stood next to him, also looking down the road but obviously not seeing it in the same way.

"With all due respect, sir," Gates protested, "this is the dumbest damn thing I've ever heard of."

The colonel's face flushed red. He wasn't accustomed to being questioned by subordinates, especially not by *Negro* subordinates who were supposed to keep their mouths shut, follow orders, and die if they were told to.

"I didn't ask your opinion, Lieutenant Gates."

"No, sir. But I'd be derelict in my duty to my men if I didn't give it."

"I don't give a rat's ass about your 'derelict,' Lieutenant," the white colonel snapped. "We're ordered to take Honskirch, and that's what we're going to do."

Gates controlled his temper with an effort. To send tanks in file down that road on the attack, when they couldn't get *off* the road because of timber and obstacles, defied all rules of good tactics. The regimental commander either didn't give a shit or didn't know any better. Word around said he had been a finance officer, a rear echelon commando, until some idiot who didn't give a rat's ass about getting soldiers killed sent him to the front to command an infantry regiment.

Where was General Patton when you needed him? It wasn't unusual for him to relieve incompetent people on the spot. Where, for that matter, was Colonel Hunt? Colonel Bates would have been all over this man.

Lieutenant Gates patiently pointed out to the colonel various major German defenses, all of which should have been clearly recognizable to any experienced military man: the high forested ground to the left of the road, more forest on the right; additional fortified hills that overlooked the town from the rear; the road approaching Honskirch running in the open directly below all that high ground and under German guns. The tanks would be caught on open terrain and bottle-necked. What kind of an idiot would send men into a trap like that? What kind of an *idiot . . . ?*

"Sir, it's suicide for my company to charge down that road,"

Pop Gates argued. "It's poorly organized to attack like this. It's not an effective way to use tanks. We won't make it halfway there."

"*I'm* the one who decides that, Lieutenant Gates. Mortars and artillery will take care of the Germans. You get your men ready to go, mister."

"Yassuh, yassuh," Gates acceded, pouring on the cotton field accent.

The colonel twisted on his heels and stormed off, leaving Gates alone gazing down the road to Honskirch. Rain in sheets slanted across his vision, brightening the macadam road so that anything on it stood out like cockroaches on white porcelain. Tendrils and snarls of early morning fog mixed with smoke from earlier mortar bombardments oozed out of the menacing high ground forest and seemed to sneak and curl among the trees on either side of the road, like ambushers.

The colonel thought shelling would weaken the Germans and destroy their resolve to fight. Gates knew better. He had been up since 0200 hours when the battalion's 81mm Mortar Platoon went to work in the dark. Due to enemy minefields, the terrain, and the weather, the gunners were unable to operate from half-tracks. Instead, they had had to set off on foot in the dark, slogging through mud with gun tubes on their shoulders and ammo in sacks in order to get within range of Honskirch and its defenses. The batteries had been firing in continuous waves ever since, banging away for fifteen minutes at a time, then a lull like the one in which Lieutenant Gates had had his conversation with the regimental colonel.

The mortars were at it again now, along with heavier artillery, prepping the target. A deep red glow from fires in the town reflected ominously against the lowering cloud cover.

Even as Pop Gates studied his intended route of attack with growing trepidation, Germans retaliated with a ten-minute pounding of Panther mortar positions. The whine and whir and scream of enemy mortars, 88s, and Moaning Minnies preceded the terrifying *Wrack! Wrack!* when the rounds impacted. Five men of the Assault Guns Platoon, which Gates had previously commanded, were wounded and evacuated.

The Krauts had plenty of venom left. More significantly, they were undoubtedly saving most of their bite for when the attack began.

Pop Gates would never send men to their deaths; he would lead them. He was determined to wait as long as he could, however, hoping the Paddy finance colonel would realize his error of judgment before it was too late and come to his senses. All he could think to do was resort to the old slave methods of his Deep South ancestors when they disliked the master's orders— delay, drag feet, delay some more, make excuses, bumble around, delay some more . . .

The finance colonel returned, hopping mad.

"Lieutenant, this is a direct order," he shouted in Gates's face. "Stop dragging your ass. I want those goddamned tanks on that road in ten minutes. Is there anything about this you don't understand?"

"No, sir. But I've told you what will happen."

He took a last look down the bright road. The road to hell was paved as much with ignorance and arrogance as with good intentions.

47

Dear Moms . . .

—CORPORAL E. G. MCCONNELL

Corporal E. G. McConnell dreamed the night before Honskirch that he was going to be hit and killed. Now promoted to corporal, he had left the relative safety of HQ to volunteer for forward duty as a tank crewman, filling in for a wounded man in Charlie Company. The dream was so vivid that he felt flames searing into his flesh and smelled burning gasoline and oil, heard brother tankers screaming and crying. He awoke in a cold sweat, trembling in his sleeping bag while rain and sleet pattered on the canvas roof of his pup tent. This, he thought, must be the way it was every day with Willie Devore. It had to be a special kind of hell to go through each day knowing you *were* going to be killed but not knowing the precise hour and place of death.

He rolled over to his side and held a flashlight close to his diary to make a final entry to his mother. *Moms, I may not be coming home. If I don't, know I love you and I'll be waiting for you on the other side . . .* He read a comforting passage from his prayer book, prayed, and went back to sleep.

The feeling of impending doom remained with him the next dawn on the road to Honskirch. Lieutenant Pop Gates had tapped Lieutenant Thomas Bruce's platoon to lead the assault and ordered it forward to wait at a crossroads kickoff point for further word. A French pub and a couple of rock-and-mortar houses sat abandoned at the crossroads.

While they were waiting, E.G. and some of the other tankers entered the pub's dim interior, hoping it would be warmer and dryer inside. The room was full of storm troopers. E.G. dived for cover, swinging his grease gun around for action before he noticed the Krauts weren't moving.

Someone exhaled in loud astonishment. "Jesus God!"

E.G. stared. The Germans were all dead. A half-dozen of them. The tankers had seen corpses before. Nothing unusual about that anymore. What made this scene eerily different was the way most of them had died. It reminded E.G. of Harvey Woodward's "Ghost Tank" at Morville where all hands had expired in their buttoned-up tank, and not one of them bore obvious injuries.

The pub seemed hardly damaged at all. The proprietor was nowhere in sight, but bottles and glasses remained undisturbed on the bar. Half the German dead lay on the floor, where they had bled very little, but it was the one table that attracted all eyes. Three uniformed Krauts were seated at it, almost as though in the middle of an all-night poker game. Two had their heads down on their arms, resting, while the third was reared back in his chair with his legs straightened underneath the table, chin resting on his chest and his eyes wide and staring directly at E.G., accusing him. Their glasses hadn't even been knocked over.

Rain beating on the roof contributed to the surreal atmosphere of another of war's little mysteries. E.G. had no heart to try to explain it. Let God take care of it.

"I'd rather be standing in the rain," he said, leaving.

For nearly four hours, until about midmorning, Lieutenant Bruce's platoon and the rest of Charlie Company a few hundred yards back waited anxiously for orders to advance. No one knew what was going on. To keep busy, McConnell, a mechanic and trained in armaments, gave his tank an overall inspection. To his surprise he found the cannon had jammed in recoil. Its malfunction in combat could have been fatal for the crew. He repaired it.

The discovery made him feel as though he had rooted out

and thwarted death as revealed to him in his dream. Maybe it was God's way of telling him He had changed His mind about calling E.G. home.

48

The thing I told him would happen, did.

—LIEUTENANT CHARLES "POP" GATES

D eathly quiet settled over the soggy countryside as Lieutenant Bruce's platoon set off in single file leading Charlie Company down the bright road to Honskirch, the attack no longer possible to delay. Watchful and apprehensive, his nerves taut, Able Company's CO, Lieutenant Pop Gates, rode the lead tank with TC Tech Five Lane Dunn from Kentucky. Radios had gone silent. Everything that needed to be said had already passed through the platoon. Five, six, eight, ten, twelve tanks strung out on the road like little mechanical ducks at a county fair shooting gallery. Infantry trotted along behind the tanks, using them for cover, or they spread out in the woods and fields to either side.

The rain slacked off to a miserable spitting drizzle of mixed sleet and snow. Forest and mud prevented tanks from leaving the road, kept them channeled into what Pop Gates considered a kill zone. Fog and smoke snarled around the dark monsters, the big white-now-gray stars on their sides blending with the color of the sky. Thudding engines throbbed against the fringing forest, the sound absorbed quickly into the stillness after abrupt and distant echoes. Even the artillery had hushed, waiting until the attack formation reached Phase Line before starting up again.

The assault elements failed to reach Phase Line.

Lieutenant Gates was dazed but not surprised when the Germans opened up with everything in their arsenal and caught the Americans in the open. He knew it was going to happen.

Exploding shells in volleys first struck the road in front of the lead tank occupied by Gates, halting the procession. More shells vibrated the air, passing over to land on and around rear tanks to prevent retreat. The world turned upside down. High explosives hammering the road and its convoy of infantry and vehicles created instant chaos, confusion, and terror. Shrapnel, bolts of fire, tank treads, rifles, packs, smoke, bloody portions of bodies filled the air with unearthly sights and sounds and smells. Tanks caught in the deadly crossfire were smashed, broken, and erupting in flames all along the road, the attack having turned into a bloody disaster before it even got started. Shrieks and moans and cries of fright filled the smoke-laden air.

Communications went spastic. Everyone tried to get on the air at the same time, yelling, screaming, shouting orders, requesting orders . . .

Throwing AP in here . . .

Can't move up . . .

My God, they got 'em, they got 'em . . .

Cover road to the left front . . .

Fire on that wall . . .

They got a gun dug in, firing through the trees . . .

Someone screaming with his mike open.

Lieutenant Gates ordered Lane Dunn to turn the tank around and retreat. The tank weaved back down the road in the direction it had come, dodging explosions and avoiding disabled tanks. Gates got back on the radio.

Get back, everybody back. Follow me . . . Gawd damn, get back . . . !

Gates's tank went up in a fireball and a puff of smoke. The

mechanical monster stopped as though it had hit a wall. It shuddered, partly blocking the road. Smoke hissed from a neat AP hole piercing the armor.

Inside, the crew compartment was a gory mess of blood and torn flesh. Specialist Dunn absorbed the main impact. There was hardly anything of him left.

Shrapnel peppered Pop Gates and the other crewmembers, but they managed to extract themselves and run for the cover of a water-filled ditch. Machine gun fire chased after them.

Six tanks were wiped out in the matter of a few minutes. Surviving crews, many wounded, merged with terrified doughs, everyone darting and flopping about seeking a hole to crawl into. Some were either dead or too seriously wounded to get out of their tanks. Among them were Corporal Ardis Graham and Corporal Coleman Simmons, Jr., who not so long ago while crewing for Sergeant Johnny Holmes had thought killing the enemy was murder. He had since lost that inhibition.

A few of the tanks in the kill zone and those toward the rear escaped. The fifth tank in the column, driven by Corporal Leon Hopton, pulled a little two-wheeled trailer stocked with extra ammo. It seemed the Germans were shooting every other tank, working their way down the line. The machine in front of Hopton got it, its front end leaping into the air in a flash ball of fire. The tank behind got it, miraculously leaving Hopton unscathed.

Hopton cut a U-turn and took off as if he were drag-racing from a starting line, zigzagging to make himself a difficult target while shells dropped and exploded all around. He kept the gas pedal on the floor until he reached Munster.

TC Frank Cochrane's tank failed to make it. His driver, Private James Welborn, was killed instantly. His body slammed forward and jammed the control levers, causing the tank to reverse as quickly as a goosed cat. Engine revving, banging apart, smoking, the tank bounced over the roadside drainage ditch and smashed backward into a tree. Its engine continued to wind up as Cochrane helped survivors evacuate.

The cannoneer, Private Frank Greenwood, was critically injured. Both legs were blown off, leaving little but ragged shreds of flesh and crushed bone from the knees down. His shrieks of pain and terror filled the "Sears & Roebuck coffin." To further complicate matters, what remained of his legs had melted into steel and iron and wires and levers to become part of the mangled tank. Cochrane was afraid he would have to leave him behind. Smoke filled the cockpit and made breathing difficult.

"This is gonna hurt, bro'," he apologized, hacking as arid smoke filled his lungs.

As if he weren't already hurting.

Driven by desperation, Cochrane gripped Greenwood's stumps one at a time and yanked them free. It was either that or leave him behind to burn. Germans would have had to be deaf not to have heard his howls of pain. The TC got underneath his friend and pushed him up and out of the open turret. Greenwood's blood flowed over his face.

Fortunately, the wounded gunner rolled off the slanted tank and into the mud before a burst of machine fire skipped clanging across the armor. Cochrane followed and dragged him to a ditch half-filled with icy water. Greenwood had lost consciousness. Cochrane stuck his booted foot underneath his head to keep him from drowning while at the same time clawing himself as deeply as he could into the mud and water. Total fear is an emotion that cannot be sustained uninterrupted, but for Cochrane it seemed the terror might go on forever.

Nearby, a small group of doughs and other tankers cringed in the same ditch. Mortars walked toward them, slinging mud, water, and hot shrapnel. Cochrane buried his face in his arms. He recited the Twenty-third Psalm, lips quivering, while he waited for the end.

"The Lord is my Shepherd, I shall not want. Yea though I walk through the valley of the shadow of death, I will fear no evil, for Thou art with me. Thy rod and Thy staff they comfort me . . ."

The mortars kept coming. Explosions shook the ground and dropped chunks of mud and hot steel in on them. Shrapnel sizzled when it landed in the water. Cochrane continued reciting.

"The Lord is my Shepherd, I shall not want. He maketh me to lie down in green pastures; he leadeth me beside still waters . . ."

KIA (Killed in Action)

Tech Five Lane Dunn
Corporal Ardis E. Graham
Private Coleman Simmons, Jr.
Private James Welborn, Jr.

49

It's pretty tough to be in a place where you don't want to be, and still be unable to leave the damned place.

—PFC WILLIAM KISER, JR.

When the 761st mortars and the Assault Guns Platoon had moved up in the predawn to begin shelling Honskirch, the 105mm-mounted Sherman operated by Sergeant Robert "Motel" Johnson and his gunner, Elwood "Hometown" Hall, got separated in the dark from the rest of the Guns Platoon. A few hours after daylight, the battalion's exec, Major Russell Geist, came through in a half-track and found Sergeant Johnson's howitzer tank stranded in an isolated pocket and lost from the rest of the platoon.

Major Geist pointed out the correct route. By then, Charlie

Company was bottled up and in losing contact with the Germans. Motel and Hometown cranked up and blazed away to help relieve the beleaguered company. They soon ran out of both HE and AP.

"We done fired all our ammo except white phosphorus smoke, Sergeant Johnson," Hall reported.

"Fire that."

Dropping WP on the action turned out to be a lucky break for doughboys and tankers of Able Company trapped on the battlefield. It provided a smoke screen under which hundreds of men were able to withdraw and medics and litter bearers could get back in to bring out the wounded. Men in little knots and in singles, limping or dragging limbs, assisting each other, materialized from out of the roiling white clouds of smoke, looking stunned and disbelieving.

Nothing would ever convince Sergeant Frank Cochrane that something as simple as Motel Johnson's getting lost and running out of other ammo was responsible for the contrails of white phosphorus streaking across the sky, exploding against nearby enemy positions, and cloaking the killing fields with white, congealing clouds. God had answered his prayer. Motel Johnson was merely the vessel.

"Thank you, Lord," Cochrane murmured, truly grateful. "I promise you, Lord, I am gonna be a better man."

He hoisted Greenwood's mutilated, unconscious body into his arms and began running and staggering with him through the smoke toward the rear.

Dozens of tankers and doughs not caught in the ambush volunteered or were drafted to assist in finding the wounded out there in No Man's Land and bringing them to the rear. Corporal Buddie Branch, Baker Company, joined a litter team. Under continuing heavy fire, he inspected disabled tanks for casualties and ran carrying stretcher cases nearly three hundred yards to safety while Jerry peppered away with both direct and indirect fire.

The commander's driver for Dog Company, Corporal George Blake, used his Jeep to haul dozens to field aid stations set up behind the lines. Bullet holes magically appeared in his vehicle as he drove about the field like a madman picking up the wounded, stuffing them in the backseat, and heading for home with aidmen hanging on for dear life.

Wounded men, both black and white, lay on makeshift OR tables and on litters in and around the aid tents. Most were silent now. Some cried softly. Others moved their lips in prayer. Still others simply stared off into a thousand yards of void.

Lieutenant Pop Gates had turned bitter within the span of those minutes when his company had been caught in the open. His dark eyes burned furiously as he lay on a litter at the aid station.

"That sonofabitch, that honky sonofabitch," he murmured. " I *told* that motherfucker what would happen."

50

I remember the crying and the moaning of the wounded.

—CORPORAL E. G. McCONNELL

Platoon leader Lieutenant Thomas Bruce took command of the battered and much decimated Charlie Company after Pop Gates was wounded and evacuated in the initial disastrous approach on Honskirch. Later in the afternoon, following another softening up of the objective by artillery and mortars, Charlie tried it again.

Half of Bruce's company seemed to be missing. The men who remained were exceptionally quiet and cheerless. Rain ceased falling. The sun even peeked out a few minutes before promptly disappearing again, as though in dismay at the destruction it witnessed. Sergeant Harding Crecy nursed a simmering rage.

"They are gonna pay for this," he vowed.

Corporal E. G. McConnell had made it out of the kill zone unscathed that morning. Still, he felt apprehensive about being placed in the vanguard as the attack rapidly unfolded in the afternoon, and as a TC at that.

None of the tanks was taking any chances this time. They moved in so quickly the doughs almost had to run full-out to keep up. E.G. flipped open the turret hatch and laid in with the .50-caliber machine gun until its barrel glowed. All tanks came in hot, belching fire at every haystack, every barn, every house, and every other thing along the way big enough to conceal a German, following the advice General Patton gave E.G. to "shoot every gawd damn thing you see . . . every gawd damn thing you see. This is war. You hear me, boy?"

E.G. had heard him.

The road lifted into a hill straight ahead, a kind of embankment. Germans began dropping shells as E.G. in the lead tank reached this feature. The last tank in the column shuddered and rode high on a flashball before thudding back to the road, its wheels spinning wildly and flopping broken tread. A shell struck the center of the hill, spraying E.G. with dirt and mud and road materials. He ducked into the turret, then immediately popped up again.

Krauts were working on the tanks in earnest, but this time nothing was going to stop them. The dark war wagons kept going through the smoke and explosions. It was clear they would break through and extract the satisfaction of some payback.

It occurred to Corporal McConnell that last night's prophetic dream had become today's reality. He might have made it out this morning, but he was once again living his own nightmare. Maybe God was going to take him after all.

The half-expected blow struck with such a terrific jolt that it twisted E.G. completely around in the turret and shot him straight into the air, like the clown propelled from a circus cannon. He glimpsed flash fire.

"Moms . . . !"

51

If you want me you can always find me in the lead tank.

—GENERAL GEORGE S. PATTON, JR.

General Patton came around while Lieutenant Pop Gates was recovering in a field hospital and asked him why he had lost so many tanks in such a short period of time the day Honskirch was seized. Gates always figured Patton had as little use for a Negro soldier as the next white commander. He nonetheless respected the man as a fair man and one hell of a combat leader. He related the story of the regimental colonel, a former finance officer.

"Motherfucker," Patton said and walked out.

Gates's estimation of Patton went up a notch when he learned General Patton immediately relieved the colonel of his command and had him shipped to the United States. Presumably, he ended up back in his old job as a finance officer where he belonged, and where he would send no more men to their deaths.

52

For the next couple of days I didn't know if I was coming or going.

—Corporal E. G. McConnell

Corporal E. G. McConnell existed in a hazy nether world somewhere between earth and hell. He smelled wet earth and grass and the odors of unclean men. He heard what seemed to be the demented moans and cries of sinners being tormented by hell's eternal flames. Had old Satan gambled for his soul and won it after all this?

After some time during which he simply drifted in ether, he slowly became aware of his surroundings. He was relieved to find he was still on earth but shocked to see what earth had become. He lay on a poncho spread over mud outside a large OD tent. Other soldiers lay all around him, broken, twisted, mutilated bodies, blood everywhere, trampled into the earth so that the mud turned a rusty red color. People cried in anguish and torture, they prayed, and some even laughed because it was all over for them at last.

Excruciating pain shot through E.G.'s head, like the Devil was poking his brain with a red-hot pitchfork. Dried blood had glued his helmet to his skull. He tried to remove it. That simple effort proved too much for him, and he passed out again.

Nothing seemed to have changed when he revived. Moments later? Hours? He called out feebly to get someone's attention. Medics and doctors bristled about looking harried. Honskirch had generated a shitpot full of casualties.

"Where . . . where . . . what . . . ?"

He wasn't sure he could speak anymore.

"We'll get to you as soon as we can, boy." The surgeon kept going. He wore rubber gloves smeared with blood up to his elbows.

Gradually, bit by bit, details leading up to the poncho and the tent returned to the young corporal. They were vague and ephemeral, almost like a part of the dream he had about being killed.

He remembered being hit and ejected from his tank. The next thing he knew he couldn't open his eyes because dried blood had sealed them shut. He thought he must be on his way to the Great Hereafter, until he heard the chatter of machine gun fire and the occasional *Crump!* of a mortar shell exploding. Surely the Great Hereafter would be free of those.

He lay on soaked ground. He felt the chill seeping into his bones.

He found he could move one hand. He rubbed crusted blood from his eyes and tried them again. This time they opened.

He lay in a water-filled ditch, but his head was out of the water. Someone must have dragged him there and left him. It was getting late. A moment of panic shot through him at the prospect of remaining out there after nightfall.

Moaning. Someone nearby.

"Who's that?" he demanded, alarmed.

The moaning continued. He turned his head.

Strobe flashes of explosions in the distance. A reddish glow against the far sky from fires in Honskirch.

Maybe it was a German moaning.

After a while, after the panic subsided, he became cognizant of other men sobbing and groaning all around. So much pain, so much misery. It was as if he were a tiny component of a larger cesspool of common suffering that filled him with immense sorrow and sadness.

Medics finally appeared at the casualty collection point and started to roll him onto a stretcher.

"No, I'm okay," he resisted. "I'm okay."

He didn't want to appear helpless and admit he couldn't look out for himself. Someone helped him off the ground, escorted him to a Jeep, and again offered him a stretcher.

"I'm okay. I'll ride on the back."

The Jeep started off. E.G.'s head whirled, and he toppled off the back.

The next thing he knew he awoke at the aid station piled up with other GIs. He drifted in and out of consciousness on a cloud of painkiller. Somewhere along the way he was told that a chunk of shrapnel had lodged between his helmet and his skull. V-mail stashed inside his helmet had probably saved his life by absorbing some of the impact. Moms and God were still looking out for him.

A three-quarter-ton ambulance loaded him and three white doughboys from the 26th into the back and sped further toward the rear. Some German POWs unloaded them at a hospital. E.G. hoped it was the 14th Field Hospital where the colonel's lady was a nurse.

"Her name is Lieutenant Taffy," he explained. "I know it 'cause one of our tanks is named *Taffy*. One is *Cool Stud*, one is *Detroit*, and one is *Taffy*."

"There's no Taffy here, tank or otherwise. This is the 100th General."

The baby-faced corporal was transferred to a tent ward where he felt completely out of place as the only black man. However, the guy in the bed next to him was one of the three white doughs with whom E.G. had shared the ambulance ride. His name was Holt. Holt wasn't much more than a kid, either. Like E.G., he had lied about his age in order to join the army.

A doctor told E.G. he would soon recuperate and be sent back to the front. On the other hand, Holt's war was over. As soon as his strength returned, he would be flown to England and then transported home to America. His entire body was in a cast from the soles of his feet to his armpits. Even an arm was encased in plaster. He would wave his free arm about exaggeratedly and make everyone laugh. Holt was going home. He was in good spirits.

"At least they left me one good arm," he bugled. "I can still hold my dick when I got to pee."

"I think it's in a cast too," E.G. teased him.

E.G. and Holt became friends from long hours of idleness with nothing to do but sleep, eat, talk, and wait for the nurses to come around with more pain pills.

One day a two-star general entered the ward to pay a visit and cheer up the heroic wounded. No one knew who he was except that he was a general and therefore important. He walked down the row between the facing lines of beds, shaking hands and making obligatory small talk. *How are you, Sergeant? How are you doing, Private? How're you feeling? Getting enough to eat? What unit you with? Where are you from?*

He reached the only black face in the ward and looked E.G. over. E.G. lay there with his head encased in a roll of bandages the size of a helmet.

"What's wrong with you, boy?" the general asked in an attempt to be funny. "Got the claps?"

An old negative stereotype pertaining to supposed Negro promiscuity. The remark cut E.G. like a rapier. He hadn't even had a sweetheart before he went away to the army at age sixteen. He lay dumbfounded, speechless and helpless while the general grinned.

The ward went completely quiet. The duty nurse stiffened. A voice suddenly sliced out of the bed next to E.G.'s. Holt was in a lot of pain and just didn't give a damn. His war was over anyhow.

"Hey, General," he said. "If he got the claps, he got 'em from your mother. Go ahead and send me back to the front, you asshole."

E.G. turned his head and eyes away and lay there soaked in humiliation. While grateful to Holt for coming to his defense, all he wanted was to get out of there and go back to the front lines to be with his own kind, his black brothers. He felt lost and out of place in the rear with all the whites. Much as he dreaded returning to the war, it was better to live in danger with friends than out of danger with white men who felt free to come by and insult you.

53

You can't imagine what it was like to be black in World War II.

—TAFFY BATES

A rmy nurses in the European Theater of War landed on the Normandy beachheads only four days after the D-Day invasions. By the end of the war, army nurses in Europe would number more than seventeen thousand. Most of them served in mobile field and evacuation hospitals that moved nearly every month, sometimes sooner, following the troops as they fought their way across France toward Germany.

Field hospitals like the 14th could accommodate up to 150 patients at a time and generally had about eighteen nurses assigned. These hospitals normally occupied tents, but also set up in schoolhouses, churches, public buildings, or abandoned houses whenever they were available. Constant relocation meant nurses were always scrubbing, cleaning, and disinfecting in order to provide comfortable, sanitary facilities that could handle large numbers of critically wounded or sick patients. During those times when their equipment and supplies failed to keep up with them, they often slept out in the open, sharing the discomfort of the troops while they spent days looking for lost gear.

Nursing experiences ranged from intense boredom during

lulls in the fighting to periods of exhausting activity whenever the units were engaged. A nurse had to be flexible, innovative, patient, adaptable, and highly skilled.

As Allied forces pushed the German army eastward through France, high numbers of casualties occurred in pockets of resistance. Litter bearers and ambulances filtered the wounded through front-line aid stations and battalion aid stations to field hospitals. Wrecked young soldiers with their bodies horribly maimed, limbs severed, paralyzed, destroyed physically, emotionally, and mentally, passed through in sporadic heartbreaking streams of blood, gore, and tears.

Sometimes a field hospital performed up to eighty surgeries a day. Patients judged strong enough to travel were taken by ambulance to evacuation hospitals located further back of the front lines and near transportation facilities. Postoperative patients too weak to travel were nursed until they could be moved. Others were allowed to recuperate and then sent back to their front-line units. White and black wounded shared hospitals, although Negroes complained they were not treated with the same care as white soldiers.

As the 14th Field Hospital trailed Patton's Third Army across Europe, Taffy grew accustomed, if not exactly inured, to suffering. A nurse who wore her heart on her sleeve could not function. However, she continued to hold a special place in her heart for the black men of the 761st, even after her Paul had left it. She was appalled when nurses, all of whom were white, refused to bathe injured black soldeirs who could not tend to their own bodily necessities. She stripped these men herself the same as she did other patients and sponge-bathed their torn bodies, for which effort she earned their gratitude and a reputation as a "White Angel."

"What would you have them do?" Taffy scolded the nurses. "Have them lie in their own contaminated filth just because they're black? You treat injured Germans better than you do them."

"You're a nigger lover, Taffy."

"If I can bathe a white soldier, why can't I bathe a black one? It has nothing to do with race."

Wounded black tankers kept Taffy abreast of the 761st and the men she had come to know so well through Paul—who was dead, who had the million-dollar wound and was going State-side, how the battalion fared in Colonel Bates's absence.

"Colonel Hunt is all right," tankers coming through the hospital informed her, "but he don't care about us the way *the* colonel does."

"I get letters from him," she relayed back. "His leg is busted up pretty bad, but he wants you to know he'll be back with you in a few more weeks."

Aside from letters, Taffy hadn't spoken to Paul since early November shortly after he was hit. She yearned to see him again, although that would become possible only when and if he returned to France and combat. As long as he remained in England, she didn't have to worry about some terrible day when a new load of casualties came in and there lay her Paul.

As early winter set in, the beginning of the hardest winter in years, combat casualties actually declined while more men arrived at the hospital suffering from trench foot, exhaustion, and exposure. Specialist Kenneth Hamm of Able Company was one of them.

Extreme cold and wet had slowly cut off circulation to his extremities. His boots froze to his feet at night. One night he made the mistake of removing them. His feet swelled, and he couldn't get his boots back on without cutting them. He had to wriggle his toes all the time in an effort to keep his feet from going completely numb.

His feet died a slow death apart from the rest of his body because he could never get them warm and dry. They turned gun-steel blue. They swelled something awful in the first stages. Then the swelling left and his feet became almost flat. Gangrene set in. Great chunks of skin and flesh fell and peeled off. They stank of putrefaction. He had to be carried into the field hospital on a stretcher. He would not be going back to the front. He would be lucky if he escaped amputation. His war was over.

"My million-dollar feet are sending me home," he said. "Still, I sure do wish I could be here to see the colonel when he gets back. I feel like I done be letting him down."

54

The thing that kept them going was their determination to show the world that they could fight in tanks and win.

—PHILLIP W. LATIMER

Combat stripped away the everyday business of skin color, religion, and social class. White soldiers and black soldiers lived together—or at least side by side—in a common condition of discomfort and danger. Having little time for personal sanitation, they wore the same woolen shirts, trousers, and long underwear for days at a time. Clothing grew so raunchy it could almost have been sent out on its own to engage the enemy. Sometimes it was more than a man could do to simply brush his teeth, wash his face, or shave out of a canteen cup of cold water.

In addition to problems of hygiene were those of the senses—the pressure of enduring German air and artillery attacks, the constant shock of seeing buddies slaughtered, the fear that drove the mind to strange and desperate psychological places. It reached the point where a man was almost immune to further trauma.

During normal times, the mind readily distinguished among the multiple layers of past, present, and future. In combat, all concepts of future disappeared first. There might never be a future beyond the next hour, the next minute, even the next second. Death became a constant companion, an overpowering presence.

The demanding need for survival in the present gradually diminished the past. The past became faded memories revived, if but incompletely, with the aid of snapshots and small keepsakes.

Only the immediate present held any real meaning. Life existed moment by precious moment. This *very moment,* this *very instant,* had value. Nothing else mattered.

The entire battalion suffered tremendously during the first month of combat. Charlie Company, almost decimated at Honskirch, was reduced to a total of fifty-eight men, much less than half-strength. The other three companies weren't doing much better. Still, the battalion fought on, determined that once it had "Come Out Fighting," it could not, would not, shame itself. The only man so far to show cowardice in the face of the enemy was Major Wingo, a *white* man.

Many top brass in the military, assuming black inferiority, still felt that Negroes were not fit for combat duty. The stereotype of the untrustworthy, indolent, thieving Negro who ran at the first shot fired in anger persisted. It may have been precisely because of such stereotypes, of low white expectations, that Patton's Panthers of the 761st became determined to prove they were warriors equal to if not superior to their white comrades in arms.

"Damn you, don't let me down!" Patton had exhorted.

Most of all, they mustn't let themselves down.

Sergeant Horace Evans of Baker Company watched with consternation as a company of white infantry refused to get up off the ground to accompany tanks into a skirmish. Officers and NCOs pleaded with the broken, sobbing doughs, coaxing them, begging them, finally cursing and threatening, shoving packs on their backs and weapons into their hands and kicking them.

Damn them, sergeants warned, they'd be shot for desertion if they didn't get up and go.

"Fuck it! Shoot us," the doughs cried. "We're going to be killed anyhow. We're not going to fight anymore."

It was called combat fatigue. Evans shook his head. "Pitiful. Just plumb pitiful," he murmured. This would never happen to Patton's Panthers.

Lieutenant Horace Jones of Battalion Supply was speeding down the road in his Jeep helping Captain Phil Latimer coordinate delivery of combat provisions when he saw a white captain run up to where infantry were sprawled in various positions alongside the road awaiting orders.

"Off your butts and on your feet!" the officer shouted. "We're moving out."

"By God, I'm not going," decided an emaciated dogface with a hillbilly twang.

With that, he lifted his foot off the ground, jammed the muzzle of his M1 against it, and pulled the trigger.

Black soldiers experienced the same emotions of despair, sadness, and fear as white soldiers. Centuries of coping with slavery and subjugation in many different parts of the world, however, seemed to have bred into the race a special form of resiliency. The black man's innate ability to joke and laugh, his self-deprecating humor, went a long way toward keeping up morale on the front lines, toward helping build a well-knit family that made each man feel needed and secure.

Hardly had a tank column stopped before men were jumping out to socialize with crews in front and back, talking trash and laughing to reduce anxiety.

"Hey, nigger? Know one thing? I dreamt about your mama last night."

"That wasn't *my* mama. That was *your* mama."

Talking trash like that was something whites found difficult to understand. But it was a game, a rib, nothing meant by it. It got them cracking and laughing, elevated their spirits.

Humor and laughter served as a safety valve for maintaining sanity in the midst of insanity. They howled with mirth at the incongruity of some pint-sized black tanker marching a large Nazi POW to the rear, kicking him in the butt at every step, and hollering, "Move it, move it, you ole Super Race you. Get along!"

Krauts mortared Sergeant Eugene Matthews of Headquarters Company in his Jeep on the approach to Sarre-Union. As the barrage closed in, he abandoned ship and sought cover in the rear on foot. Tall and lanky, a high-school basketball star, he poured on the steam. Men teased him from then on about the Jeep not being fast enough.

"Last sighting showed him seven miles west of here and still going strong," his buddies exaggerated. "He wouldn't have stopped at the English Channel except he figured out he couldn't swim."

A German "Bedcheck Charlie" reconnaissance plane spotted Charlie Company bivouacked in an abandoned village. He notified the Luftwaffe. A fighter-bomber zoomed in, dropping five-hundred-pound bombs. Sergeant Johnny Holmes crashed straight through the closed door of the building in which he considered sleeping the night in comfort. He raced into wide open country at full foot speed, really pouring it on, until he came to an old bomb crater and jumped in. It was half-full of icy water.

"When you gotta go, you gotta go," he gruffly responded to teasing about the alacrity with which he exchanged a dry, warm building for a pothole full of ice.

"He misses sleeping with his feet in the water so much," someone cracked, "that he can't hardly wait to get back to it."

Two light Stuarts from the Mosquito Fleet were assigned to protect the flanks of the Assault Guns Platoon. During a midday lull, the crews built a fire to dry out their boots and socks in an attempt to ward off trench foot. They were backed up to the flame talking trash and grabassing when Jerry decided to drop in an 88. It exploded about twenty-five yards from the fire, splattering everyone with mud. The tankers made a beeline for their iron horses, but the Germans weren't through with them yet.

Bursting geysers put out the fire and crashed down nearby timber. The men held onto the earth for dear life, faces down in the mud, as though they were wet fleas on the back of a dog trying to shake them off. Each time they started to jump up and make a run for the tanks, Jerry lobbed in more rounds to pin them down. A few minutes of shells screaming in was guaranteed to reduce the most gung-ho trooper to quivering gelatin and clacking teeth.

Assault Guns observers located the source of the fire and retaliated with their 105mm howitzers, silencing the enemy incoming. Sergeant Willie Brent dusted himself off, walked over to where the fire had been, and began collecting burning embers and faggots to start a new fire. He sighed dramatically.

"Just another day on the Western Front," he quipped.

55

At times, Johnny Long was so daring I thought he was out of his mind.

—SERGEANT EDDIE DONALD

Like him or not, every man of whatever high or low rank who encountered Lieutenant Johnny Long, Baker Company's commander, had to respect him. He was known as "the Black Patton" for a very sound reason. Like Patton, he never attempted to *push* a string of wet spaghetti. If you wanted him, you found him up front, helmeted head stuck up from the turret of the lead tank, cussing a streak blue enough to scorch the ears of every enemy soldier within a mile. He never asked a man to do something dangerous without getting out and showing the way.

"The Panthers are fighting," he said. "We have a legacy to build."

"He is one mean, evil bastard," Sergeant Horace Evans opined every time the company received a new mission and his sensitive "secret weapon" stomach started churning. "Sometimes I hate the man's guts."

Evans thought the lieutenant must have the luck of the Irish. Tanks battened down, shells falling all around, Lieutenant Long would be out there alone in all that hell calmly walking about to survey the situation. If the column came upon a minefield that blocked the way, the commander leaped from his iron ride and walked ahead to guide his tanks safely through.

During the assault on Honskirch, an exploding 109 shell had knocked Long's tank off a high embankment. By the time someone reached him, he was already climbing out uninjured and burning the air with invective over how much time the blankety-blank inconsiderate Krauts had caused him to lose.

"That crazy, glorious sonofabitch," Evans conceded.

Sarre-Union fell to the Americans after a hard battle on December 2, 1944. Doughs dug in for the night, but the Germans counterattacked the next morning and drove them out. Enemy armor gained strong positions in the town. The fight to retake it promised to be as bitter as the first battle. At 1310 hours, the 761st Battalion was dispatched to start the attack by engaging the enemy in a wooded area on the eastern outskirts.

As was his usual routine, Lieutenant Long assembled his men to brief them on the mission. It was a blustery afternoon with low scudding clouds and spitting rainfall. Wind rattled the skeletal arms of trees that hid the assembly from the view of enemy only a short distance up the road. All around, the company's tanks sat parked with engines idling and ready. Long pointed.

"That stretch of road is the only way to get there," he said, blunt and honest as always. "It's probably mined and the Jerries have set up machine guns and mortars to crossfire it."

November had been a tough month of combat. The Black Panthers had lost twenty-four men KIA, eighty-one WIA, and had had a total of fourteen tanks shot out from under them. December seemed to be starting out the same way. As veterans, the tankers had lost some of their initial gung-ho and were becoming by nature gun-shy and more cautious. Only fools rushed in.

"I don't like it, Lieutenant," Sergeant Eddie Donald objected.

"Neither do I," Long agreed, "but it's the best plan I can see. It's our job to take that town and, by God, we're going to do it."

He left it at that and walked off out of earshot to let his men talk it over and get the bitching out of their systems. He stood next to the road looking down it toward the enemy, his back to the company. Tall and broad-shouldered, his entire bearing suggested a heroic statue carved out of stone. The man could be as stubborn and exasperating as the real Patton. A charge of dynamite could not move him once he made up his mind about something.

He strode back to the gathering once it quieted down some. Sergeant Donald seemed to have been appointed spokesman.

"Lieutenant Long, ain't none of us like this," he said. "It'll be just like what happened to Charlie Company at Honskirch."

Long had already given the briefing and his point of view. The discussion was over as far as he was concerned.

"Are you going with me?" he forthrightly demanded.

Sergeant Horace Evans thought of the white doughboys who refused to get up off the ground to go out and fight. He thought he would never see the day when the Black Panthers did the same thing.

"Pitiful. Just plumb pitiful," he muttered to himself.

Lieutenant Long delayed for another heartbeat, his eyes sweeping the company. Men shuffled about, uncomfortable and embarrassed under the weight of his fierce gaze.

"Okay. You're not going," he said.

He pushed his way through and snatched the handset of a field telephone hanging on a tree limb. He rang battalion headquarters. Every eye in the company watched him, assuming he was speaking to Colonel Hunt. No one ever knew for sure if he actually put the call through or not.

"Sir, I am proceeding as ordered. The men have refused to go. I'm court-martialing every damned one of the sorry bastards as soon as I get back."

Sergeant Mike Ward and his crew lolled around on their tank. Lieutenant Long ordered him to get down. He took over the tank and its crew personally. The tank took off toward town alone, clanking and squealing and crunching on frozen mud. The lieutenant obviously wasn't kidding. He was going to attack by himself. Stunned, Baker Company's left-behind tankers watched. Eddie Donald broke the spell.

"If he's fool enough to go it alone," he blurted out, "then I'm big enough the fool to follow him."

Tankers scrambled into their iron monsters and took off down the road after their leader.

Long's tank hit the first mined antitank ditch at full throttle and cleared it, guns blazing. The others dutifully followed, guns spitting back at Kraut machine gun nests. Donald's was the only tank lost. An exploding mine put it out of commission without seriously injuring the crew. The others made it and permanently silenced the enemy machine gun nests, allowing infantry to advance and retake the town after two hours of savage combat.

Donald, Sergeant Evans, and the other three crewmembers from their disabled tank walked into town to catch up with the company. They came upon Long's tank parked in front of a little cottage. In the kitchen they found Lieutenant Long sitting comfortably at the table smoking a cigarette and drinking a cup of coffee.

56

One must never sit still.

—General George S. Patton, Jr.

Allied forces hit the much-touted failed French Maginot Line on December 9, 1944. It proved a much tougher nut to crack for Allied forces going east than it had four years earlier for German forces going west. Straight infantry could accomplish little against the large number of pillboxes, blockhouses, trenches, minefields, and booby traps that made up the German-occupied Maginot. Successful operations called for coordinated efforts among U.S. Army Air Force dive bombers, armor, and combat engineers.

Bombardment from the big guns of the 761st Battalion, both the 76mm tank cannon and Assault Guns' 105mm howitzers, bounced off the thick pillboxes like rubber balls. However, concussion shock waves dazed pillbox defenders long enough for engineers to rush in with explosives to blow the Germans to bits. It was noisy, dangerous, savage business.

Sergeant Johnny Holmes's ears rang for days afterward, not only from explosions and the numbing constant roar of artillery and big guns but also from having lost another tank when he ran over a mine. He went around mumbling, "Huh, huh? Whatta ya saying? Damn it, speak up so a man can hear you."

"I *am* speaking up, you deaf nigger. I'm yelling at you now."

He got out of his replacement tank to inspect one of the smaller concrete and steel fortresses minutes after Germans abandoned it. He was curious about its construction.

"Man, don't do that," his crew cautioned him. "Man, you got more brass than a brass-ass monkey."

The little stronghold was ingeniously constructed with steel-reinforced concrete walls nearly a foot thick. Inside, it was about six feet in diameter and six feet tall, sufficient for machine gunners or mortars. The front and rear were shielded with extra protection while the sides were thinner and weaker. Johnny Holmes pointed this out. From then on, the battalion tankers maneuvered to lay shells in from the sides, with far more success than they had had charging the pillboxes head on.

Germans abandoned some of the Maginot towns without a fight. Others they defended to the last man. There seemed to be no rhyme or reason to how they selected those they tried to hold. Bellevue Farms Village, for example, appeared worthless both strategically and tactically, but the Krauts dug in to fight.

Able Company fanned out to the right of the village, Charlie Company to the left, Assault Guns and its tanks dispersed across a line, and the bombardment began, aided by Allied fighter bombers dropping munitions and strafing fortified positions. They pounded the Germans all morning until not a single house was left standing, the village having been turned into a great smoldering pile of ruin. People wandered about in the debris like rats, some sobbing, others simply gazing about in bewilderment.

The 26th Infantry Division and attached tank battalion moved approximately sixty-five miles in one week, crushing heavily fortified positions and breaking through the Maginot Line. Captain David Williams's Able Company attacked in the vicinity of Aachen; Lieutenant Johnny Long's Baker Company smoked through at Etting; Lieutenant Thomas Bruce, still in command of Charlie while Pop Gates recuperated, hit Oermingen.

Engineers expanded bridgeheads over the Saar River at Saarlautern and Easdorf and over the Blies River in the Sarreguemines area. Attacking forces crossed the major highway leading from Sarreguemines and entered German territory. A SHAEF (Supreme Headquarters Allied Expeditionary Forces) communique read in part: "Lt. General George S. Patton's Third Army infantry and armor slammed into German territory at a new point after crossing the Blies River above Sarreguemines."

Able, Baker, and Charlie of the 761st all rolled onto German soil. Sergeant James Nelson commanded Able's first tank to cross the border. With him were Tech Five Willie Young, Corporal Robert Kitchen, PFC Willie McCall, and Private Joe Singleton. Staff Sergeant Moses Dade was TC of Charlie's first tank, accompanied by Tech Four Roosevelt Whittaker, Tech Five William Donaldson, PFC Nathaniel Dyson, and Private Twyman Bentley.

Willie McCall got out and looked around. "So *this* is the home of Superman," he said, spitting contemptuously.

"This war is about over," Willie Devore decided, "but they still got time to get me."

A SHAEF operational directive sent to Patton stated that the Third Army would continue to advance northeast to seize the Mainz-Frankfurt-Darmstadt region. Commanding generals of the Ninth U.S. Air Force and the XII and XIX Tactical Air commanders conferred with Patton and representatives of the Seventh Army to coordinate aerial bombardment of the Siegfried Line, Germany's own Maginot Line, constructed to defend the Reich. The attack was scheduled to begin on December 19.

However, events were beginning to unfold that might postpone further advance into Germany. On December 9, G-2 intelligence reports indicated increased enemy rail activity and estimated the Germans were collecting at least six and a half divisions in the Eifel area, indicating a possible offensive in the Ardennes. SHAEF ignored the report.

On December 12, G-2 again warned SHAEF of the very great probability of a German buildup for a major offensive in the Ardennes. Yet a third warning followed on December 13. Four reconstructed divisions of the Sixth Panzer Army remained west of the Rhine River in the vicinity of Cologne despite the growing threat of Patton's Third Army. A fifth panzer division was being held in reserve north of the Moselle River near the boundaries of the First and Third U.S. armies.

G-2 Colonel Oscar Koch wrote in his report to SHAEF that "the situation north of the Moselle demanded special attention." He was again ignored.

57

The battalion was unfortunate in that the Battalion Commander (Lieutenant Colonel Paul Bates) became a casualty early in the day and as a consequence considerable confusion resulted.

—COLONEL GEORGE W. COOLIDGE,
WAR DEPARTMENT OBSERVERS BOARD

Mechanical failures and enemy action dwindled the strength of both men and machines in the 761st. Yet, while the 26th Infantry Division pulled back for rest and refitting following penetration of the Maginot Line, the weary Black Panthers were reattached to the relatively untested 87th Infantry Division for further combat. After only one month in command, Lieutenant Colonel Hollis Hunt turned the Panthers over to Major John F. George and returned to his former assignment at the 17th Armored Group, a higher command.

The War Department was particularly interested in how well its experiment with Negro armored troops was working out. It sent observers into the ETO to question officers, virtually all of whom were white, about their opinions and observations. The War Department Observers Board asked Colonel Hunt about his command time with the 761st, a period during which the battalion had been in almost continuous combat and had suffered a large number of casualties. A single month had witnessed the heroic deaths of such men as Ruben Rivers, Sam Turley, and Roy King. Black company commanders like Lieutenant Johnny Long, Lieutenant Pop Gates, and Lieutenant Thomas Bruce had demonstrated exceptional leadership.

Yet, in his response to the Observers Board questionnaire, Colonel Hunt seemed to have little good to say about the Black Panther Battalion:

Lt. Colonel H. Hunt (W)
CO, 761st Tank Battalion

Q: How did the Negro enlisted men conduct themselves in combat?

A (Hunt): Obeyed orders when properly led. Tank returned from front line to battalion when platoon leader was killed but went back when given specific orders as to what to do. Were short on initiative.

Q: What was the combat performance of Negro officers? Initiative?

A: Poor on average.

Q: Sense of responsibility?

A: Poor on average.

Q: Ability to elicit the confidence and respect of the men?

A: Fair, varied directly with (above).

Q: Instances of fear and cowardice, including pre-battle sickness?

A: One lieutenant lost weight, couldn't sleep and admitted fear and was incapable of leading men in actual combat.

Q: Specific instances of valor?

A: One lieutenant fought his tank until out of ammo when blocked on roads by enemy tanks. One lieutenant had his tank disabled and was wounded, then mounted another tank and fought on. Platoon sergeant dismounted under fire, removed road block and continued attack. Excellent man.

Q: Were any companies led by Negro officers committed to combat? Under what circumstances and with what results?
A: Yes. Both against enemy opposition. One did well, the other very poorly.

Q: How did the performance of companies having only Negro officers compare with companies having some white officers of your command when operating under similar conditions?
A: Companies led by white officers were much more successful and showed more initiative and control when under fire.

Q: What percentage of the Negro officers of your command who were committed to combat would you say measured up well in all respects?
A: 15%.

Q: Based on combat performance, what percent of your colored officers do you regard as field grade potential?
A: None.

Q: Was there any noticeable improvement of colored units and colored officers as they acquired combat experience?
A: Yes.

Q: Were there any instances of white officers manifesting fear of their Negro troops? Any instances of troops attacking their officers or vice versa?
A: One. XO (executive officer) had been Summary Court (Major Wingo) and was afraid men might try to kill him.

Q: Was there any noticeable breakdown of racial barriers in the theater of operations? Any intermingling of white and colored officers in messes, athletics, barracks? Any instances of drinking together, gambling together, etc.?
A: Yes, at the front. On the front they live, sleep and eat together. Unobserved any social activities.

Q: How did the rate of promotion of colored officers overseas compare with that of white officers?
A: Depended on vacancy. If proven in combat then promoted regardless of color.

Q: What were the principal recreations of Negroes overseas?
A: Resting and eating.

Q: Considering both combat and non-combat phases of overseas experience, what is your evaluation of the Negro private with reference particularly to the following: Interest in soldiering?
A: Little.

Q: Care of equipment?
A: Poor.

Q: Pride in personal appearance?
A: Poor

Q: Loyalty to superiors?
A: Excellent.

Q: Observance of orders and regulations?
A: Fair.

Q: General proficiency as a soldier?
A: Poor.

Q: Considering both the combat and non-combat experience overseas, what is your evaluation of the colored NCO?
A: Generally lacks initiative.

Q: Considering both the combat and non-combat experience overseas, what is your estimate of colored officers, with reference particularly to the following: Sense of responsibility?
A: Poor.

Q: Observance of the code of conduct commonly recognized as being applicable to officers?
A: Fair.

Q: Extent to which racial sensitiveness impairs effectiveness as leaders?
A: 30%.

Q: Pride in self and in organization?
A: Excellent.

Q: Percent who measured up well in all respects as leaders?
A: 15%.

Q: How did the Negro soldiers get along with the natives?
A: Well.

Q: Do you think that it would have been better not to intermingle white and colored officers in the same unit? Why?
A: Yes. White officers tend to lower standards to that of colored troops unless they predominate in numbers.

Q: Based on your observations and experiences what are your recommendations as to the organizations, command and use of Negro soldiers in a future emergency?
A: They should be commanded by white officers and should not be used in Tank, Tank Destroyer, or similar units requiring a high degree of technical knowledge, sense of responsibility, and initiative.

58

*The 761st was a bastard outfit. We fought with any-
body who needed us.*

—Sergeant Johnnie Stevens

Not even cigarettes were more ubiquitous in the military than rumormongering. "Even a rumor is better'n know-ing *nothing*," Black Panthers insisted with a laugh. In retrospect, breaking the Maginot Line wasn't as tough as rumor said it would be. However, taking on the Siegfried Line might be something else. The Siegfried, Germany's answer to France's Maginot Line, a final homeland defense against invasion, was said to be the most heavily defended line the world had ever known, manned by rabid, desperate troops who still believed in the Third Reich and were willing to sacrifice their lives for the mad Führer.

Rumors about a possible German offensive, a huge buildup of panzer divisions on this side of the Rhine River, also made troops "nervous in the service." Just when it appeared the Krauts were getting their asses stomped, they seemed to have nursed their strength in the middle rounds in order to come out strong in the final rounds. Even Patton, it was said, was concerned.

The intensity of combat not only destroyed all normal sense of time, it also selectively enhanced or diminished certain as-pects of the war so that almost no one in the lower rank and file had any idea whatsoever of what might be going on. That proved particularly true of the 761st because it was so frag-mented much of the time that rumors were brought back from all over the Third Army and built upon until they became "true," in some sense. For example, one rumor reported that

Hitler was dead, another that he had built a bomb that would destroy the world, starting with Allied armies in Europe.

Sometimes companies of the 761st, even the members of a single platoon, might not see each other for days at a time. A company would be sent to one of the regiments of the 87th Infantry while three or four tanks might be chopped out of another company's platoon and sent to still some other division for a few days. Sergeant Horace Evans opined that powers above kept the battalion split up because they didn't want Negroes to share in the honors of battle.

Rumors aside, the Allied strategy seemed clear and simple enough for even the lowest-ranked assistant driver or loader in a Sherman tank to understand: move forward until the enemy resisted, counter, then start moving forward again until the enemy resisted. It became almost routine, another day on the factory assembly line.

The Krauts seemed to have developed their own "day at the factory assembly line." Withdrawal for them was simply another delaying tactic. For the big offensive they were planning? Roadblocks, strongholds, defense of a city, all appeared to be part of some strategy to wear down the Allies a piece at a time. Even when the Black Panthers weren't in direct combat, they heard infantry and other armor fighting in the distance to mop up pockets of resistance.

Not so long before, the tankers had watched distant fighting with fascination and horror. Not anymore. Man is so universally adaptable that he can get used to even the vilest circumstances. Ensconced on the top of a hill, Captain David Williams's driver, Big Tit Richardson, slumped over the wheel of his Jeep while a mile or so away in the valley below tanks jousted with each other.

"Sir, wake me when we start moving again?" he requested, not as interested in the outcome of the skirmish as he was in catching a few much-needed winks of sleep. Someone would tell him if it ended the wrong way.

Vinton Hudson smoked a cigarette. "I am getting so tired of this war," he said.

58

All along the front the drive was taking on the proportions of a giant contest.

—Historian Cornelius Ryan

In the crazy, zigzagging patchwork skirmishing that the front had become in many places, tankers never knew where the enemy was or when he might appear. Kraut armor would suddenly emerge from over a hill, out of timber, from between two buildings or a barn, prompting a point-blank confrontation while literally looking down each other's gun barrels. Anything went when it came to fighting. You dealt with the bad guys with the quickest and most effective means available. Shoot them in the balls or the back, shred them with machine guns or tank guns when they ran, skewer them when they slept or got careless, and send them to hell when they stopped to eat or take a dump in the woods. Trick them, cheat them, deceive them, and have no respect for them in the morning. Winning the game was the thing, and it didn't matter how you won it.

Of course, Jerry did the same thing back because he wanted to win too.

During a cold and blustery afternoon, Charlie Company spearheaded an infantry advance on the fringes of another of those nameless little towns and villages that dotted either side of the French-German border. Lieutenant Tom Bruce, still Charlie's CO, led the way. Several hundred doughs ready for combat trotted along with the armor.

Suddenly, chickens and pigs in a barnyard scattered as a *Jagdpanzer,* a small tank destroyer armed with a 75mm cannon, shot out from behind the barn and scurried toward Bruce's war horse like a vicious dung beetle, muted flashes blinking from its main gun. Its first shot caught Bruce in the rear sprockets and disabled the tank.

Lieutenant and crew unassed the machine in a split instant and sprinted in a pell-mell race for the rear. At the same time, a machine gun nest in a nearby patch of timber opened up, weaving tracers among the doughs and popping geysers all over the field.

Sergeant Johnny Holmes's tank was the nearest to the threat. It could be suicide to confront a TD (tank destroyer) head-on at such close range. Not only did the *Jag's* armored sides slope upward to deflect hits, it was also a sturdily built little fighting machine that could sustain immense damage and keep going. In contrast to American armor that used gasoline and was therefore quite explosive, Germans burned diesel fuel, difficult to set afire.

"Get the hell out of here, Miller!" Holmes barked at his driver. "Let's flank the bastard. Go up the draw to your right, and we'll come up and around."

Advantage lay in catching the dung beetle from the side.

A TD was not equipped with a turret, which meant its main cannon could swivel only a few degrees to either side. Although it had to turn on its tracks in order to fire a new azimuth, it could do so with amazing quickness.

The terrain was hilly and grassy and fairly open among scattered clumps of brush and trees. Yesterday's light snow had melted off the ground except in the shade, leaving the earth still frozen solid enough to provide the tank solid traction. Holmes cut a wide fast circle to the TD's right, hoping to catch it by surprise.

"Keep her loaded, lad!" he shouted at Thomas Ashly, who served as both loader and assistant driver/bow gunner because of short-handedness.

"Raleigh, face to the sights!" he barked again. Gunner Raleigh Hill, who occupied the turret forward of and just below the TC, *had* his eyes to the sights of the 76mm cannon, his fists clenched on the triggers of the coaxial .30-caliber, and his foot ready to tromp the firing solenoid on the floor.

Holmes kept his head and shoulders stuck up through the open turret hatch to gain a good view. He saw some of the other Shermans fire a few rounds at the *Jag*, forcing it to dart back behind the barn, out of their sight. Holmes saw it start down the reverse side of the hill. He lost sight of it then.

The draw opened into a field. The Sherman roared out onto the other side of the hill. The TD was waiting, having apparently anticipated the attack. Fifty yards away, it opened fire at what was literally point-blank range for such monsters.

Keep her moving. Don't stop . . .

Ain't stopping, Sarge . . .

Flank the bastard . . . Gunner! Fire!

On the way!

It was the OK Corral all over again, ironclad gunmen squared off and banging away at each other.

Damn! Missed the sonofabitch . . .

The *Jag* swapped ends like a cat. Its cannon flashed. The AP round struck the ground short, bounced, hit, skipped, and sheared off a tree at ground level.

Fire . . . !

Damn. Missed him again . . . !

Don't stop, kid. Move to the right . . .

Holmes was so busy with the TD that he failed to notice the enemy machine gun until green streaks shot past his head and lead started clanging against steel plating.

Machine gun to the left . . . Ignore the bastard . . .

He ducked into the turret and stuck up a hand periscope to keep track of the TD. The machine gunner shot it out of his hands. It stung like crazy.

Goddamned . . .

Miller kept the tank moving at full speed, circling the *Jag* to keep it off-balance. Holmes's view was now restricted to the slit periscope built into the tank. Raleigh Hill traversed the turret to keep the scuttling little enemy monster within his sights, depending on the gyro-stabilizer to hold the gun steady at such speed.

Survival for one depended on eliminating the other as expeditiously as possible.

Move again, Miller . . .

Shit, Sarge, I am moving . . .

Fire!

The AP ricocheted off the enemy's hull in a streak of fire.

That's the last AP . . .

What!!!

There was nothing worse than running out of ammo in the middle of a fight.

So give the mother HE . . .

High explosives could incapacitate enemy armor even if they failed to penetrate.

Hill opened up with the coaxial machine gun to find and fix the target with tracers, holding up on the 76mm until he felt sure of a hit. The two metal beasts scurried about on the open hillside, *mano a mano,* each seeking the advantage and a soft underbelly, throwing exploding shells at each other.

Holmes scored first, a death blow.

Bingo!

In spite of its diesel engine, the TD burst into flames. It was amazing how a vehicle constructed almost entirely of steel could burn. Actually, it didn't. What caught fire were fuel and oil, supplies inside, personal gear, and other combustibles either inside the tank or attached to it.

The German crew remained buttoned up, grilling as ammo began cooking off and exploding. The dung beetle shook violently as pressure and ordnance tore jagged holes in the plating.

Chalk one up for us on that cocksucker . . .

Germans on foot hauled ass out of the area.

Let's go for the machine gun nest . . .

Bingo! Bingo!

Some of the doughs watching from the top of the hill stood up and cheered.

It was a good day's work.

60

We had a rule in A Company not to leave wounded out there to die alone.

—CAPTAIN DAVID WILLIAMS

A Kraut observation post and machine gun nest armed with *Panzerfausts* smoked one of Able Company's tanks on a drive, blowing a track and knocking the tank lopsided next to a strip of winter-bare timber dripping icicles. In the excitement of bailing out for the rear, the crew overlooked one of its members. Corporal Vinton Hudson managed to escape the tank but now lay alone and semiconscious in No Man's Land. Someone would have to go back for him before the Jerries shot him. He lay less than 150 yards from the nest of vipers that had done in the tank.

Captain Williams quickly organized a rescue patrol. He would lead it, since a company commander had to set the example The group included Big Tit Richardson, Henry Conway, Chico Holland, a stretcher bearer, and a battalion aidman named Ray.

"Where the hell is your vest?" Williams asked Ray.

Medics were supposed to wear bright vests inscribed front and back with a Red Cross to identify them as noncombatants.

"I gave it to the infantry," Ray said. "They needed it worse than we do."

"Damn. The Krauts can't see that cross on your helmet."

There was no time to scrounge up more vests. Ray and his assistant secured a stretcher, and the party set off on foot, using a shallow draw for cover as it made its way in spurts toward the disabled tank and Hudson. To Williams's surprise, they took no incoming fire. The Germans seemed to have deduced the purpose of the mission and decided not to harass it.

Either that or the sneaky bastards were waiting until the Americans made clearer, nearer targets of themselves.

As the band approached the tank, now crawling on bellies, Captain Williams heard a weak cry as Hudson tried to attract attention. Chico Holland spotted him collapsed behind a tree. He and Conway pulled security with their carbines while the others slithered across the cold ground to the wounded man. A dead German lay face down a few yards away. After taking one quick look at the body, no one paid any further attention to him.

Hudson's arm was shattered. Shards of bone poked out of the bloody mess.

"Am I going to die, Captain?" he asked.

"What makes you think that? You're on your way home."

He wasn't bleeding that much, considering all that damage. Ray dusted the wound with sulphur powder, bandaged it, splinted the arm, and then indicated that he was ready to go.

"Maybe you'd better give him morphine, Ray," Williams suggested. "The stretcher ride back could get a little rough."

The Germans still had not opened fire, not a single shot.

Medication promptly brought a euphoric smile to Hudson's face. Ray and the litter bearer started dragging the heavy stretcher across the ground, crawling on their bellies. A slight noise, *something*, caused Captain Williams to look back.

The "dead" German raised a hand. He seemed too weak to lift his head. He simply looked at the Americans, silently pleading.

"Ray, hold up a sec. Follow me."

The stretcher bearer dragging Hudson returned to the shallow draw and headed home. Captain Williams and Ray crawled to the wounded German. They couldn't just *leave* him. He'd die without care.

"Was ist los mit dir?" Williams asked. He spoke some German.

"Ich bin verwundet."

He had at that. His shoulder was smashed and bloody.

Ray cut away the man's tunic, dusted the wound, and used a compress to stop bleeding. Williams signaled for another stretcher to be brought up. The cease-fire persisted. Apparently, the Germans realized that the Americans were caring for their soldier and that he was better off in a prisoner of war camp than if recovered by his own side. Hitler's armies were running critically short of all supplies, including medical.

As the Americans started away with the German on a stretcher, a Kraut officer stood up in the machine gun nest and smartly saluted his thanks. Captain Williams returned the salute.

Both wounded men—Hudson and the German—survived.

"Krieg ist endet für dich," Williams told the German. The war was over for him. "You'll like Camp Hood, Texas."

The poor sonofabitch had been given the luckiest break of his life. Somewhat later, Captain Williams received a letter from him.

Dear Hauptman. You were right. I like Camp Hood, Texas . . .

61

I was a tank mechanic; cleaning out those wrecks went with the job.

—SERGEANT CHESTER JONES

The Sherman required a lot of TLC, tender loving care, else it simply gave up the ghost at the worst possible moment. Having a tank break down in combat, a common occurrence with all tanks, was almost as bad as having it knocked out by the enemy. Therefore, much of a tanker's spare time went into maintenance.

Fouled spark plugs were the most common problem. Ordnance shop trucks with sandblast cleaning machines kept constantly busy with them.

Tracks posed the next major problem. Tracks were constructed of rubber blocks instead of steel. They lasted approximately two thousand miles of highway driving, more or less, including one reversal, before the constant pounding started to break them apart. Rubber marks and pieces of rubber littered France and had now started to appear in Germany. Sergeant Floyd Dade quipped about how he must have personally left at least a truckload of rubber in his wake.

A high percentage of Black Panther tankers came from the rural South and therefore had had experience with tractors, cultivators, and other farm machinery. They and the city boys had also spent a great deal of time in the motor pool during armored basic training where they maintained and serviced their mechanical war horses—replacing tracks and wheels, spark plugs, belts; checking oil, water, and other fluids and lubricants. The driver and assistant driver took responsibility for such first-echelon maintenance.

During lulls in the fighting, engine housings were opened and black grease-smeared tankers could be seen everywhere with wrenches and hammers pounding, tinkering, *coaxing* their temperamental beasts to keep going. The tune of an old Negro spiritual, "Dry Bones," had been modified and used in basic training as a learning aid. Its quick melody drifted among the sounds of hammering and frustrated curses.

> *The wheel bone's connected to the axle bone;*
> *The axle bone's connected to the differential.*
> *The differential's connected to the propeller shaft,*
> *And it all goes round and round . . .*
> *Them bones, them bones, them dry bones . . .*

The M4 was supposed to be pulled off the line every one hundred hours for routine maintenance and an operational check. It didn't always happen, not in combat. Combat action and attrition claimed so many that companies often operated on less than half their allotted complement. Many of those were patched-together pieces of junk. Master tank mechanic Sergeant Ernest Hill, Service Company, went around bartering for deadlined tanks from other outfits.

"Don't junk that," he pleaded. "I can fix it."

Some tanks simply quit at crucial stages of a battle. TC Sergeant Floyd Dade experienced one of those frustrating and harrying occasions while Dog Company was screening against a town being prepped by U.S. P-51 dive bombers.

The little aircraft swarmed in the sky above the town like vicious wasps, darting in to repeatedly sting targets. Fire and smoke from the pounding created a weird, phantasmagoric scene in the gray morning light.

Sergeant Teddy Weston, acting platoon leader, found Dade

pacing back and forth in front of his tank, blistering it with the cussing of its inanimate life.

"These pieces of shit is gonna get us all killed," he exclaimed in disgust. "Damn battery has gone dead."

"I'll radio somebody to bring up a battery," Weston offered. "Get a machine gun set up over in them trees to provide some cover."

Dade set up the machine gun. A mortar round impacted nearby as he returned to his stalled tank for a box of ammo. The concussion knocked him to the ground, splattered him with mud, and elicited a new round of cursing.

As though all that were insufficient to ruin his day, he noticed a P-51 break off from strafing and bombing the town and head toward him. It circled the tank, sniffing suspiciously. Germans often used captured Shermans.

Dade jumped up from the ground and waved frantically. So did the rest of the crew, everybody shouting as loudly as he could: *"We're Yanks, we're Yanks!"* The aircraft swung out and then back in, as though the pilot couldn't make up his mind.

Thoroughly pissed by now, the TC ripped off his field jacket to use as an eraser and ran to the tank. He hurriedly wiped off caked mud to reveal the large white star on the side. This seemed to convince the P-51. It wagged its wings and flew off to resume its business around the town.

Many of the Yank tanks resembled rolling junk piles. Tankers attached sandbags, wooden timbers, old auto tires, spare track blocks, and about anything else they could find to the face plates of their tanks as added protection against murderous German antitank guns. On top of *this*, mounted to various and sundry parts of the monster's body, went duffel bags, 10-N-1-ration boxes, water cans, and other personal items. Mud crusted everything equally while enemy action ripped and tore everything. A tank battalion could be followed solely by the gear left discarded and lost along its route.

Maintenance people with T2 recovery vehicles ventured onto

the field after each fight to locate, evaluate, evacuate, or destroy shot-up, stalled, and damaged equipment. Tanks could not be replaced without the proper paperwork. Maintenance men found some of the most ghastly sights imaginable whenever they opened the hatches of wrecked vehicles.

The enemy possessed many means of cracking a tank like an eggshell and scrambling its inhabitants. German tanks were mounted with 88mm and, for the great Tigers, 128mm cannon, both of which could reach way out and slap a Sherman before it even came within range of its own 76mm gun. Although the electric-system turret on the Sherman, referred to as "Little Joe," made it possible to swing the gun and turret into position faster than Jerry's hand-operated one, the Sherman first had to get within range in order to make sure the fastest draw won the gunfight.

Antitank ditches, mines—*always* mines—and deadly hand-held *Panzerfausts* extracted a toll perhaps even greater than did tank destroyers or other tanks. At least enemy armor could be *seen* and fought. Mines, although sometimes deadly, were pretty much considered a nuisance. Tankers feared the *Panzerfausts* as much as they did armor. They could be fired from anywhere at any time to spray the inside of a target with molten metal.

When a tank hit in battle was opened, often there were remains all over the interior—parts of arms and legs, amputated hands, intestines draped about like colored Christmas tree garlands, spattered brains and blood. Everything was tossed into plastic containers for the Graves Registration people to root over. The tank was repaired, if possible, but men were squeamish and a bit superstitious about taking a machine back into battle in which others had already died.

Maintenance people were always busy after an engagement. Sergeant Ernest Hill and his mechanics recovered a Charlie Company tank hit and gutted in the same fight during which Sergeant Dade's light tank quit because of battery problems. One of the crewmembers turned up missing and was presumed killed. Hill expected to find what was left of him inside the tank. There was no corpse inside when he reached the tank. Everyone then presumed he would be found later the way Ivory Hilliard had been found in Guebling—dead in enemy territory.

The next morning after fighting ceased and the targeted village had been taken, Sergeant Hill led a recovery party into town. Allies had moved on through in pursuit of retreating Germans. Inhabitants had departed before the battle started and so far had no reason to return. There wasn't much left to return to.

Not an intact building remained standing. Nothing but smoldering rubble, a partial wall sticking up here and there like a broken rib, total silence as though in hushed tribute to the memories of horses, cows, dogs, and men whose mangled carcasses lay everywhere. So much quiet gave Sergeant Hill the creeps.

Ice water crept down his spine when, as though at a great distance, he heard in all that destruction the unearthly tinkle of piano keys.

"Do you believe in ghosts, Sergeant Hill?" a mechanic inquired.

"Ain't no ghosts. Just people who go crazy."

The cautious little band followed the sound. It grew louder until Hill recognized the tune.

"My Mama Done Told Me."

It came from up ahead, from a shell-exploded house with its roof collapsed and only half of one wall standing. As the mechanics edged nearer, they discovered the source of the music. Among the debris of shattered furniture and dishes, the remnants of someone's former life, sat a broken piano. And at the piano sat the missing tanker from Charlie Company.

He was decked out in a black silk top hat and tailcoat he had scrounged from somewhere in town. And he was playing that broken piano, playing it in the early morning grayness, playing it with total concentration as though he were the only living thing left in the world, playing a concert for the dead and, perhaps, for God.

"My Mama Done Told Me . . ."

62

We gave infantry regiments or divisions we worked with the best protection possible. It meant their lives.

—SERGEANT EDDIE DONALD

With relief and some surprise, the 761st received orders to stand down in the rear to refit, relax, maintain equipment, receive and train replacements, and shake off some of the battle mud. It was a rare opportunity for the tankmen to feel like ordinary human beings again. They set up pup tents by platoons, shook out their gear, washed clothes, played take-down football, grabassed, talked trash, and enjoyed shaves and "showers" out of their canteen cups. PX rations were even issued—cigarettes, fresh cakes of soap, shaving cream, candy, gum, aftershave lotion.

"Ooooh, you stink so good!"

Replacements arrived to fill out the battalion roster again. Casualties had reduced the 761st to bare bones. Shermans were going into battle with only three or four men of the customary five-man crew. Some of the new men had hardly even *seen* a tank, having been dispatched from repple depples (replacement depots) with scant regard to their training specialties. Bodies were needed *here* more than *there,* so they were sent *here.* They joined their new units feeling alone and disoriented.

Black soldiers had few choices anyhow; they *had* to go to a segregated outfit where vets trained them quickly not only in tank operations but also in battlefield survival. If they made it through their first firefight or two, they stood a chance of becoming veterans themselves, useful members of the battalion, and making it through the war. The battalion was suffering far fewer casualties now than it had when it was green in the beginning of the French campaign.

Sergeant Motel Johnson looked around at all the new faces and chafed, "Lawdy, the Black Panthers is turning *green.*"

"Lean, mean, green fighting machine," Johnny Holmes corrected.

"It just ain't normal," Johnson said, talking trash around a bonfire, "to go blowing up cities, burning things, and cheering—*cheering*—when our side kills the other guys."

"Kill 'em all before they kill us," said mild-appearing Sergeant Harding Crecy, addressing a number of wide-eyed replacements standing nearby. "Remember this, boys, and don't forget it: You kill them bastards, you kill them as fast as you can, as many as you can, any way you can—or else they'll kill you."

"How many you kilt so far, Sergeant Crecy?" someone asked.

The little man adjusted his glasses and walked off.

"That guy don't look like no killer," one of the Panther vets explained to the new men, "but I reckon he's that all right. Jerries kilt his best buddy when we first come over. Since that day Sergeant Crecy has been on a tear to destroy every German he can find. Something happened to change the sergeant the day Scotty died."

Sergeant Johnnie Stevens, who rejoined the battalion after recuperating from wounds sustained on Hill 309, was tapped to give instruction to white infantry and black tanker replacements regarding joint operations between tanks and doughboys. Blacks gathered around on one side, whites on the other. An infantry lieutenant introduced the cocky Black Panther.

"Sergeant Stevens is a tank commander with the 761st Tank Battalion," he said. "These men have done a lot of fighting. They've lost a lot of men and they know what they're doing. They are experienced combat soldiers and I want you to listen up."

It was Stevens's assertion that if a replacement could fire a machine gun, there was a job for him in the 761st. He could always be taught to be a bow gunner or a cannoneer.

Stevens sauntered over to the nearest tank and vaulted on top of it.

"Smoking lamp is lit," he said. "Smoke 'em if you got 'em. But if you want to live, you'd better listen."

He paused while men nervously shook cigarettes out of packs. Poor bastards. Scared shitless. Had he and the other vets been *this* green when they first came on the line?

"You have to learn what to expect from a German tank and you have to learn how to fight with a tank," Stevens began. "The only way I can teach you is to tell you what we fear. The German tanker fears the same thing. If you go into combat tomorrow and you meet eight or ten German tanks, you're going to die. If you learn from what I tell you, then you might come out of this alive.

"What do I fear as a tanker? I fear the guy who has guts enough to run out there and take his rifle and shove it in my sprocket. You can stop a tank with a rifle. The sprocket isn't going to bust that damned rifle. No way.

"I worry about the guy who has guts enough to run up from the rear of my tank, climb aboard, and drop a hand grenade down my hatch.

"I worry about the guy who has guts enough to run up there, pull the pin, and drop a grenade in my gas tank.

"I worry about these things."

He spent the rest of the day talking, demonstrating, showing the new guys how things worked.

"This is the deck plate, the lower escape hatch," he said, showing them. "If you're in a foxhole and you're being machine gunned and can't get out, don't raise your head up. We will see you. I got a tank. We will run right over the foxhole and open the deck plate. We are going to bring you up and take you inside the tank. We are going to get you out of that damned field . . ."

He went on and on.

"If you find yourself in a minefield, don't lose your head. See them tank ruts, see how deep they are? All you have to do is get in them ruts and you follow 'em . . ."

The most attentive man listening to the crusty sergeant's spiel was one Private Christopher Navarre, a strikingly handsome, light-skinned twenty-four-year-old from LaFayette, Louisiana. Navarre was no ordinary replacement. He had been a company *first sergeant* before taking a bust to private in order to go to the front lines and fight. That was only one part of his colorful background.

He was born into a traditional southern household of six brothers and sisters where "Mama was never wrong." Being a Negro in the Deep South where remnants of Old Dixie hung on well into the twentieth century, he knew Jim Crow on a first-name basis and grew up in rigid segregation.

He attended a segregated Catholic high school and studied for the priesthood afterward at a segregated Catholic seminary. Negroes were not allowed to drink from public water fountains, eat in a white restaurant, or enter a white tavern or café. They had to go to the rear of any place where they *were* allowed to go—the back of the Catholic church, small balconies in the rear of movies, the back of the bus, and when they died they were buried at the back of the cemetery. There were three rest rooms in his hometown bus station marked as *Men, Women,* and *Other.* Negroes, both men and women, were *Other.*

In 1940, Christopher went home on a visit from the seminary and never returned, having decided he wasn't cut out to be a priest after all. He briefly enrolled in Louisiana's State Barber College before enlisting in the army. Japs bombed Pearl Harbor while he was serving with the 15th Infantry Division (Buffalo Soldiers) at Fort Huachuca, Arizona, a unit composed of white officers, Indian scouts, and colored enlisted men. Dogs, mules, and horses were assigned military rank and often outranked Negro soldiers.

When the United States Army mobilized after Pearl Harbor, Navarre's mama wanted him to marry before he shipped overseas. She already had a bride picked out for him—a pretty local girl named Bernice Breaux, whom Christopher knew only slightly. But . . . Mama was never wrong. She scheduled the wedding and the young groom-to-be wrangled a weekend pass three days before his outfit was scheduled to move out. He left on Friday for a big wedding on Saturday and had to be back on post for movement by Monday morning.

"You know what I'll do if you don't come back," his company commander warned.

Navarre shipped to France with the 590th Ambulance Company, promptly advancing to become one of the youngest first sergeants in the Regular Army. He remained near the front lines of the invasion, moving continuously through France driving a camouflage-painted ambulance. White soldiers seemed to resent being transported by black medics and ambulance drivers. Christopher requested a transfer from his service unit to a combat outfit. He wanted to go into armor.

His CO resisted at first, turning down his requests. "We need you here, First Sergeant."

"I want to fight, sir. I want to do *something.*"

"Believe me, Navarre, you don't want to go on the line."

"I'm volunteering, sir. I'm going to keep requesting a transfer until you sign it."

Finally, the CO threw up his hands. "All right. All right! Navarre, you are one stubborn man. But the only way you can go is to give up your first sergeant rank and start all over again as a private."

Navarre saluted smartly. *"Private* Navarre requests transfer, sir."

He was assigned as a fledgling replacement gunner to the 761st Tank Battalion, Charlie Company. He would learn through OJT, on-the-job training.

"So *this* is what you wanted, *Father* Navarre?" Sergeant Stevens asked. "Well, Father, you are going to see plenty of action soon enough."

"You are crazy, *crazy,*" said little Willie Devore, who couldn't understand why anyone would want to leave a cush job in the rear to ride around in a Sears & Roebuck coffin and risk getting killed.

63

I don't ever recall a black soldier in my outfit crying.

—CORPORAL HORACE EVANS

It was a commonly accepted reality that anyone who spent any length of time in combat was going to become a casualty sooner or later. The casualty, as if by a miracle, immediately went from a frozen, brutal wasteland to a warm, kind world with a gentle touch. If the man was lucky, his million-dollar wound bought him a ticket back home. If not so lucky, he suffered permanent injury, say as an amputee or an invalid. If downright unlucky, he ended up dead—or returning to the front.

Many black soldiers, however, dreaded even the thought of going to a hospital with white soldiers. There was no such thing as race on the front lines, where black and white soldiers desperately wanted to live and had to depend upon each other for their survival. But back in the rear area with its "gentle touch," race once again reared its head to bite the balls of Negro soldiers. Most could hardly wait to return to their front-line families, even if it did put them back in danger.

So it was with Charles "Pop" Gates, Sergeant Johnnie Stevens, and Corporal Horace Evans. Pop Gates, now promoted to the rank of captain, returned from his Honskirch wounds and resumed command of Charlie Company. Stevens had gotten back just in time to start training replacements when the battalion went on stand-down. Evans, the "Secret Weapon" of Baker Company, had been wounded in the arm during one of the battalion's countless little skirmishes and came walking back into his company area one morning just before the 761st went back on line after its rest.

"Hey, hey, the man is back. You poor nigger."

A bright smile split Evans's dark face. "*Au contraire*," he said.

"Listen to *that*. This country boy done learned French while he was gone."

Evans seemed downright ecstatic to be back, having, he said, been treated so poorly in the hospital.

"On the front line," he said, "there is so much more freedom."

Overworked hospital staffs often assigned walking wounded to help those patients less fortunate. Evans had been asked to attend a white infantryman suffering from a leg amputation. For a week he stuck with his charge, wheeling him around, taking him to chow and the pot, even tucking him into bed and helping him bathe.

One afternoon he entered his patient's ward unobserved and overheard him fretting to another white patient. "I'm hungry. What's holding up my nigger?"

The amputee looked up in time to catch Evans's eye. They stared at each other.

"Fuck it!" Evans spat back in retaliation, turned on his heels, left, and never came back. The remark stunned, infuriated, hurt, and surprised the tanker, all at the same time. Johnny Holmes was right: You couldn't trust a Paddy to be anything except a Paddy.

That was the one time Evans cried, the only time he ever personally knew of a Black Panther actually crying. He went off by himself and suffered out his hurt and anger. After that, he sneaked off from the hospital before doctors released him and caught rides to the front. One Black Panther might call another *nigger,* but joshing wasn't the same thing as a white man using the word, especially a white boy to whom had been offered nothing but kindness and friendship.

Injury followed insult as Evans worked his way back to the 761st, hitching rides from unit to unit on his way forward. One night MPs picked him up and made him stand in a lineup for a black soldier accused of raping a local white French girl. His stomach was a real wreck by the time he reached Baker Company.

Sergeant Eddie Donald embraced him. "Welcome home, boy," he said.

64

Nuts!

—GENERAL ANTHONY MCAULIFFE, WHEN ASKED TO
SURRENDER AT BASTOGNE

General Dwight Eisenhower still gave little credibility to intelligence reports warning of a German buildup for a possible counteroffensive in the north. In his opinion, such a major move seemed beyond Germany's capability. Patton, however, assumed a different stance. In early December he noted in his personal diary that "the 1st Army is making a terrible mistake in leaving the VII Corps static, as it is highly probable that the Germans are building up east of them. . . . Had the V and VII Corps been more aggressive, the Germans could not have prepared this attack."

Patton instructed his staff to prepare two different plans of operation that could be quickly implemented in case the Germans did push westward. He, alone of major commanders in the ETO, predicted the epic struggle that became known as the Battle of the Bulge, because of the way it bent back the American lines.

Americans stationed in the Ardennes Forest were enjoying themselves tremendously while the Germans were getting ready. The war had not come to the Ardennes and, better yet, was not expected to. GIs stationed there played poker, improved upon their winter quarters, chased local skirts, and received passes to nearby rest and recreation centers. Someone observed that the Americans were like the grasshopper in the old fable—playing his fiddle and enjoying his days while the Germans kept busy as ants getting ready for the winter games.

"We are billeted as comfortably and safely as we were in England," Private Joe Schectman wrote to his parents on December 15. "Of course there's no telling how long I'll be in this paradise. But as long as I am, I'll be safe."

In the predawn of December 16, 1944, at precisely 0530 hours, an American sentry on the quiet Ardennes front radioed his HQ to report innumerable "pinpoints of light" suddenly flickering along the German line. He was still on the radio when, an instant later, German shells began crashing around him. The "pinpoints of light" were the muzzle flashes of hundreds of German artillery pieces. All along the eighty-five-mile front from the medieval city of Echternach in the south to the resort town of Monschau in the north, thunderous artillery bombardments jarred American units from their sleep and cut great black gashes in the six-inch blanket of snow.

In desperation, the Führer had launched Operation Autumn Mist in an attempt to push Allied forces back through Belgium to Antwerp and across the River Scheldt and thereby compel the Allies to sue for peace. He threw a quarter-million German soldiers into the Ardennes against eighty thousand Allies, catching them completely by surprise.

General Eisenhower ordered George Patton to assume command of VIII Corps south of the enemy breakthrough and attack toward the north to stop the German penetration. The Third Army began moving north along four separate routes with nearly twelve thousand vehicles.

The 761st Tank Batalion had been poised in the vicinity of Saarbrucken and Zweibrucken, waiting to strike against the Siegfried Line, when it received orders to dash to the Ardennes with the rest of the Third Army. One contingent traveled by train while the bulk of the battalion negotiated steep and icy roads on the way to battlefields in Belgium, encountering snow slides, downed and weakened bridges, and enemy bombing and strafing, all of which resulted in the loss of ten tanks and one man. Tech Five Horace Johnson died when the battalion came under hostile artillery fire.

General Eisenhower issued an Order of the Day to all troops in the Ardennes: "Let everyone hold before him a single thought, to destroy the enemy on the ground, in the air, everywhere to destroy him."

KIA (Killed in Action)
Tech Five Horace G. Johnson

65

We were more expendable than most.

—Private Christopher Navarre

The Ardennes Forest was Christmas card perfect. Evergreen trees grew so thickly a man couldn't walk among them without dislodging snow and being smothered in it. Icicles three feet long tinkled merrily when the wind or a careless hand loosened them. While it may have been picturesque, it was hell on both men and machines and threatened the very limits of the 761st's character and patience.

Temperatures plummeted to as low as twenty below at night. Snow covered the solidly frozen ground in depths up to two feet, burying narrow roads, heavily wooded hills, mountainous cliffs, and deep ravines in a mantle of white. It was an Ice Age world where primordial fog hung thick and low, where every day began and ended cloudy and foggy, where snow fell so thick and continuously that a man had to cover his mouth just to breathe. Walking to take a dump in the woods became a concentrated effort.

The long convoy of Black Panther war wagons clanked, crunched, and shrieked over roads made almost impassable by snow and ice. Head stuck up out of his turret hatch, TC Eddie Donald's eyes watered from the wind, his nose ran because of the cold, and everything wet froze on his face.

"Didn't your mama never teach you to wipe your nose?" Horace Evans asked.

"Don't make me laugh, man. My face'll crack and fall off."

Almost everything a tanker wore to keep warm was made of wool—OD woolen trousers and shirt, long woolen underwear, woolen sweaters, double woolen socks under combat boots, and wool-lined parkas. Some of the men cut leg holes in their sleeping bags and drew them on like a pair of trousers.

The only disadvantage of wool was that once it got wet it took forever to dry. And the men were always wet, even inside the refrigeratorlike tanks. They were constantly having to get out into the weather for one reason or another. Snow sifted into their clothing and melted from body heat, wetting them to the skin. Water sloshed in their boots and froze in their canteens. The experience wasn't always miserable; sometimes it was torture. Nights were worse, especially as the battalion neared the Bastogne area and had to leave their tanks to bivouac at nights because Germans shelled tanks wherever they found them.

"Let 'em have the tanks," was Sergeant Johnny Holmes's philosophy. "Save your black butts."

Ground was frozen so solidly that it took a quarter-pound block of TNT to loosen the ice crust before a pickax could be used to further enlarge a foxhole. Tankers on bivouac sought protection in the trees where they dug their holes and covered them with logs, rock, dirt, and snow as a shield against artillery. But if the snow was a curse, it also became a blessing during the frequent artillery barrages by absorbing much of the blast and fragments. It was possible to avoid injury from a shell strike as near as a yard away if the target threw himself prone in the snow.

One evening during a shelling, Private Thomas Ashly was observed taking hurried leave from his dugout after a near miss.

"Where you going, Ashly?" someone called out, taunting.

"Just going for a walk."

"Walk, you say? Then where the hell is your boots?"

The tankers paired up for warmth in order to sleep. Each pair lay down and snuggled as close as they could get to each other to preserve and share body heat and keep from freezing, like dirty, smelly twins in a womb.

"I suppose you expect me to marry you after this is all over?" Eddie Donald cracked as he hugged Horace Evans close.

"You are so ugly. Forget it."

Lt. Colonel Paul Bates, commanding officer of Black Panther Battalion. TAFFY BATES

Nurse Taffy Bates. TAFFY BATES

Company commanders in England (commands changed later). Clockwise from left: Captain David J. Williams, Able Company; Captain J. R. Lawson, Baker Company; Captain Irvin McHenry, Charlie Company; Lt. Richard English, Dog Company; Captain Ivan Harrison, Headquarters Company; Captain August Bremer, Service Company. NATIONAL ARCHIVES

General George S. Patton, Jr.
U.S. ARMY

Ruben Rivers, 761st Medal of Honor
winner (posthumously).
JOE WILSON

Tank Commander Warren G. H. Crecy, "the baddest man in the Black Panthers."
JOE WILSON

James Mason and Sergeant Johnnie Stevens.
JOHNNIE STEVENS

Dog Company, 761st, preparing equipment in England prior to going into combat. Front row, left to right: Maxie Henry; Judge Favors; Jack Gilbert; Albert Fullwood; John Wimbush. Rear, left to right: Elmo Johnson, Matthew L. Johnson; Arthor E. Richie. NATIONAL ARCHIVES

Captain Phil Latimer, Supply Office for 761st.
U.S. ARMY

Black Panther Battalion Patch.
U.S. ARMY

A Sherman tank and infantry maneuver in France.
U.S. ARMY

E. G. McConnell (left) with crewmembers of the "Cool Studs" tanks.
E. G. McCONNELL

Sergeant Harvey Woodward's tank shortly before the entire crew was killed without a mark on the tank or its crewmen. NATIONAL ARCHIVES

Remains of four German tanks and two 761st tanks near Guebling, France. NATIONAL ARCHIVES

Private Clark, Charlie Company, tank driver, sports his newly captured German Luger pistol. E. G. McConnell

Lt. Moses Dade in Germany. Joe Wilson

Sherman tanks and infantry enter a destroyed German town. U.S. ARMY

Tech 4 Eddy Jones celebrates the end of the war.
JOE WILSON

The doughboys built more elaborate digs, since they moved about so much less than tankers. Some were little underground chambers whose floors were covered in straw. Blankets hung over doorways to keep out wind and snow. At one end might be a small wood-burning stove pilfered from an abandoned house. The holes were surprisingly warm and comfortable with a good fire going.

The cold did strange things to the dead—and there were always plenty of dead lying about where earlier battles and skirmishes had been decided. Men froze in the exact grotesque positions in which they fell and died. Sometimes the only way to get them to stay on a stretcher was to break their limbs loose with a board or a rifle butt.

Sergeant Crecy fired two rounds from his Tommy gun into a German lying at the side of the road with his rifle before he discovered the trooper was frozen as solid as a block of ice. The bullets chipped and cracked his flesh as if it *were* ice.

"It won't do him any good to thaw out in the spring," someone commented.

The Mosquito Fleet bivouacked one night in a monastery, the woods around which were littered with corpses. Corporal George Blake didn't know if they were German or not and didn't care to go out and look. He didn't get much sleep.

"I'm not much on dead bodies," he said.

Weather and conditions were such that Captain Phil Latimer in Supply gave up on using trucks and turned to Dog Company's light tanks to deliver provisions. Sergeant Jack Gilbert's Stuart broke down on the road about dusk during one supply run. He removed the engine cowling and found he needed help with wrenching off a particularly stubborn part in order to replace it. As the rest of his crew had gone on with the company, he looked around and spotted a doughboy standing nearby next to a half-track.

"Hey, buddy. Give me a hand with this, willya?"

"No problem."

The guy called out to two other GIs. All three rushed over to help. Gilbert got a shock when he took a closer look and saw that the first soldier wore the stars of a major general and the other two were colonels. He thanked his helpmates after he was finished. They smiled. He jumped back into his tank and roared and shrieked off into the night, chuckling over how he had finally gotten to order a general around.

Snow in great wet flakes frequently fell so hard and thick that visibility was cut to almost the length of a Sherman's main gun. During such a snowfall, Sergeant Johnny Holmes led a Charlie Company platoon along a narrow lane bordered in quiet snow-laden conifers. Piled snowbanks on either side rose shoulder high to a man on foot.

Head protruding from the tank, eyes squinting, Holmes was directing his driver along the lane when the damndest thing happened.

A file of German soldiers materialized out of the storm, appearing suddenly, as ephemeral as ghosts. The American tanks and infantry were going one way, the Storm Troopers the other way. They passed each other not fifteen yards apart. Neither side looked directly at the other, for to have acknowledged the presence of enemy meant something would have to be done about it. It was just too damned cold and miserable to start a fight.

The surprise of the encounter, the unexpectedness and sheer implausibility of it, kept the guns on both sides still. The Germans vanished wraithlike into the mist and blowing snow. Holmes exploded the breath he had been holding.

"Damn! Did you see that?" he asked his gunner. "Germans!"

The gunner was tongue-tied from astonishment. He shook his head vigorously until he finally dislodged words. "No, Sergeant. I ain't seen nothing. I *ain't* seen *nothing.*"

On Christmas Eve, the men of Able Company cut down a small cedar, brought it into camp, and decorated it with cotton, boot strings, gauze bandages, and anything else they could find. They built a big fire. Everyone seemed unusually subdued, pensive as they thought of home and families an ocean away. Christmas to Americans would always mean going home.

Someone began to sing in a soft, sad, baritone voice. Others joined in until the chorus rose gently into that cold dark night.

Silent night, holy night,
All is calm, all is bright . . .

Mobile field kitchens prepared the traditional turkey dinner on Christmas Day. Orders came to move out before the meal finished cooking. Panthers grabbed hunks of half-raw turkey and ate Christmas dinner on the road.

"Lousy Krauts must have caught ole Santa and kilt him," Willie Devore complained. "He didn't bring me shit."

"Here, Willie," Private Thomas Bragg offered, "you can have my last pair of dry socks. Merry Christmas, Willie."

"Merry Christmas, Thomas."

66

During the Ardennes operation we had very little armored unit support, but of that we had the 761st was by far the most effective and helpful.

—GENERAL WILLIAM MILEY, COMMANDER
17TH AIRBORNE DIVISION

The Battle of the Bulge dashed hopes that Hitler might be ready to give up. It seemed the Germans were getting a second wind. They drove forward for ten days, pushing "the Bulge" deep into Belgium and inflicting dreadful casualties on the Americans. Nearly nine thousand surrounded Americans surrendered in one pocket near the Schnee Eifel, the single largest mass surrender in American history outside Bataan. At Malmédy, the SS executed seventy-one captured Americans in a field. Some thirty-three English-speaking commandos led by Otto Skorzeny infiltrated Allied lines to create chaos, as if the offensive itself were not already doing so.

The Allies reestablished air superiority on December 23. That same day, American forces launched a counterattack against the southern flank of the Ardennes bulge. Germans fought desperately to stop the move and prevent their having to withdraw to their own Siegfried Line.

Letter of Instruction No. 12 from Twelfth Army Group directed General Patton's Third Army to: attack northeast to seize Houffalize and link up with the besieged First Army; destroy Germans in its zone of operation; launch an offensive toward St. Vith to protect First Army's flanks. At the same time, General Patton made a bold attempt at slashing through to relieve American troops faced with annihilation at Bastogne.

The 761st Tank Battalion joined the American counteroffensive on December 31 after it had already achieved notable successes spearheading for the relatively untested 87th Infantry Division and the more battle-hardened 17th Airborne Division. That same night, hampered by terrible weather that included bitter cold, deep snow, and freezing ice, Patton's Panthers led the way in recapturing the villages of Rondu and Nimbermont. Tanks rumbled through the snowy streets of Nimbermont at exactly midnight, New Year's Eve.

"Happy New Year's!" Sergeant Johnnie Stevens called out, to which no one responded.

On New Year's Day, the 347th Infantry Regiment and the 761st began an offensive to cut the Bastogne–St. Hubert road, a main German supply line. Heavy enemy artillery and antitank fire slowed the attempt as, for the next several days, the units fought to recapture towns that guarded the route.

On January 2, 1945, the black tanker battalion left four of its tanks burning in the woods. However, in subsequent days Baker Company with Lieutenant Harold Gary leading the attack killed 150 enemy infantry at Bonnerue; Charlie Company knocked out three machine gun nests at Remagne and killed fourteen enemy gunners; and the Mosquito Fleet destroyed eight machine guns, killing seventeen gunners, and captured seventy prisoners even as it ferried supplies to the rest of the battalion.

Casualties remained surprisingly light. The battalion suffered only one KIA. Sergeant Robert "Motel" Johnson of Assault Guns Platoon, who had helped save Charlie Company's bacon at Honskirch by firing white phosphorus smoke to allow the pinned-down and wounded tankers to escape, died when his 105mm howitzer tank slid off a slippery road and crushed him.

Low casualties while inflicting high casualties on the enemy was one indication of a good fighting unit. Battalion commander Major John George thought the 761st had compiled an out-standing record for itself in the weeks since its first battles in early November, considering the heavy fighting in which it had been involved.

The enemy gradually fell back from Bois-de-Lambay Fays and Pironpre. Fighting along broken roads and trails moved toward the town of Tillet located some fifteen miles or so west of Bastogne and less than three miles from the Marche-Bastogne Highway, another major German supply route. The 761st and the 87th plowed through heavy opposition to cover twenty-five miles toward Tillet in six days of combat. Roads through the icy hills were reduced to little more than crushed and broken paths and tank tracks across open fields and through timber where the enemy concealed artillery posts. German armor was sometimes dug in and sometimes marauding. Storm troopers fought savagely to hold each town and village or, if they were unable to do so, to make the Allies pay dearly for taking it.

The 761st was assigned to support elements of the 87th Infantry in recapturing Tillet.

Germans had fortified the area, turning smaller villages and other real estate around the town into a killing ground. The elite Führer Begleit Brigade of the 13th Panzer Division, whom the Black Panthers had fought before in the Saar Basin in France, waged a grueling defense in dense pine woods south and east of the town. Enemy positions were carefully planned and backed by numerous machine gun nests, self-propelled guns, mortars, and armor. Within past weeks, Allied tanks, artillery, and infantry had tried repeatedly to take Tillet and end the see-saw battle to win the St. Hubert Road. All had failed, beaten back by stubborn German defenders.

On January 4, Patton's Panthers and doughboys of the 87th began their own drive to reach the town and take it.

KIA (Killed in Action)
Sergeant Robert A. Johnson

67

You can find Tillet in many books on WWII, but you won't find one word about us.

—SERGEANT EDDIE DONALD

Artillery flashed almost continuously as the intensity of German fire increased around the villages and towns on the way to Tillet. It rumbled like thunder in a summer storm as shells crisscrossed the sky like deadly lightning. Sergeant Eddie Donald said he knew after the first hour of fighting that the 761st was up against SS troops, old adversaries from France. These guys knew how to fight. Infantry doughs scattered among the tanks and moving with them suffered horrendous losses from mortars and machine guns.

An infantry captain ran up to Sergeant Johnny Holmes's tank and pointed to a timbered hill covered in deep snow.

"There's a fucking sniper up there and he's already shot three of my men," he shouted above the growl of the tank's engine. "Sergeant, can you see him?"

Holmes glassed the hill with a pair of binoculars from his higher vantage point in the turret.

"Yeah, I think I see him."

"Can you get him for us?"

"You ask, we deliver."

He pointed out the target to gunner Raleigh Hill.

"HE," he said. "Smoke the bastard."

Hill laid two rounds on the sniper's position. High explosives erupted snow geysers and toppled a tree. The sniper abandoned his hide and fled.

"Good shooting, kid."

Holmes walked .50-caliber fire up the running man's ass, then through him and past him, shredding his body and tossing him to the snow like so much garbage.

"Thanks, Sergeant."

"We aim to please, Captain.

The tanks moved from town to town, village to village, playing follow-the-leader along frozen and disintegrating remains of roads, rushing inexorably toward Tillet. Many streets in the little towns were cobbled, often narrow, sometimes spanned by stone archways. Tanks and doughs dispersed along different avenues, always alert to the unexpected appearance of German firepower, fighting hand to hand against the recalcitrant Germans, street to street, building to building.

Sergeant Harding Crecy saw a German fire a *Panzerfaust* point-blank from a house window at a tank loaded with doughs. It exploded and flung GIs in all directions. The Kraut then emptied a burp gun at the survivors as they scrambled for cover. Only after he ran out of ammo did he throw up his arms and jump out through the window, shouting, *"Kameraden!"*

"Kameraden my ass!" Sergeant Crecy retorted and filled the Kraut's gut with machine gun bullets.

He might have let the guy live if he had surrendered in the beginning. It was bad form and bad judgment for him to have shot up everything in sight and then tried to give up when he was out of bullets.

"Screw the bastard," Crecy said. "He had it coming."

He wished the Kraut could have died a slower, more painful death.

"No more Mr. Nice Guy," Crecy declared, his eyes burning from smoke that fogged everywhere. "Blast all the windows. Give these sonsofbitches something they won't forget."

Sheets, rags, and anything else white hung out many windows as civilians attempted to indicate their presence and their capitulation. Wads of German soldiers staggered and limped out of the smoke with Belgian and Belgian-German citizens, everyone waving white flags and yelling *"Kameraden!"* Sergeant Johnnie Stevens stopped firing because he couldn't tell combatants from noncombatants. Occasionally, white flag decoys were used to lure Americans into letting down their guards.

On an evening before an attack on one of the few towns left between the advancing Americans and Tillet, Private Thomas Bragg came to see Captain David Williams as Able Company bivouacked. Bragg, loader in the tank TC'd by Sergeant James Nelson, had been a popular member of the 761st Orchestra before the battalion shipped overseas. A talented musician, he was a small, sensitive man of medium dark complexion and good manners. Although he stayed shyly in the background, he was not a shirker and did more than his share of volunteering.

"What's on your mind, Tommy?" Williams asked. He made a point of knowing the first name of every man in his company and something about their lives and backgrounds.

Williams, his driver, and several other noncoms were in a discussion. Snow dusted their shoulders and the hoods of their parkas. Fighting rumbled in the distance, but the world immediately around seemed to have settled in for the night.

"Captain, I got to talk to you in private, if I could?"

They walked off together. Bragg rubbed the side of his nose, looked away, and seemed uncomfortable.

"Out with it, Tommy. What's bothering you?"

He blurted it all out in a single pent-up breath. "Captain, my wife is about to have a baby, and I know I'm going to be killed."

Premonitions of death were not uncommon with men in the constant presence of the Grim Reaper. It was easy enough to say, "I won't be coming out of the next battle," when you kept seeing buddies fall, when every day you kept thinking that the next one, the next dead soldier . . . is *me*. A premonition, however, didn't mean it *would* happen. Look at Willie Devore, who had been predicting his own demise from the time the 761st sailed out of New York Harbor.

Still, such feelings often preceded a deeper depression, a sinking feeling of the soul in which life lost its meaning, the world went dark, and death tagged every footstep. Premonitions left unanswered even led to death *wishes*.

"Go back to the rear," Captain Williams offered. "I'll put someone else in."

A man afflicted with such intuitions often lost them if he had a chance to rest up for a few days.

"Captain, I ain't telling you this so I can Wingo out and go back. I know it's going to be mean up there tomorrow. I'm just telling you so I can ask you to write a letter to my wife."

"Tommy, don't say that. I'm giving you an order to go back."

"Please don't order me, sir. I'm needed. I'm going to fight. Will you write the letter?"

A lump formed in Williams's throat. He thought of Ruben Rivers, who wouldn't quit either.

"Tommy . . ."

"Will you, Captain?"

These magnificent men. They would do anything, even confront what they thought to be certain death, in order not to let down their buddies. He had seen so many of these black men die.

He nodded mutely, overcome with deep sadness and a weariness of the soul.

"Thank you, Captain. Be sure to tell her I love her."

Infantry of the 87th Division died by the score the following morning. Able Company joined the fray with all guns firing. Lieutenant Teddy Weston's platoon laid down such a fierce base of fire after the 87th had been stopped in its tracks that the enemy withdrew toward Tillet. In what could almost be considered a last act of defiance, a German TD hurled an 88 Ripsaw that struck Sergeant James Nelson's tank a bull's-eye blow. Nelson, who had commanded the first tank of the 761st to roll onto German soil at the beginning of December, was killed instantly.

So was his loader, Private Thomas Bragg. Captain Williams had to write two letters home.

KIA (Killed in Action)
Staff Sergeant James W. Nelson
Private Thomas S. Bragg

68

Quite often in life, nothing goes as planned.
—Private Joseph E. Wilson, Sr.

Tillet was a town under siege. As picturesque as a post-card—"Wish you were here"—it nestled in a natural terrain bowl surrounded by fir- and pine-covered hills. Thick mantles of snow cloaked the hills and shrouded the town in an eerie, hazy fog composed of a mixture of smoke and thin cloud cover sparkling with ice crystals in the first rays of the morning sun.

The small hilltop village of Gerimont looked down into the Tillet basin. Able Company's commander, Captain David Williams, and his driver, Big Tit Richardson, stood in the middle of the ice-sheeted road and studied the objective. For the present, the guns on both sides lay silent, as though waiting.

According to all accepted defensive tactics, the Germans should have abandoned the town in favor of high ground elsewhere. Normally, a defender wanted the enemy to have to climb to get to him. Yet Captain Williams had to admit SS tactics under the circumstances were brilliant.

The town bristled with armor and artillery, but its real defensive power lay in a well-fortified hill that rose to overlook the Tillet basin. From the top of this hill, even taller than the one on which Gerimont was built, artillery, armor, and mortars could shoot right down on top of attackers, sort of like medieval defenders on a wall dumping boiling oil on invaders.

Tanks and troops descending steep, icy slopes to get to Tillet would have a tough time withdrawing once they engaged. The return route up the hill was too steep and slippery. Once the assault consigned itself to that pit of a Roman gladiator's nightmare and found itself in crossfires from both below and above, one side or the other would have to win decisively.

Patton's Panthers had received their orders: Spearhead the taking of Tillet. *How* that was to be done was left up to the commander of the 761st and officers of the 87th elements. They were reluctant to commit to battle on the Germans' terms; the Germans were equally disinclined to fight other than on their terms. The siege had therefore turned into a waiting game. Baker and Charlie companies of the 761st had dug in on Able's flanks, 87th Infantry companies dug in around them—and everybody waited.

For the past two days, Germans had tried to get the Americans to come down and fight by probing them with mortar fire and foot soldiers camouflaged in white sheets. The Americans had not taken the bait. None of the German probes was a serious counterattack. The fight was more like two punch-drunk boxers, each of whom refused to leave his corner on the bell and stood his ground while throwing air punches at shadows.

Resupplies and reinforcements were urgently needed. The battalion had moved so rapidly in recent days that its supply lines, already plagued by weather, had been stretched unacceptably thin and made vulnerable to the enemy. The wooded terrain of the Ardennes offered ideal sites for enemy raids on supply trains. While the light tanks of Captain English's Dog Company continued to move fuel, food, and ammo to its sister companies at the front, returning with wounded infantrymen and tanks, often driving through gauntlets of machine gun fire, it was never enough. Captain Williams had been forced to conserve both ammo and fuel.

"We're getting low on gasoline," he told his platoon leaders, "but there's not much we can do about it. Don't idle the engines any more than you have to. These monsters use too much gas as it is."

The 87th Infantry was made up of relatively green troops

with limited combat experience. The battle-tested 17th Airborne was supposed to be on the way—but it was currently out there doing something else. Jerry in the basin was getting restless. The American troops were getting restless. Worse yet, it was reported that General Patton was getting restless. Word came down that higher Headquarters was tired of waiting.

"Take Tillet."

Where was Colonel Bates when the battalion needed his strength of will and personality?

Captain Williams had offered his plan for seizing Tillet. Wouldn't a feigned attack on the Kraut's hill draw the enemy out into the open from their town fortress, at which time Baker and Charlie companies could move in quickly with their doughs and take the town while it was at its weakest? Major George thought it worth a try.

There was only one way to find out if it would work.

After a last troubled look at the apparently sleeping town in the basin, Captain Williams abruptly turned away. "Let's do it," he said.

He got in the Jeep with Richardson and raced back into Gerimont, where attack forces waited to be unleashed. Sergeant Johnnie Stevens had dozed off in his turret seat. Engines revving woke him. He gave a start.

"Is it over yet?" he asked of no one in particular. "One of these mornings I'm going to wake up and there I'll be back home in my own bed—and all this shit won't be nothing but a bad dream."

Doughs jumped onto the tanks for the ride into battle, clinging to the backs of the monsters, as Emerson Hadnot put it, like baby possums to the fur of their mamas. The tanks roared off, leaving fading echoes and whirls of snow blasted up from their downward-pointed exhausts.

The infantry dismounted when the hill loomed directly in front. Able's tanks moved out ahead with the inexperienced doughs of the 87th trotting along behind. Captain Williams spotted uniforms in the snowy woods an instant before hell erupted like a volcano.

"Holy shit!" came an exclamation over the radio.

The deep woods were full of Krauts armed with deadly tank-killing *Panzerfausts*. Tanks couldn't get to them through the heavy timber, although Able did knock out a TD in the initial skirmishing and sent two other small Kraut tanks scuttling back up their hill. Tanks were particularly vulnerable in such close combat and depended upon infantry to shield them. Infantry in this case, however, had gone to holes wherever they could find them and were too frightened to get up and fight.

An ambush such as this offered two choices, neither of which was altogether palatable: Either you fought your way out of it, or you lay down and got slaughtered.

Shouting sergeants ran amok among the cowering soldiers, kicking them and blackguarding their ancestry all the way back to the beginning of time. Sergeant Stevens and Lieutenant Weston jumped out of their tanks and, in between firing their personal weapons at converging shadows in the woods, joined the melee to get the doughs on their feet.

"What the motherfuck is the matter with you people?" Stevens yelled. He scurried about in the flying lead yanking doughboys off the ground and tossing them toward the woods.

It was a clusterfuck, a deadly clusterfuck.

When the doughs finally got off the ground in some numbers and charged into the woods, the Krauts broke contact and pulled back deeper to allow Moaning Minnies and 88s to work over the Americans. The tanks were momentarily ignored. Jerry evidently figured they could do little damage in this environment. Although the tankers were unable to see the fighting in the forest, they certainly heard it.

Soon, infantrymen came running and shambling out of the trees with visceral horror written huge on their faces. Large numbers of Germans appeared chasing them, firing as they came.

Tanks and infantry retreated, leaving a considerable number of dead doughboys in the woods.

69

I shall never forget that place.

—SERGEANT EDDIE DONALD

The battle for Tillet continued. Krauts showered Gerimont with artillery and mortar fire, then trudged up the hill to engage Able Company. Captain Williams threw them back into Tillet. By this time he was running so low on fuel and ammunition that he dared not exploit the situation and launch a counterattack. The 87th was dispirited after its defeat in the woods and content to lick its wounds. Williams sent a runner back to Major George with a message that he feared the Germans might have guessed his men were short on supplies and would launch a full attack. He wasn't sure if he could hold out.

Night fell. An atmosphere of apprehension as thick as ground fog collected around the tankmen of Able Company. Captain Williams called a meeting of his platoon leaders and noncoms in the village house where he had established his CP. First Sergeant Bob Linzy, platoon leader Teddy Weston, platoon leader Sam Brown, Sergeants Johnnie Stevens and Henry Conway, Sergeant Walter Lewis, gunner Joe Kiah, Big Tit Richardson . . . they gathered in the kitchen.

Light from a pair of burning candles reflected flickering on black skin and against the makeshift blackout curtains over the bungalow windows. Corporal Richardson boiled some coffee and poured canteen cups full of it on demand.

"I'm not going to mince words," Williams said, looking as tired, ragged, filthy, and unshaven as all the other men in the room. "If the Germans attack us, we can't hold them. I guarantee you that if we resist, they'll kill us all. I'm the company commander, but I'm going to bow out of this one. This is one decision you guys have got to make. Do you want me to wave my underwear, or do you want to fight it out?"

For a long minute no sound came except the guttering of candles and the low moan of the winter's wind at the panes. German tank destroyers lurked in the forested hills to the north. The situation to the east and west looked no brighter. The slope leading down to Tillet was already strewn with disabled American tanks and the snow-dusted corpses of the fallen. Sergeant Conway thoughtfully slurped hot coffee from his cup.

"What about the 17th Airborne?" someone finally asked.

"They're supposed to get here tonight or first thing in the morning," Williams said. "They may be too late."

What Captain Williams told no one was that he had received seemingly impossible orders only hours ago in response to his own message. If the battalion survived the night, it was to assault and take Tillet the following morning with the 87th. With or without the 17th Airborne.

Sergeant Walter Lewis, the quiet man, suddenly slapped his cap on the table with a forceful bang and stood up.

"We can't give up, Captain," he said. "It wouldn't be right. I say we fight it out."

That broke the tension. Walt was the last man anyone expected to speak up. Nervous laughter filled the kitchen. The vote was unanimous. Everyone agreed with Lewis. Besides, they had all heard about the massacre at Malmédy.

"Done!" Captain Williams concluded. "If Walter wants to fight it out, then we'll fight it out. Fifty percent alert all night. Get ready. Meeting adjourned."

70

It was a strange thing. You are trained to do a job,
even to the killing of men, but you do your job.

—LIEUTENANT JOHNNY LONG

To the relief of the 761st and especially the 87th, the 17th
Airborne arrived overnight, pulling in to Gerimont in
their vehicles and on foot over snow so frozen it cracked
and popped under pressure. The Germans knew of the reinforcements and held what they had in Tillet and on the overwatching hilltop.

The final decisive action against Tillet launched at dawn with
tanks creeping through the early morning fog and snow. Major
George contributed all three medium tank companies to the effort.

Sergeant Walter Woodson, TC of an Able Company lead
tank, found communications with other tanks jammed. The
Krauts had scrambled radio transmissions in order to put on
Axis Sally, the generic name applied to the various women who,
in perfect English, broadcast propaganda to the Allies. Her
voice came in loud and clear through Woodson's headset. She
gave him a peculiarly eerie start when he realized she was talking directly to the men of the Black Panther Battalion in a soft,
soothing voice.

Good morning, Negro soldiers of the 761st. I am sorry that
you will die today in Tillet. Our fight is not with the Negroes in
America, and your fight is not with us. Your fellow Negroes are
rioting in Cleveland. Your commander, Captain Williams, is
leading you to death and destruction. He is white and not one of
you. Your battalion commander, Major George, is also white and

not one of you. Leave your tanks now and return home to Cleve-
land where you are needed and you will not be killed . . .

On and on.

"Fuck you, bitch!" growled driver Walter Lewis.

Sally played Louis Armstrong's "I Can't Give You Anything But Love, Baby" to accompany Patton's Panthers into combat.

Able Company hadn't traveled more than one hundred yards downslope out of Gerimont before a slight breeze stirred across the face of the hill, lifting the fog's skirts. And there the Germans were. Right in front and everywhere. Already beginning to fight.

Sergeant Woodson's tank got it first. His hatches were still open when the Ripsaw struck with the noise of heavy plate glass bursting into a million ear-shattering pieces. Somehow, the force of the concussion, all that pressure built up inside, shot Sergeant Walter Lewis straight into the air out the driver's hatch.

He hit the snow and rolled to his feet, stunned and hardly knowing which way was which. His clothing hung in bloody shreds, his ears rang, his head whirled. Only one thought entered his mind: *Get the hell out of here.*

He ran. *Ran.* Not knowing in which direction, he ran. *Ran!* Ran from the pulsing crescendo of sudden all-out battle. Through the snow and through the bullets that grazed across the terrain. Ran until his lungs burned and his eyes seemed to freeze up in his skull. Ran right on past Gerimont and didn't even see it. Ran until he came to a monastery, tall and red brick and undamaged and sitting in undisturbed snow among snow-laden conifers.

No one in sight. Refuge.

He ran toward it. He heard the air shrieking as Germans shelled the monastery too. Geysers erupting, mussing and churning the clean snow.

Sobbing, he ran past the monastery. Ran until he blacked out and collapsed.

The next thing he knew he was on a litter being evacuated in

a convoy of ambulances moving slowly through minefields and
booby-trapped roads. The quiet man who had spoken up last
night—his war was over. In the distance he heard the thundering roar of dueling artillery and tank guns, the hard chattering
spatter of small arms . . .

The final battle for Tillet was under way.

71

*In my opinion, the Battle of the Bulge was the tough-
est.*

—LIEUTENANT JOHNNY LONG

Infantry, airborne, and all three companies of Black Panthers
hurled themselves against the iron ring of the German defenders in a fight that was most notable for its raw savagery.
It was never clear at any one moment to the men doing the
fighting whether they were winning or not. Both sides were losing men and equipment. Meat wagons kept busy hauling
wounded back from the sound and fury of battle. Captain Pop
Gates's Charlie Company was down to about 50 percent again.

Platoons led by Sergeants Moses Dade, Frank Cochrane, and
Teddy Windsor accounted for eight machine gun nests, one
Mark IV panzer, three antitank guns, an ammo dump, and more
than one hundred Germans—but they were still unable to make
headway and enter the town. An antitank round clipped the turret off Dade's tank and sent it caroming through the air for more
than fifty feet. Fortunately, the crew had hunkered down out of

the turret when it happened. Although the .50-cal was gone, Dade and crew continued to fire their remaining weapons, refusing to pull back out of the battle.

German antitank fire repeatedly lit up Sergeant Frank Cochrane's tank. Pop Gates watched the Sherman zigzagging through a hail of machine gun bullets and *Panzerfaust* rockets.

"What's your condition?" he asked.

"They've hit me three times," Cochrane responded, "but I'm still giving 'em hell."

Sergeant Harding Crecy, turret hatch open to allow him access to the heavy machine gun, was busy mowing down Krauts and cranking up his body count numbers. He paused every so often long enough to adjust his glasses, give orders to his driver, and look for fresh targets.

"*Sonsofbitches!*" he shouted. "*Sonsofbitches!*"

These were all part of the same *sonsofbitches* who had killed Scotty.

Tech Five Willie Devore, driver for Sergeant Teddy Weston, chanted at the top of his lungs, "This is it! This is it!"

We put HE in there. I think we did some good . . .

The doughs want us to lay some big ones in there. There's a pillbox or something . . .

Watch out to your left . . . your other left . . .

Get ready to move out when we get some room . . .

There are friendly doughs a hundred yards to your right . . .

Don't get any of our doughs, but if you spot Jerries . . .

Someone saw a tanker jump out of his wagon right in the middle of a fight, drop his trousers, and dump a load in the snow. He scrambled back into his tank without wiping, his pants still halfway off.

Eddie, was that your Secret Weapon . . . ?

Whassa matter—already filled up his helmet?

True to habit, the Germans dispatched an occasional artillery barrage at support personnel in the rear. One salvo killed Tech Five Jessie Bond of Headquarters Company. No one saw him die. His lifeless body lay sprawled out in the open among trucks and other vehicles near the battalion CP.

Sergeant Henry Conway and his crew got separated from the rest of Able Company on a low hilltop on the outskirts of Tillet. Sixteen German panzer tanks surrounded him, all banging away with their 88s. He backed his Sherman around the corner of an abandoned factory where he could command the only avenue of approach along the road. Only one or two panzers at a time could come at him.

He waited, waited for a panzer to stick its ugly snout around the curve in the icy road.

Ready! Ready! Fire!

Shot out . . .

Bingo! That son of a bitch . . .

Sergeant, these motherfuckers never learn . . .

Soon, they had burning tanks stacked up on the curve, spreading clouds of dense black smoke.

Sergeant Johnnie Stevens's voice came over the air. "Henry, you winning this war all by your lonesome or can anybody get in on it?"

"I figure there's enough fighting for everybody to get some."

"Move over, Rover. The big cat's back in town."

KIA (Killed in Action)

Tech Five Jessie J. Bond

72

The whole thing moved so fast we could hardly keep up.

—SERGEANT ERNEST HILL, MASTER TANK MECHANIC

During the thick of the Tillet fighting, a Sherman limped off the battlefield and was eventually abandoned in a wooded draw. Four Service Company mechanics driving two light Stuarts went out to recover it. Captain William O'Dea and Tech Five Bill Love led in the first tank with Lieutenant Bill Griffin and Tech Four Lewis Smith trailing in the second.

The two speedy little tanks circled wide of the main sounds of combat, ducking and buttoning up only once, when a mortar tried to home in on them. They approached the draw from the south and located the tank sitting upright at the bottom, apparently undamaged, hatches left open from when the crew unassed it. There didn't seem to be anyone around; the roar and chatter of battle, ebbing and flowing, remained on the far side of a range of hills. Falling snow hissed in the evergreens and piled on the tank's decks.

"I'm going down," Love said. "Keep me covered."

He skittered down through the trees lugging a box of tools and shaking loose mini-avalanches of snow. He crouched near the tank and observed it for a few minutes, looking for tracks or other signs that Jerries might have discovered it first. Satisfied at last, he rose and quickly climbed inside.

The crew compartment was as cold as a tomb. Snow drifting down through open hatches covered the seats and the floor. A loose round of unfired 76mm HE jammed the gear levers. He extracted the shell and tried the engine. To his surprise, it started right away, its only problem, he determined, a loose transmission. He thought he might be able to herd it back to the battalion VCP under its own power.

He popped his head out the driver's hatch and motioned for the others to lead the way. Captain O'Dea started down, but Love waved him off. He could do it better alone.

It turned out to be one wild ride. All the hatches were frozen open. The transmission slipped, limiting the tank's top speed. A German forward observer spotted the three tanks when they were halfway home and directed artillery fire down on top of them. Speeding, darting targets were difficult to hit. With the assistance of a P-47 Thunderbolt that happened to be in the area and dive-bombed the German artillery, the little convoy shot on out of the kill zone and onto the final stretch.

Love reached the VCP driving like a bat escaped from hell. When he applied brakes the tank skidded for more than fifty yards across the frozen ground, nearly wiping out a maintenance tent and another parked tank before it plowed into a snowbank. He jumped out grinning and flashing the V for victory for the benefit of his audience of other mechanics and HQ personnel.

73

The Negro tank battalion attached to my command fought bravely in the critical Battle of Bastogne.

—GENERAL GEORGE S. PATTON, JR.

Captain Pop Gates, the crusty "old man" of the 761st, personally led, on foot, a ten-tank assault on one of the German hilltop outposts overwatching approach routes to Tillet. Suspecting enemy ahead, he grabbed his grease gun, climbed out of his tank, and darted up through clumps of trees to take a look for himself. He crept to the edge of a clearing and counted three Mark IV panzers, a 75mm German assault gun, an 88 antitank Ripsaw, and about a company of SS. They occupied strong bulwarks, but their defense was oriented in the other direction. If he hurried, he could surprise the poor bastards and catch them from the rear.

He scooted out of sight and returned to where his tanks waited. He burst out of the trees covered with so much snow that he resembled a yeti with a black face. He pumped his arms.

Come on, come on, *come on!*

Remaining on foot to better guide his iron war wagons, Gates led the way through the scattered trees. Tanks growled softly after him like a pack of giant trained predators. Doughs from the 17th Airborne stretched across a wide front, dodging and trotting uphill through white fairyland forest.

A German sentry hiding in the woods happened to spot them. He jumped out and started back to spread the alarm. Gates started the fight by dropping him with a spray of rounds from his grease gun.

Accesses to the hilltop had alternately frozen and been covered with drifting snow so heavy and deep that even the tanks found footing precarious. They blazed away, engines roaring as they toiled up the long, gradually rising slope, on-line like a troop of charging cavalry mounted on great fire-belching steeds.

Inspired by the sight of the big black man leading the way shouting encouragement and firing bursts from his little submachine gun, slipping, sliding, and falling only to jump up again to repeat the process, infantry caught up in the excitement and frenzy of the moment stormed the enemy redoubt.

The hill posed one of the last obstacles to taking the town. Again and again, Charlie Company and the 17th Airborne threw themselves at it. Chilled to their bones, the weary men followed the black captain each time he waved his grease gun above his head and shouted, "Them sonsofbitches are going *down!*"

The fight was all but over, nothing left but the mopping up, when a land mine nailed Sergeant Teddy Windsor's tank, a pop of smoke underneath his forward treads. The tank humped into the air with the impact, jarring the teeth of the four-man crew. Many of the tanks were undermanned.

Barely had the smoke and snow settled before an HE followup round walloped the tank a good blow and enveloped it in a ball of flame.

"My God! My God!" driver Willie Devore shrieked.

Dazed by the dual knockout punches, crewmembers chased their way out of the dead behemoth only to find themselves out of the kettle and into the fire. German artillery batteries in Tillet opened up final protective fires in an effort to keep the critical hilltop from being overrun. Explosions walked back and forth, chewing up ice and snow and tearing doughboys apart. Equipment and body parts flew in all directions. Foot soldiers seemed to vanish from the earth in a blink of bright light. A bloody severed hand dropped out of the sky and almost hit the fleeing tank crew.

"Run! *Run!*" Windsor shouted.

The others needed no further encouragement. Gunner Bill

McBurney and loader Leonard Smith zigzagged down the slope behind Windsor, taking long leaping downhill strides and windmilling their arms to maintain balance, dodging explosions while their brains seemed to be bursting with the horror and racket of the devastation.

The three managed to stay together during their wild flight from the heights. They ran, crawled, and wriggled on their bellies for nearly two miles through mortar, artillery, and small arms fire. Hours later they stumbled onto the battalion CP in the rear. They were half-dead from concussion wounds and exposure to subarctic temperatures.

"What about the rest of your crew?" they were asked.

Windsor shook his head, half-numb from the ordeal.

"Did anybody see if Willie got out and which way he went?" he asked the others.

No one had seen Willie Devore after the hill.

74

Seeing that death, a necessary end,
Will come when it will come.

—SHAKESPEARE

For two days the 761st Tank Battalion fought side by side with the 87th Infantry Division and the 17th Airborne before finally wresting Tillet from German hands on January 7, 1945. Successful American operations split the enemy lines at three vital points—the Houffalize-Bastogne Road, the

St. Vith–Bastogne Highway, and the St. Vith–Tries Road—and thereby helped prevent the resupply of German forces encircling American troops at Bastogne. The exhausted Black Panthers assembled in a field east of Tillet to regroup, refit, and catch their breath. Most were so tired they didn't even want to eat.

The kid of the outfit, E. G. McConnell, who had been wounded and evacuated from Honskirch, returned to duty while Allied forces were still mopping up and cleaning up after the battle to take Tillet. Lane Dunn, Johnny Holmes, Isiah Parks, the correspondent Trezzvant Anderson, and a few others from the battalion brought McConnell up to date on who had been wounded, who got killed, and how things had been going. They were sitting around on gas cans and water cans at the assembly area while they somberly assessed the events of the past few days. Willie Devore, they told E.G., was MIA, missing in action, for the past four days. It was believed he might have been captured.

"This war goes on and on," Dunn said. "It ain't ever gonna stop until there ain't none of us left."

"It's worse sometimes than it is at others," Holmes said philosophically. "We gotta keep going until the fat lady sings."

"That fat bitch never could sing," Parks said. Nobody laughed.

Holmes threw up his hands. "I don't understand these German folks," he said. "How can they keep fighting on and on when we are kicking their asses?"

A three-quarter-ton truck interrupted further conversation. It pulled up and stopped in Charlie Company's area. Two black soldiers from Battalion HQ got out and walked around to the back of the truck. They dropped the tailgate and lifted the tarp.

"Hey!" one of them called out. "I think we got one of your guys here."

They dragged out a corpse. It fell to the snow with a dry crunch. There in the snow, body grotesquely twisted and frozen in that shape, lay the remains of little Willie Devore. His eyes were frozen wide open, as though the death he had been expecting since New York had finally caught him by surprise. E.G. reached for his prayer book and held it tight as he stared at what was left of his friend.

KIA (Killed in Action)
Tech Five Willie J. Devore

75

We must make certain that the German is not free behind his strong defensive Siegfried Line.

—Captain Harry C. Butcher, naval aide to
General Eisenhower

It wasn't until after the turn of the year and after having successfully beaten back the enemy in the Ardennes Bulge that General Dwight Eisenhower and the Combined Chiefs of Staff (CCS) could again start thinking about penetrating the Siegfried Line and crossing the Rhine River, the last major barriers to the Reich's heartland.

The CCS estimated the Germans to be exhausted but still dangerous in spite of Allied pressure in the west and pressure from the Russians in the east who had already crossed the Oder River and were menacing Vienna. Eisenhower contemplated a Rhine crossing that would eliminate the industrial capacity of the Ruhr region and open a path to the north German plain, excellent territory for mobile armor operations.

The Rhine, wide and treacherous in its northern reaches, posed a major geographical obstacle as well as a military one. Further, the Germans controlled several dams on tributaries that allowed them to manipulate the level of water and speed of the current. Plus, the Germans had not been exactly routed at Bastogne. They were retreating, but retreating in an orderly fashion, making the Allies pay in blood for every yard of territory gained. There was still much fighting to do before the Allies reached the Siegfried Line, penetrated it, and headed for the Rhine and the final thrust to Berlin.

76

The spirit of comradeship between the men of the 761st and the men of the 17th Airborne was a beautiful thing, and they willingly risked death for each other on many occasions.

—TREZZVANT ANDERSON

As always, the average GI knew little of the war's Big Picture. He seldom knew what was going on outside his limited scope, where he was going next, or what he would do when he got there.

"How much longer is this war gonna be?" medic Howard Brown worried.

Milton Dorsey from 761st Supply smoked a cigarette, shivering hand cupped to shield it from freezing rain. "There's gotta be an end to it somewhere, brother, and it ain't far away. It just can't be much longer until we sees ole Hitler come marching in with his hands over his head."

"If we make it that long," Brown said.

During the month of January, Patton's Panthers, operating with the 87th Infantry and the 17th Airborne, pushed the enemy back from the center of the left flank of the Bulge for approximately sixty miles. Towns fell one by one. Horresbach, where Pop Gates's Charlie Company accounted for twelve enemy *Panzerfausts,* one pillbox, one Mark IV tank, a mortar position, and eighty Germans. Huem, where Johnny Long, now promoted to captain and awarded a Bronze Star for valor, led Baker Company in destroying machine gun emplacements so the 345th Infantry Regiment could take the town. Into Luxembourg, the fourth country in which the 761st had fought, and a fight at Espeles where the Assault Guns Platoon fired up a large patch of woods that concealed heavy enemy forces and armor, prompting Germans to come out with their hands lifted in surrender.

Sergeant Frank Cochrane and Sergeant William Kitt, both of whom distinguished themselves at Tillet, became the first men of the battalion to be awarded battlefield commissions. Lieutenant Maxwell Huffman kept the leadership of Able Company white when he replaced Captain David Williams as CO. Williams was hospitalized with such a severe case of trench foot that his driver, Big Tit Richardson, had to help him in and out of his Jeep. The "blackest white man" the men of the 761st had ever known would not be coming back. Big Tit's eyes moistened as Williams was loaded into a three-quarter-ton ambulance. Able Company solemnly congregated for an event that seemed to be the end of something.

"Keep knocking 'em back, Jack," Williams called out in the Harlemese that had become his calling card before every engagement. And then the ambulance with Williams in it was gone, vanishing in the fog and blowing snow.

People in Belgium spoke both French and German. Many

Germans had lived in the buffer zone of eastern Belgium even before Hitler seized it in 1940. Many remained strongly pro-Reich. Still, as Patton's Panthers fought their way across Belgium, white flags waving from house windows signaled that the German nationals living there were willing to surrender peacefully. They had suffered terribly in the war, as had most civilians all across Europe.

Yesterday's houses were today's rubble piles. Bullets had pockmarked and artillery shells and bazookas had gouged out the walls of those houses left standing. Abandoned vehicles, weapons, equipment, and trash littering the roads left evidence of the German retreat. People were often quite willing, even eager, to warn advancing Allies of German roadblocks and defenses.

"*No me Boche. Français, me Français.*"

"Parley-vous English?"

"*Un petit. Beaucoup Boche en le bois, beaucoup Boche.*"

Snitching on the Krauts. *Many Germans in the woods.*

The fighting seemed interminable. There was always another town lying ahead. Another hill to climb and take. A river to fight across. Life, the world, became a succession of bitter days. One battered town after another, each of which offered some form of resistance before it invariably fell.

Take the town, mop up the region, secure the area, establish medical tents and prisoner facilities—and then move on to do it all over again. A routine filled with noise, mud, fatigue, anxiety, and a constant struggle to keep going. A grim nightmarish existence in which survival depended only on dogged determination and luck.

Trench foot. Hands and face filthy. Haunted eyes sunk into skulls. Skinny. Filthy uniforms too big. Chain smoking. Trembling hands. Fingers and lips split and raw with blood and suppurating sores and scabs. Sleeping in bombed-out houses, in the tanks, in the snow, sitting on the ground, sitting down, standing up, leaning against a wall, walking even. Sleep that rarely satisfied and never cured the bone-deep weariness. The only escape was through death, wounding, capture, mental breakdown, desertion—or the end of the war.

"All right, cats! Get ready to go. Let's make some noise. Get them engines revved."

Doughs trudging through the weather, looking as miserable as starving, mangy curs kicked out into the winter rains.

"I wouldn't trade places with y'all tankers for nothing," said a dough with a Mississippi drawl.

"You're kidding."

"Huh-*uh!* Them tanks attract Kraut fire like magnets. You get trapped inside that tin can and you ain't got no place to hide and they ain't no point in ducking. Y'all might be safe from bullets and mortars, but you ain't escaping them big-ass 88s."

"I still feel safer in a tank."

Dead Germans. GIs kicking them over with their boots to search for rings or watches or other booty. Cutting off fingers to get the rings.

"Shoot 'em and loot 'em."

"I suppose they're shooting and looting us, too."

A man couldn't help thinking that the next fight might leave him out in the cold for some German to come along and find. Sergeant Harding Crecy took off his wedding ring and stuffed it deep into his pocket.

A German POW seemed stunned to see black men in uniform. "What are you doing here?" he asked in English. "This is a white man's war."

Sergeant Johnny Holmes offered him a cigarette. "You ain't got no black or white when you're over here and the nation's in trouble," he said. "You only got Americans."

Chilling drizzle turned the landscape as dreary as the men felt. More snow fell. Fog hung low over the roads. Sullen skies. The sun seemed to have been rationed out of existence. Biting wind. More snow. Nights as black as a black man's midnight asshole. Pelting rain. More snow.

Swampy ground lay underneath the snow on open ground. Tanks bogged down. Recovery vehicles and other tanks pulled them out of the mud and muck. Eight tanks were lost to the battalion at one time because of terrain conditions.

"How can it be almost over," Corporal Joe Kiah lamented, "when we just keep on keeping on day after day?"

On February 3, the 761st rolled into Jabeek, Holland, near the German border and set up a command post in the land of windmills, dikes, and wooden shoes. There would be a brief respite while Allied units regained strength for the assault against the Siegfried Line and the Rhine River.

Black Panther enlisted men were starved for the important things in life, like girls, French fries, girls, hot dogs, girls, going to town on Saturday nights to boogie, and girls. They set up a "joy house" in the basement of the two-story house Major George selected as his battalion CP and furnished it with two or three jaded local whores. Every horny tanker in the outfit knew at least two words in perfect French: *couchez avec.*

77

Taffy, don't you understand? What I am is a teacher. I teach men how to stay alive.

—LIEUTENANT COLONEL PAUL BATES

Colonel Paul Bates's nurse of the 14th Field Hospital had followed the Third Army and thus the 761st Tank Battalion all the way across France and into Belgium. Although Taffy and Paul corresponded daily via slow V-mail and managed an occasional telephone patch call, they had not been together since that rainy night when Paul sent a staff car for her. Taffy missed him, but for her part she would just as soon he stay safe in England until the war ended.

One morning in mid-February, she was busy catching up on paperwork at a field desk when the flap of the hospital tent opened. It was a rare day when the sun shone with such brilliance that its reflection on snow was enough to blind. The silhouette of a tall soldier filled the opening. The sun against snow blasted an aurora all around him. She blinked, squinting against the glow.

"Taffy."

"Paul! Oh, my God!"

She sprang to her feet and threw herself across the tent and into his receiving arms, crying and laughing all at the same time in her joy.

When they caught their breath, Paul explained that they had only a few hours together as he was on his way to Holland to resume command of the 761st. He had turned down a promotion to full colonel and command of an infantry regiment in order to return to his black tankers.

"The job's not over, Taffy," he said. "From every report, the Panthers have acquitted themselves well and honorably since I've been gone. But what kind of man and officer would I be not to return to men I've trained for over two years to do a job?"

"I wouldn't question it, Paul. Let's go to my tent. I'll grab a coat and warn my bunkmates to stay away on penalty of having their throats choked."

On February 17, Lieutenant Colonel Paul Bates resumed command of the Black Panther Battalion. Major John F. George was promoted to light colonel and transferred to an infantry staff. Sergeant Moses Dade became the third Negro in the battalion to win a battlefield promotion to lieutenant.

The battalion had changed considerably in Bates's absence.

Not only was it now battle-hardened, but many of the old-timers from the days at Camp Claiborne, Camp Hood, and England were also gone, some of them dead and many of them wounded and shipped Stateside. More than 30 percent of the battalion had been replaced. More than two hundred recent repple-depple replacements joined the battalion in Holland. All of them were greenhorns and required training in tanks; replacements were assigned out of service and ground forces with little consideration for previous experience. Staff Sergeant Walter Sadler had been a cook, for example, and Sergeant O. D. Collins a military policeman.

The two-week training course Major George had set up under instructors like Sergeant Johnny Holmes and Johnnie Stevens and the platoon lieutenants was busy making hands of the new men and sending them out on OJT cleanup combat missions in Holland. Sadler soon became a gunner in Baker Company; Collins took over a war wagon as tank commander.

Word of the colonel's return spread rapidly through the battalion even before change-of-command ceremonies. A line of tankers, veterans who knew him from the beginning, formed outside the CP tent to welcome him back with grins and handshakes.

"Who is that white man?" a young repple-depple asked.

"He ain't no white man," Corporal Joe Dixon shot back. "That man is Hard Tack. That man is *the colonel,* the best commander in the U.S. Army."

78

*The more Germans we kill west of the Rhine, the
fewer there will be to meet us east of the river.*

—SUPREME ALLIED COMMANDER
DWIGHT EISENHOWER

Hitler counted on the formidable barrier of his West
Wall—the Siegfried Line—and the Rhine River to stop
an invasion from the west. He retained only about a
million soldiers on his Western Front to pit against 3,750,000
Allied troops while he funneled reinforcements to the east to
stop the Russians.

The Wehrmacht had suffered nearly four million casualties
during five years of warfare. Manpower resources were dwin-
dling. In mid-January 1945, Hitler ordered all men under forty-
five to be drafted into the armed forces. He also ordered the activation of eight new divisions composed of seventeen-year-olds
and *Volksgrenadier* (people's infantry) scavenged from rear-echelon units and stray airmen and sailors. While these lacked
training, they retained the discipline to keep fighting in the face
of clearly hopeless odds. Officers constantly reminded troops
that anyone who indulged in "defeatist talk" ran the risk of being
shot.

Although the Germans had neglected maintenance of the
West Wall since their early victories in 1940, they were now
hastily refurbishing it. Hitler depended on tenacious troops dug
in on the Siegfried Line to delay the Allies long enough to permit him to deal with the Russians and then throw a counter-
punch at the Americans and British.

Germany had begun construction on the Siegfried Line in

1936 and eventually stretched it four hundred miles from the Swiss border in the south to Holland in the north. The fortification system was three to twenty miles in depth, depending on terrain, and included more than three thousand pillboxes and blockhouses with interlocking fields of fire. Minefields, newly dug fieldworks, antitank dragon's teeth, wire, artillery, armor—everything would be thrown into stopping Eisenhower's advance at the West Wall.

Unlike France's Maginot Line, which had been designed for World War I–type static fighting, the steel-and-concrete West Wall was designed for a new type of highly mobile warfare. Small towns and villages were incorporated into the system. Many innocent-looking farmhouses were actually fortified pillboxes with basements of twelve to eighteen inches of reinforced concrete. Ventilation openings disguised narrow gunports. Houses built around these pillboxes were so well camouflaged that their true purpose was hard to determine from a distance.

Zigzagging trenches connected many of the farmhouse bunkers with major pillboxes in the towns and in the countryside adjacent to towns. These pillboxes were either rectangular or in a polygon shape to merge with the lay of the land. Some blockhouses contained underground bunkers sixty feet across and capable of accommodating up to fifty men.

At a distance of from twenty to ninety miles behind the Siegfried Line lay the Rhine River's great natural moat against attack. The river flowed 450 miles through Germany from Alpine sources in Switzerland before joining the Old Maas River at Rotterdam and emptying into the North Sea. Until the Allies controlled both the West Wall and the Rhine, the way into the rest of Germany was effectively blocked.

In early March, with spring scenting the air and snow beginning to melt, with Colonel Paul Bates once more in charge, its ranks fleshed out and its equipment repaired and replaced, the 761st Tank Battalion entered German territory in the north with the 79th Infantry Division to mop up pockets of resistance. The operation had hardly begun, however, before the 761st received orders to proceed by train through Luxembourg to Saverne, France, where it would be temporarily attached to the Seventh Army, commanded by Major General Anthony McAuliffe. McAuliffe had received recent wide notice in the United States when, as deputy commander of the 101st Airborne Division at Bastogne, he replied "Nuts!" to a German surrender ultimatum.

The Panther mission: Break through the Siegfried Line and go to the Rhine.

79

Any man who is captured without being wounded or having fought to the last will be disgraced and his family will be cut off from all government support.

—ORDER FROM ADOLF HITLER

The worst of the winter was over. Snow had melted and spring was redolent in the air. Black tankers of the 761st and other elements of Task Force RHINE assembled in a snow-melted field west of German-occupied Reisdorf and prepared to assault the Siegfried Line. The large field lay at the foot of an escarpment, the Hardt Mountains, running generally south to north. A road wound up and on up in the forest toward the West Wall.

Task Force RHINE, formed on March 19, 1945, was part of a concerted effort by the Allies to crack the Siegfried Line and pour through the crack to the Rhine River. In addition to the

761st Tank Battalion, it was composed of the 2nd Battalion of the 103rd Infantry Division, a recon platoon of the 614th Tank Destroyer Battalion, and a detachment of combat engineers whose main function was to take out pillboxes and blockhouses. Some sixteen hundred to seventeen hundred men total. Colonel Paul Bates was task force commander, a selection that delighted the Black Panthers. They trusted Hard Tack to put their welfare first whenever he could.

The 42nd Rainbow Division and the 36th Infantry Division flanked Task Force RHINE on the left and the right. They were also kicking off toward the West Wall, supported by the 10th Armored and 14th Armored divisions. The 10th and the 14th had operated in the sector for the past week probing for an opening but had so far failed to break through. A few days before, the 14th had even reached as far as Bobenthal in the middle of the Hardt Mountains before being kicked back by stubborn German resistance.

The field was a hive of activity and excitement. The 761st had spent most of February in Holland scrubbing up local German resistance, receiving and training replacements, and preparing for the campaign that would take it through the Siegfried Line, across the Rhine River, and into the enemy's heartland.

"I led you across France," Baker Company's CO, Captain Johnny Long, said. "Now I'm gonna kick your asses all the way across Germany." He was one hardcore sonofabitch.

Participating in the birth of such a force of armor and infantry, being a part of it, was an awesome experience. The roar of engines and the rattle and squealing of tanks. Men shouting. Boots tramping. Officers' Jeeps darting about. Captains and lieutenants standing on top of things getting their soldiers straightened out. Checking vehicles, weapons, ammo, food, water, each other. Last-minute well-wishing between buddies. Company and platoon meetings and briefings. In the air the odors of excitement, menace, and fear.

At first, no one noticed a faint sound like the distant drone of bees. It grew louder and louder, attracting the notice of first one man and then another and then groups until the entire field went into freeze motion. All heads lifted toward a clear first-day-of-spring sky. E. G. McConnell said it for everyone.

"God Awmighty!"

Most were awed into simple silence, heads lifted and motionless to watch as formations of U.S. heavy bombers escorted by fighters blotted out the light of the sun, their shadows flitting menacingly across the countryside below. The combined roar of engines rattled the earth's teeth.

"I am so glad we ain't on the other end of *that*," Corporal Bill McBurney said.

The giant armada passed. The din of its passage faded into a hush. Soon, the men shook their heads in amazement and went about their business of getting ready.

Movement to contact began at 1600 hours with tanks leading the way. Ahead in the Hardt Mountains, themselves a natural barrier to the Rhine River, lay the Siegfried Line dotting the rugged landscape with pillboxes, machine gun emplacements in wooded hills, antitank sites, mortar positions, minefields, and plenty of enemy infantry.

Captain Pop Gates's Charlie Company took point. Captain Max Huffman, Captain Williams's replacement, took drag with his Able Company. Colonel Bates and his staff took middle-march positions for better command of both ends of the column. Infantry were scattered throughout. They rode clinging to the tanks' deck plates as the iron monsters in dispersed single file took the secondary road that led through the mountains.

Forest hugged the edges of the road. Conifers stood dark and ominous while beeches and oaks stood out as bare as skeletons from one of the hardest winters on record. Mountain peaks towered ahead. The long green line snaked upward past threatening overhanging cliffs and sheer dropoffs falling down to fast-moving streams gorged by snow melt.

The giant armada of American bombers returned from its

mission before sunset. The distant drone went unnoticed in the drama of battalions on the move until it grew loud enough to dominate land and sky. Soldiers looked up and immediately noticed a difference in the formation. There were ragged gaps in it from missing aircraft. Smoke trailed from damaged airplanes, black and curling and etched against the bruised-red sky of approaching darkness.

It was clear that not all Americans were returning.

80

I killed so many Germans until I just got tired of shooting them.

—SERGEANT WARREN G. H. CRECY

The fight for the Siegfried Line began early the next morning. The Germans had placed pillboxes and camouflaged artillery and machine guns in the woods and in the hills on both sides of the narrow road leading to the key towns of Nieder-Schlettenbach and Reisdorf. Doughs hastily dismounted whenever the columns encountered an obstacle and moved up through the high ground to comb enemy infantry from the feet of the steeper mountains while General Sherman tanks confronted the Krauts head-on.

Two tanks would rush the enemy fortifications at high speed, guns blazing, while other tanks laid down protective fire with machine guns and turret cannon. The first pair split off. A second pair immediately charged, then a third pair, working in timed coordination like a violent, choreographed Wagnerian opera. Engineers moved in afterward to blow up the little fortresses to prevent their being used again. Detonation blasts rocked the Hardt Mountains and reverberated through canyons as Task Force RHINE fought to break through.

It was a slugfest all the way. Black Panthers knocked out seven pillboxes and one antitank gun, killing fourteen Germans and capturing ninety more.

Sergeant Harding Crecy, "baddest man in the 761st," seemed to have a single thought: Kill! Kill! *Kill!* While dispatching literally hundreds of enemy soldiers, more than any other tanker in the outfit, more perhaps than any other tanker in the ETO, he had not lost a single crewmember to enemy action. Other men vied to fight with him because of his primitive combat prowess and because he appeared to live and fight under a protective charm. When Crecy moved over out of Dog Company's light tanks to Charlie Company, First Sergeant Bill Burroughs gave up his rank in order to ride with Crecy as his gunner.

When a pillbox pinned down a platoon of doughboys near Nieder-Schlettenbach, Crecy got out of his tank and stood on top of the turret to get a better view of the situation. The pillbox sat almost hidden inside a copse of evergreens about one hundred yards away. Its firing ports flickered like eyes in the head of a demented giant as they hurled death rays of tracers at Americans gone to ground in a narrow ravine.

Crecy nodded, satisfied with what he had seen, and slipped back into his turret.

Driver, flank to the left. Don't spare the horses . . .

The Germans built their fortifications to withstand direct frontal assault; the sides were more vulnerable. Crecy's tank flew through the woods, sliding around the larger trees while simply crushing the smaller ones underneath its treads. David charging Goliath.

Bill, AP followed by HE. Don't miss . . .

Harding, I don't miss.

A Ripsaw inside the pillbox turned its attention to the speeding war wagon. Shells burst all around the tank, but it kept going through the smoke, trailing tendrils of it. Crecy hung on to the .50-cal, his head stuck up out of the turret and his fists gripping the butterfly triggers.

Keep her loaded, boys. Bill, keep your face to the sights. We're getting there . . .

The tank charged directly at the side of the pillbox, machine gun clattering. Tracers streaked past Crecy's head.

Get ready . . .

Gunner ready.

Loader ready.

Gunner. Fifty yards. AP. Fire . . . !

Shot out . . .

The pillbox shuddered with the impact of the armor-piercing round thudding into its flank, penetrating. Smoke and dust puffed from its seams.

Gunner. HE. Fire . . . !

The high-explosive round rattled the pillbox to its roots. Flames shot out the firing ports as ammo inside began cooking off. Surviving Germans scurried out of it like ants from burning oil. Crecy mowed them down without mercy, chewing at them with the heavy .50-cal, sweeping devastating fire back and forth through their fleeing ranks and piling them up in bloody clumps and mounds of shredded cloth and butchered meat.

"Sonsofbitches!"

In the meantime, not far away, Sergeant Teddy Windsor's tank dropped nose and big gun down into a camouflaged anti-tank ditch. German gunners zeroed in on the sitting duck. The crew scrambled out of the tank as mortar explosions walked toward it cracking down trees and erupting earth, only to encounter volleys of enemy MG-42 bullets.

Bonded together by need and habit, Windsor and his men crawled several hundred yards on their bellies underneath furious grazing fire before they came to a wooded draw. The five men raced along it, strung out in a fast line like long-distance racers. The sound of gunfire receded.

Corporal Mozee Thompson was the first to climb out of the draw when it dead-ended.

"Goddamn!"

He dropped to the ground. A quick chop of the hand warned the others. Windsor made his way forward. He brushed aside shrubbery to observe a pillbox not one hundred yards away camouflaged onto the walls of a cliff. Here they had survived by sheer luck a gauntlet of death only to encounter an even more formidable opponent. They couldn't go back and they couldn't go forward. The pillbox commanded a view of the entire downslope. Enemy behind, enemy ahead.

Sweat oozed from Windsor's dark face even though it was a cool afternoon.

"Now what?" Mozee asked.

Private Bob Thrasher's eyes rolled wide. He summed it up in one word. "Trapped."

Among the five of them they possessed two grease guns, an M1 carbine, and a pistol, not much of an arsenal to go up against an entire Kraut army. They huddled together at the blind end of the draw like mice cowering from a circling raptor, trying to make up their minds what to do.

Their best option, perhaps their only option, was to stay where they were in hiding until other elements of the task force caught up with them. Windsor formed his crew into a three-sixty to cover all approaches. He was most concerned that Jerries from the first clash might be pursuing them.

Minutes passed. Nothing moved around the pillbox, which made it all the more remarkable when the fortification suddenly exploded spontaneously right before their amazed eyes. They were still blinking away concussion and astonishment when American combat engineers rose up in the smoke and walked up to look over the mangled pile of concrete and rebar sticking up like dinosaur ribs. Americans who had already taken the pill-box must have left engineers behind to blow it up.

"It's our guys!" Mozee Thompson hooted. "I ain't never been so glad to see white men in my life."

81

The first stage of our operation has been brilliantly completed.

—GENERAL ANTHONY C. MCAULIFFE

On the way to the formidable Siegfried basin town of Nieder-Schlettenbach, TC Floyd Dade's tank got stuck in a muddy field. He and his crew scavenged posts from a nearby rail fence to stuff under the tank for traction. He was hurrying back across the brown meadow with a second post on his shoulder when an 88 antitank emplacement bracketed him for annihilation.

One shot howled over his head, the other landed short. He ran dodging through other explosions that chased him all the way across the field. The tank was out of the enemy's sight and therefore relatively safe for the time being. He and his crew waited for more than an hour until elements of the 761st and its doughs swept the front past and a retriever came and pulled him out of the mud.

Able and Charlie companies reached Nieder-Schlettenbach after six hours of fighting. The last stretch of road ran under-neath overhanging cliffs studded with pillboxes that had to be destroyed one by one. After the breakout into the basin, the companies discovered Jerry had blown the only bridge over the Lauder River.

Dark had begun settling by the time engineers erected a Bailey bridge. An Able Company platoon led by Lieutenant Harold Kingsley and a second platoon composed of the battered remnants of platoons belonging to Lieutenant Moses Dade and Lieutenant Frank Cochrane rumbled across the hasty structure into the downtown section of the city, followed by a company of infantry. Tanks and infantry fought their way down the middle of the main street, kicking ass, as Kingsley put it. A captured German prisoner told Cochrane that troops were ordered to hold the town until nightfall and then withdraw toward the Rhine.

That intelligence seemed sound. Firing began to slacken. Krauts appeared to be running out the back of the town as American forces entered the front. The quiet periods of peace between firefights grew longer and longer until silence dominated, broken only by brief punctuations of fire from one area of town or another.

Able's commander, Lieutenant Max Huffman, stood outside his tank on a rolling hillside that looked down upon the town and the bright ribbon of the Lauder River in the forefront. Fires burned in a few places, the blazes as red in the dusk as the setting sun on the horizon. From his vantage point, the German town appeared to be weathering the attack in reasonably good condition. The battle seemed over and the town secure except for mopping-up operations.

Platoon sergeant and TC Johnnie Stevens also stood in the road, the tanks of his platoon strung out immobile behind him. Lieutenant Huffman climbed aboard his machine, calling out to Stevens, "I'm going down to take a look. Stay here in reserve."

"Sir, hold a minute."

Stevens walked over to him. "Sir, don't go into that gawd damned town. I don't like it."

"It's all over except the shouting, Johnnie."

"Maybe it ain't, sir."

"I'll call if I need you."

Lieutenant Huffman rode away into the sunset in grand style, head and shoulders stuck out the open turret hatch. Stevens and TC Sergeant Paul "Corky" Murphy watched him go. The tank hustled off the hilltop, running down the road at speed, and crossed the Bailey into downtown, disappearing from sight.

At least one pocket of resistance remained in Nieder-Schlettenbach. Huffman's lone tank and crew poked a stick into it. The fury of the attack lit up the street leading downtown in a sharp flickering light show. The noise of machine guns, mortars, and antitank weapons climaxed in a terrifying shriek.

Ambush! Bastards all around us . . .

Up front, they're up front . . .

Behind us . . .

Gawd damn, oh, God . . . We need some help . . .

"I told the man not to, I *told* him," Stevens cried in frustration. "Corky, get ready."

He mounted his tank. The crew was already aboard. Without waiting for the rest of the platoon, he charged the tank down on a mission to bail out the CO before it was too late.

Minutes later, Stevens found himself trapped in the same narrow dark street. A number of doughs had somehow ended up in the kill zone with Huffman. They were fighting for their lives and the Germans were shooting them up good. Tracers zapped about like electrical charges. *Panzerfaust* rockets caromed and ricocheted off brick and mortar and steel. Smoke oozed from the still-open turret of Huffman's disabled tank. It looked abandoned. Stevens got on the radio.

Corky, get the hell down here. All hell is breaking loose . . .

We're just turning the corner . . .

Watch out for that motherfucker up on the roof . . .

I'm burning him now . . .

Burn him some more . . .

Stevens's platoon charged like cavalry to the rescue, Buffalo

Soldiers reincarnated, guns ripping. The only thing missing was the sound of bugles. But for Murphy and the other TCs, Stevens and his crew would never have made it out of Nieder-Schletten-bach alive. The outnumbered, outmaneuvered, and outgunned Jerries quickly gave up the fight and joined their *Kameraden* in fleeing out the back of the city. A number of them too war-weary, too hungry, and too frightened to continue the war came out with their hands over their heads.

Relief, however, had come too late for Lieutenant Huffman. The Krauts had targeted him first, exposed as he was in the tur-ret of his tank. He died four days later from his wounds. He was the only white officer of the 761st to be killed in combat so far.

"I *told* him, I *told* him," Johnnie Stevens muttered.

KIA (Killed in Action)
First Lieutenant Maxwell Huffman

82

The trucks were like a band of stagecoaches making a run through Indian country. We got used to keeping the wheels going, disregarding the snipers and hop-ing we wouldn't get lost or hit.

—ARMORED DIVISION OFFICER

Supply lines were at the same time simple and complicated concerns—simple in that they existed for the sole purpose of delivering beans and bullets to the front lines, compli-cated in the way that was sometimes accomplished. As with field hospitals, Graves Registration, mess, administrative, and other "ash and trash" support units, supply depots moved up with the combat in order to accomplish their mission but stayed back far enough to be relatively secure. Army-wide, at least two men in the rear ranks supported each man with a weapon in the front ranks.

The battalion Supply officer for the 761st, Captain Phil Latimer, had worked out his own system. From his headquarters a few miles behind the lines, he sent trucks back to division distribution depots to ferry materials forward. Usually that meant trucks rolled in the morning to the depot and back, then parceled out provisions to the battalion companies in the afternoon. It was in this latter phase that difficulties often arose.

Map rendezvous points were established where companies requiring resupply could meet the trucks. Normally, these were crossroads or other prominent terrain features assigned numbers such as "Number 11" or "Number 8." Using numbers instead of saying, "Meet the trucks at the crossroads north of Nieder-Schlettenbach," kept the enemy confused should he be eavesdropping on radio communications. While these points were back of the fighting and not in a direct line of fire, it didn't mean the supply trains rolled without threat. In fact, supplies and support in general were prime targets for enemy action.

On an afternoon during the fighting around Nieder-Schlettenbach and Reisdorf, Captain Latimer dug his hands deep into his pockets, a mannerism the depth of which indicated the extent of his concern. His eyes kept drifting toward the high mountain passes through which his trains must pass in order to deliver chow, ammo, and fuel to tankers fighting to crack the Siegfried Line.

Artillery boomed in the distance, a sound to which Latimer had become so accustomed that it was as natural to his environment as mud and trees. P-47 Thunderbolts zoomed over HQ, engines thudding and rumbling. Minutes later, they could be seen looking as small as gnats up in the mountains as they strafed and bombed targets. At times, HQ dug in so near the front that the earth actually trembled underfoot like tissue paper from bombing and artillery barrages. It was an unsettling experience.

Sergeant Milton Dorsey sensed the S-4's unease. Dorsey was Captain Latimer's right-hand man as well as his driver. The two men, one white, the other black, had forged a close bond during the grueling months of making sure tanks kept rolling and men kept getting fed.

"They'll make it fine, Boss," Dorsey said. "They always do."

Latimer managed a weak grin. He clapped the slender man on the back. "I'm just an old lady," he said. "It's an old lady's prerogative to worry."

The train was lining out on a mud-encrusted half-track driven by Sergeant Leonard Keyes from Service Company. The half-track would lead the convoy of deuce-and-a-half trucks and escorting tanks from the Mosquito Fleet. Keyes would carry three passengers—Lieutenant Leonard Taylor, the S-3 (Operations) for air and commo; white motor officer Captain William O'Dea; and black Corporal James Mills, shotgun on the track's mounted .50-caliber machine gun. Lieutenant Taylor already sat in the vehicle's backseat, wearing his helmet and gripping a carbine between his knees. Captain O'Dea and Mills stood outside looking down the convoy as it lined up. Nearby, Dog Company's CO, Captain Richard English, balanced spread-legged on his Stuart, grease gun slung over one shoulder, as he directed two other light tanks to intersperse themselves into the convoy.

Truck drivers and shotgun guards waited in their cabs, engines running. Latimer walked down the line with Dorsey, personally checking every truck.

"We're just finishing up," WO Mark Henderson, assistant Supply, assured him. "This is the last can of gasoline. We're almost ready to roll."

"Get 'em out of here. Let's go."

Latimer dug his hands even deeper into his pockets.

It had been a clear, bright day with a lace of winter remaining in the mountain air. The sky was now starting to mellow out and turn pink with the approach of sundown. That concerned the Supply officer too. The train would be traveling narrow, winding, hazardous roads at night, through a "gauntlet" several miles long, where bands of enemy, still dangerous, had been bypassed by the rapid thrust of Task Force RHINE. Any activity met on the road at night would undoubtedly be Germans.

The train should be reasonably well protected, however, by the half-track and its .50-cal and Captain English's tanks.

Cold dusk was setting in when the convoy finally departed in a rush and a clatter over the mud-caked road. Latimer watched until it disappeared around a bend.

"You'd better get some sleep, Captain," Lieutenant Horace Jones recommended. "They'll be back by midnight or so and we'll have to start all over again."

Mud froze with the last of the sun's warmth, providing better traction. The road was still narrow and dark. The convoy used only narrow slitted blackout lights and thus traveled slowly. On point, passengers in the half-track rolled back the canvas top and laid down the windshield to allow more complete vigilance. Corporal Mills stood and leaned over the mounted machine gun to watch for possible road agents. The Old West had never been this hairy.

The secret to ambush success lay in surprise. That the Germans failed to achieve. As the train eased into a sharp curve, Corporal Mills glimpsed furtive movement to one side of the road. Only bad guys walked these dark shadows. Without hesitation, he swiveled the muzzle of the .50-cal and laid down on the triggers, squeezing a stream of red tracers pounding into the trees, whipping and tearing. A .50-caliber machine gun squirting a stream of two-inch-long slugs was a fearsome weapon.

Small arms flickered drumming return fire from the darkness to the side of the road and from up ahead. Tracers lashed at the half-track, spanging into it, sparking against the steel.

While Mills, supplied with two full boxes of ammo, kept the ambushers busy, his comrades bailed out of the half-track and along with Master Sergeant Willie Black worked the convoy into reverse. The road was too narrow for the trucks to U-turn.

The half-track remained behind with Corporal Mills fighting it out with the aggressors. Bullets smashed the lowered windshield, ricocheted off the hood, clapped past his head. Miraculously, Mills remained untouched. By the time the Stuarts got past the trucks and roared to his rescue, he had the enemy pinned down and ripe for the plucking. The Americans suffered not a single casualty.

Hours later, Captain Latimer awakened when he heard the convoy return after completing its mission. He crawled out of his sleeping bag and blinked in surprise as Corporal Mills and Sergeant Willie Black unloaded seven bound storm troopers from one of the trucks. Captain O'Dea grinned.

"Just another day on the Western Front," he said.

83

The colour I think of little moment.

—PETER BECKFORD, 1740–1811

German civilians quickly began to relax whenever Americans captured a Reichland community and occupied it with white troops. They were weary of the war, thoroughly exhausted and demoralized, and desired little other than for life to resume some degree of normalcy. Besides, Americans weren't that different from Germans. It would have been difficult to tell a German from an American if both were out of uniform.

It was a different story for Negro soldiers. German civilians were frightened of them. French civilians were accustomed to black people from decades of colonizing Africa, whereas a black face in Germany was rare enough to attract cautious stares. Tankers of the 761st got a kick out of hearing gasps of panic as women started to cry, men paled, and little children fled.

Lieutenant Horace Jones of Supply was a broad, dark man with an affable, fun-loving spirit. He noticed a small group of elderly men staring at the tankers as they tarried in a village to service their machines. He sauntered over to them wearing the fiercest scowl he could muster, his eyes deliberately wide and white-rimmed. As he drew near, he suddenly bent down, showed his teeth, and shouted *"Boo!"* He roared with laughter as the spooked Germans took off for cover.

Private Christopher Navarre, gunner for Sergeant Isiah Parks's tank, finally figured out why the Germans were so frightened of black men after his tank threw a tread during the assault on Nieder-Schlettenbach. The crew selected a nearby cottage in which they could wait in comfort while mechanic Ernest Hill came up from HQ to repair it. In France, American soldiers were prohibited from kicking people out of their homes. In Germany, no one hesitated in taking what he needed, including houses.

Navarre removed the firing pin from the block of the main gun while the rest of the crew set up machine guns in the cottage. Parks didn't want tank weapons turned against them in the event they were overrun by surviving bands of German soldiers.

A woman, her young daughters, and her aging father-in-law occupied the cottage. The interior was neat and clean. Other than a framed photo of a man in Nazi uniform—hubby?—there were few indications of the war that raged across the countryside. The woman apparently strove to make life as normal and pleasant as possible for her children. She and the others huddled in one corner of the living room, holding each other and staring with wide, anxious eyes as the five black tankers made themselves at home.

Parks and his crew had not enjoyed the luxury of a sofa in weeks. Jessie Glover sank onto it with a sigh of pleasure and stretched his long legs out across the floor. Willie Washington grinned his appreciation, which only seemed to further stress the occupants. They seemed to want to shrink into the woodwork.

Hungry, Navarre broke out a K-ration. He attempted to engage the woman in conversation, since he had learned French in his native Louisiana Cajun country and most Germans along the border also spoke French.

"You will rape and kill us," the woman accused, stammering.

"We certainly will not," Navarre kindly reassured her. While relentless in combat, Navarre retained the gentle soul of the priest he once intended to become. "Why do you think that?"

"We are told," the woman replied. "All the time we are told that the *Schwarze Soldaten* are coming to rape us and cut off our heads."

Navarre's brow wrinkled. *"Schwarze Soldaten?"*

She pinched her cheek for emphasis. "The color of your skin," she explained. "Dark, although you are not as dark as the Senegalese. You are the shortest Senegalese I have ever seen."

Schwarze Soldaten—black soldiers.

It was not until later that Navarre fully understood. Soldiers from Senegal, a province of France, were notorious tall warriors with black shiny skin and eyes so dark they almost glowed with fierceness. When they crossed into enemy territory, they sometimes returned bearing grisly trophies such as ears and heads. They showed little mercy to their foes. These were the *Schwarze Soldaten* whose exploits infused the German population with such terror, and to whom the American black soldiers were being compared. Most Germans failed to realize that, aside from skin color, the black American soldier was not all that different from the American white soldier.

"You won't be harmed," Navarre comforted the frightened woman.

He made the sign of the cross to bless his food before he ate. That was what convinced the German woman that black Americans were not ruthless savages. She ran over to the tanker, dropped to her knees, grabbed his hands, and gratefully smothered them with relieved kisses.

84

Man, we learned this jive from General Patton.

—SERGEANT DANIEL CARDELL

Captain Pop Gates of Charlie Company and Captain Johnny Long of Baker, along with platoon leaders Tom Bruce, Frank Cochrane, and Moses Dade, gathered with infantry commanders in the darkness on the improved road outside the small German town of Silz. Nieder-Schlettenbach, now secured and pacified, lay in the night behind them while only Silz stood between Task Force RHINE and the key Siegfried town of Klingenmunster. RHINE had been pushing hard for the last few days. Elements of the 761st were spread out in broad swaths all across the terrain. Colonel Bates had gotten little sleep for the past two days. He had to settle for a few winks now and then as he strove to maintain control and keep track of his far-flung battalions of Task Force RHINE.

Commanders standing on the road conversed in low tones as they discussed how best to seize Silz from the Germans. They had been assigned the mission; how they accomplished it was up to them. Behind them underneath a moonless night sky, worn and weary doughs sprawled on the outsides of tanks to catch a few minutes' sleep while tankers dozed in the inner sanctums. Considerations for the attack necessarily must include the mental and physical state of soldiers worn to a frazzle by the pace.

It was decided that a direct assault preceded by an artillery and tank gun prep had always worked before. The best plan was almost always the simplest. Sergeant Crecy liked to say, "What are we waiting for? Let's go get the bastards."

The town occupied a crossroads at the bottom of a gradual slope. Not a light shone anywhere. Maybe the Germans had already split.

Not a chance.

Two platoons of tanks from Baker along with two 105mm howitzer tanks from Assault Guns Platoon rolled into firing position on-line in a field adjacent to the road. They prepped the objective for fifteen minutes, pounding the town. Muzzle fire flashed and flickered like lightning, replicated in the town when the ordnance struck in ripples and waves of light and smoke.

Secondary explosions from a blown enemy ammo dump set the entire town afire. A quarter of an hour before the town had hunkered inside its own darkness. Now, there was plenty of light. Flames licked back at the darkness and cast eerie shadows against the surrounding hills and forests.

Tanks led the attack, sweeping out of nowhere so rapidly that they overran an enemy antitank gun before its surprised crew fired a single shot. It was firepower with a vengeance. Men shouted. Tanks roared through Silz, systematically and mercilessly searching every stretch of ground, every street, every building with cannon and machine gun fire. Foot soldiers kept steady streams of tracers whipping and lashing against the firelight. The barrels of M1s, .30-caliber machine guns, and Browning Automatic Rifles glowed red hot. Vikings of old could not have more completely sacked a town.

E. G. McConnell recalled what General Patton said to him before the 761st went into battle for the first time. "I want you to shoot every gawd damned thing you see—"

Yes, sir, General.

Sergeant Daniel Cardell of the "Cool Stud" tank, whose black rooster mascot rode through the melee inside his coop next to the driver, crowing mightily, thought the world might be coming to an end. Hellish fires cast weird shadows—and, my God, was it hot! Screaming from the throats of terrified civilians mingled with the agonizing unearthly din from the enemy wounded.

"My God! Has the world gone crazy?"

As Americans stormed one side of the blazing town, a Wehrmacht column of trucks, horse-drawn artillery and antitank guns, infantry, and assorted other enemy units fled out the other side heading for Klingenmunster—at least one hundred vehicles, that many draft horses, and several hundred storm troopers and support people. Frantic teamsters yelled and beat their animals to spur them to greater speed through a desperate night. Casting anxious glances over their shoulders. Calling out to each other in raw terror. Hurry, hurry, *hurry!*

Behind them, the Americans were in Silz, and Silz was burning, turning the sky a festering and terrible red. Hitler's armies were abandoning the West Wall in remnants and running for their lives. The *Schwarze Soldaten* were coming in their great iron and steel war wagons.

"*Hören Sie etwas?*"

"*Er kommen! Kommen!*"

Coming! *Coming!*

Silz barely offered a speed bump to slow pursuing Black Panthers. Tankers roared into the fire and out of the fire again in pursuit of the bolting Germans. This was a rare opportunity to trap significant numbers of the enemy and annihilate the bastards. Blood lust and animal savagery boiled through the veins of men whose only thought was to pay back those who had been killing and wounding them for the past months.

The road twisted into a series of S curves. Thick timber stepped upward on the left side of the road. Fallow fields lay to the right, great stretches of open ground that eventually abutted against more mountains. The fast-moving Shermans of Colonel Bates's battalion caught up with the German column at this choke point. Storm troopers in the rear screamed warnings as monstrous dark shadows suddenly materialized against the festering fire-red sky.

It was the Apocalypse writ smaller. Iron demons slashed into the Germans at full speed, roaring and belching flame, strewing wreckage and violent death. Cannon fire at point-blank range blasted tanks into flaming masses of twisted steel. Tanks crushed men and horses alike, their screams of pain and fear indistinguishable one from the other.

In the flow of adrenaline and blood, few of the tankers experienced anything beyond flitting images of death and destruction, images that would replay endlessly in their nightmares.

Wild-eyed Krauts in Nazi helmets firing at armor with burp guns before they went down shrieking underneath treads . . . smashing them like roadkill . . .

Tank striking a horse-drawn antitank gun, sending wheels, guns, men, and animals flying . . .

Horse with both hind legs crushed attempting to pull himself along with his front legs, dragging with him a dead handler entangled in the harness . . .

German climbing a skinny tree in panic. Tank crashing over the tree and the man . . .

Erstwhile Supermen bolting into the woods in a river of screams . . .

Krauts with their hands up attempting to surrender. *Kameraden! Kameraden!* Mowed down with machine guns where they stood . . .

The orgy of blood ended almost as quickly as it began, with

the swiftness of a Midwest tornado that dropped out of darkness, created havoc, then moved on. Debris, dead horses, shattered guns, artillery pieces, wrecked and burning motor vehicles, and dead Germans littered the road for almost five miles. Colonel Bates had to order tank dozers forward to clear the wreckage before his task force could proceed.

Sergeant Crecy got out of his tank in the aftermath and stood in the road. Fires from burning vehicles crackled around him, providing strange, uncertain illumination that disclosed freshly killed corpses singly and in little dumps. Surviving underfed horses were already starting to graze, dragging along with them whatever remained of their carriages. Horses with broken legs cried as the pitiful creatures attempted to stand. Wounded Germans pleaded for help, prayed, and sobbed in pain and hopelessness. The stench of fresh blood seemed to turn the air red and gave it taste and substance.

Pop Gates walked up beside Crecy. They stood shoulder to shoulder and looked around. Neither man spoke. What was there to say?

Crecy adjusted his glasses, then removed them as though he had seen enough. He turned slowly away, looking tired and much older than before, and walked back to his tank.

85

Over the Rhine, then, let us go. And good hunting to you all on the other side.

—British Field Marshal Bernard Montgomery

As the Allies fought their way toward the Rhineland, they rebuilt bomb-damaged roads and railways and moved up immense quantities of ammunition, gasoline, and foodstuffs from coastal ports. Nearly four million troops and 500 tons of supplies daily for *each* of 85 combat divisions would have to be sent across the Rhine. As the Allies expected the Germans to blow every bridge, they also stockpiled in forward depots 124 landing craft and 1,100 assault boats, along with enough lumber, pontoons, and prefabricated structure to build 62 bridges.

The end of the war seemed in sight. Legions that Hitler had sent out to conquer the world were now reduced to fighting for their own homeland. It appeared the war might end in at most a few more months, perhaps only weeks.

Competition to see which Allied general would cross the river first was intense, especially between British Field Marshal General Bernard Montgomery and General George Patton. On March 22, 1945, while Montgomery readied troops to cross the Rhine at Remagen the next morning, General Patton one-upped him that night. At 2200 hours, March 22, elements of Patton's Third Army made a surprise crossing of the Rhine ten miles south of Mainz at the village of Oppenheim. In 1806, Napoleon had crossed not far from here while pursuing his enemy eastward.

Six battalions of the 5th Infantry Division piled into assault boats and rafts and struck out for the opposite shore. To Patton's astonishment, only one enemy platoon guarded the east bank. Patton telephoned General Omar Bradley, commander of Twelfth Army Group, early the next morning while engineers were building bridges to hurry additional infantry and armor across.

"Brad," he said, "don't tell anyone, but I'm across."

"Well, I'll be damned. You mean across the Rhine?"

"Sure am. I sneaked a division over last night. But there are so few Krauts around there they don't know it yet. So don't make any announcements. We'll keep it a secret until we see how it goes."

Patton's gunners knocked out thirty-three German planes during the day that were attempting to disrupt bridge-building efforts. Patton telephoned Bradley again. He had changed his mind.

"Brad, for God's sake, tell the world we're across. I want the world to know that the Third Army made it before Monty starts across."

General Bradley made the announcement. Patton was first.

In the meantime, the 761st Tank Battalion fought its way through the Siegfried Line and opened a hole for the 14th Armored Division to roll all the way to the Rhine. During West Wall operations, Task Force RHINE knocked out 31 pillboxes, 49 machine gun emplacements, and 29 antitank guns, destroyed 11 ammo trucks, and seized 20 other antitank guns. It captured seven towns, destroying three of them, blew up an enemy ammo dump, knocked out 450 horse-drawn and motor-driven vehicles, captured or killed 200 horses, killed 833 Germans, and took 3,210 POWs. The 761st alone fired 300 tons of ammo and consumed 50,000 gallons of V-80 gasoline.

While wreaking such damage upon the enemy, more than during any other operation, the Black Panthers suffered the least amount of damage to themselves. Only five tanks were lost to enemy action. One officer was killed—Lieutenant Maxwell Huffman. Six enlisted men were wounded, none of whom died.

The unit's effective strength at month's end was 33 officers, 3 warrant officers, and 662 enlisted.

Rightly or wrongly, 761st tankers credited Colonel Bates for the low casualty rate. "Colonel Hard Tack is *back*."

On March 30, Patton's Third Army reclaimed Patton's Panthers. The battalion traveled 132 miles to Langenselbold, Germany, crossing the Rhine at Oppenheim, to report to the 71st Infantry Division. It lost little time getting back into action. Sergeant Alexander Bell shot down a Luftwaffe airplane with a tank-mounted .50-caliber machine gun the first day.

86

I have one hundred love letters that Paul wrote me through this period. Basically they are love letters, but always there was The Battalion.

—TAFFY BATES

Mail from home, with the possible exception of hot chow, was the GI's most welcome event of any day. No one but a GI away from home and in a combat zone could understand its importance. Excited tankers mobbed the designated mail NCO whenever he brought up a duffel bag full of mail and began waving letters in the air and shouting names.

"Crecy . . . McConnell, it's your Moms . . . Dunn . . . Taylor . . . Parks, whooo, smell that one, I ain't jiving . . . Cardell . . . Navarre, from your wife . . ."

Guys sat around reading to themselves and smiling, reading passages to their buddies, telling each other about what was happening *back home* in Mississippi or Oklahoma, Chicago or New York. Men who, perhaps only that same day, were callously shooting down other men wiped their eyes. Some whooped with joy. Laughter rang among temporarily stalled tanks.

"My wife done had our baby. It's a boy!"

"That a fact? Whose you reckon it is?"

"She say it got my ears."

"But whose face has it got?"

Talking trash always, good-natured insults that were the mainstay of battalion morale.

"Moms writes that they're letting up on sugar rationing. But they can't hardly get no gas."

"They can get all the gas they want if they was to start eating K-rations."

Mail call made a man feel good the rest of the day. The exceptions let out a curse or a groan, even spontaneous tears. Bad news, commonly a Dear John letter: " . . . I am so sorry. I was so lonesome, I can't wait for you no more. It wasn't meant to happen, but I met . . ."

"Motherfucker! That was who she met—*motherfucker!"*

A man burdened with bad news slunk off by himself to rage and lick his wounds. Buddies walked by and silently nudged him or slapped him on the shoulder. *Hey, we understand.* Sat down on a log with him and just sat there. Offered a drink from a bottle of French cognac hoarded for just such an occasion.

About one-third of the Black Panther Battalion was married. Most of the others had left behind sweethearts or fiancées who promised to wait. The numbers of waiting women dwindled as time passed.

One woman, however, rose to the minds of many 761st tankers when they contemplated feminine loyalty. The colonel's lady, Taffy, became their perfect idealized woman, one of those for whom men crossed oceans, built countries, and fought wars.

She was what all dreamed of—a beautiful woman faithful, romantic, and, the best quality of all, always waiting. Far from begrudging Colonel Bates his romance, the tankers lived it with him vicariously.

Eagerly and with good humor, they awaited news of how many letters the colonel had received this time, of what ploys Taffy might invent to talk to or see her man. Stories of her extravagant exploits circulated in the battalion, passed from old hands to the rookies with envy, amusement, and good grace— Taffy sneaking through the gates to see the colonel before they sailed from the States; Taffy visiting him in the French rain at the front; Taffy the sweet angel going out of her way in the field hospital to make sure Negro troops were treated the same as white . . .

Original members of the 761st had watched the romance blossom at Camp Claiborne and continue to grow in the years since to reach storybook proportions. They were the Prince and the Princess who, one day, would live happily ever after.

It was considered good luck to hear her voice over the field phone. She would crack the phone in the middle of the night when nothing else was happening.

"I'm trying to get the commanding officer of the 761st. His call sign is Hard Tack."

"Is this Taffy?" Tales of the romance had spread.

"Well, ummm . . ."

"Taffy, we'll sure give it a try."

Long-distance communications through field phones were iffy under even the best conditions. The signal had to be patched through a different system every few miles. Messages were relayed; person-to-person was virtually impossible. Taffy waited as one operator patched into another, then another, each voice growing weaker until finally she heard nothing except intermittent static.

Eventually, the voices returned, the relay getting stronger and stronger.

"Okay, we've got him on the phone . . ."

"He's on the phone . . ."

"He's waiting . . ."

Until: "Lieutenant Taffy, guy says we got him on the phone."

"Tell him I love him."

The message started back to the front in the same relay. "Tell him she loves him."

Then came back. "He says he loves her too."

A pause, a chuckle. "Lieutenant Taffy, we *all* love you."

87

At last we had Jerry on the run everywhere and it was just a matter of running him to death, and destroying him, and getting this damned war over, because there were some of us who wanted to get our clothes off, all of them, and get a good hot bath.

—TREZZVANT ANDERSON

The First and Third armies of the Twelfth Army Group broke the Rhine defenses and crossed the river with extremely light losses. General Patton had boasted that he would be the first American to piss in the Rhine, which he was, standing on an engineer's bridge and doing it while wearing a grin of conquest on his face.

Hitler had wasted precious strength and resources in his desperate Bulge offensive. Now he had to pay the fiddler. Allied armies manning the long front from the North Sea to Switzerland began the push to impose a final solution on the Nazi problem. Germany's only option was total and unconditional surrender.

"My dear General," Winston Churchill said to Eisenhower when he personally crossed the Rhine at the end of March, "the German is whipped. We've got him. He is all through."

Perhaps. But that didn't mean there would be no more combat.

Springtime in western Germany could often be cold and raw. However, the weather began to warm in April in spite of rain and showers two or three days of each week. Signs of spring appeared: buds on trees, sprigs of green on sunny hillsides, a lark's song, a promise of coming warmth from the sun, all welcome signs after the bitter winter of France and the Ardennes.

Black Panthers of the 761st happily stuck their heads out the turrets of their tanks to breathe the fresh air as they traveled the roads and autobahns in pursuit of the slowly retreating enemy. Everyone speculated upon their ultimate destination.

"We are on our way to Berlin."

"Gawd damn! You reckon? How about that? Berlin! Man, we is really seeing the world close up and personal."

"Once we get to Berlin, I'm gonna grab ole Hitler by the neck and *squeeze*. That'll be the end of this war."

"It has done been a long row to hoe. I can't hardly wait to get home and see my little darling."

"Is your little darling ready to see *you*? Better tell her you're coming so she can run ole 4-F out the back door when you come in the front door."

Refugees clogged the roads, walking with their heads down and their faces expressionless except for pained and haunted eyes; pulling toy wagons or pushing wheelbarrows filled with pots and pans and clothing; elderly people, frightened small children, young women with shawls over their heads, mothers carrying infants; weary and stumbling, fleeing homes to escape invasion and further devastation.

The German people were suffering immensely, as the French had suffered. Cities lay in blighted ruins all over the country, still smoldering days after being bombed or after the armies of opposing sides crashed through. Homes had been destroyed. There were almost no stores or businesses left, nowhere to obtain food except to steal, beg, or scrounge for it. The German people could not escape the war now; it had crossed the Rhine to them.

Private Christopher Navarre agonized over the suffering he witnessed. He was a fine, decent man who, as Johnny Holmes opined, would have made a "gawd damned good priest."

"Don't think about it, Father Christopher," Holmes counseled. "Ain't none of this shit our fault. Hitler did this. He fucked over the whole world, including his own people, and now it's up to us to straighten it out so we can get up and go on home where we belong."

The war had long ago lost any romantic idea that it was somehow glorious to go into combat. Nonetheless, tough men like Holmes and Sergeant Johnnie Stevens clung to a fierce, stubborn pride in doing something white Americans said Negro Americans couldn't do. They had said black soldiers couldn't master the necessary skills to fly an airplane or be a tanker. Well, stick that notion up their white butts. Black soldiers were as good as white soldiers. Better even. They had to fight harder to prove it.

It irked them that every time black tankers completed a mission, newsmen rolled in with their cameras and went right on past tanks and black faces to the white infantrymen. White GI faces appeared in the newspapers and movie newsreels back home.

"Ain't nary one of them ever ask my name or where I'm from," Stevens fumed.

"When the history of this war is written," Colonel Bates said from some great well of sadness, "it will be as though no black man ever fought and laid down his life for his country. History will ignore the black soldier."

He and his executive officer, Major Russell Geist, watched from a large storefront picked as a temporary CP. The colonel lit a cigar, puffing thoughtfully on it as white camermen filmed white soldiers while black tankers stood ignored on the sidelines. He saw Sergeant Stevens walk away in disgust.

"What I want most of all now," the colonel said with a weary sigh, "is to get these brave black men through the rest of the war without getting any more killed. I owe them that."

Many narrow dirt lanes produced savage fighting. Dogs, chickens, horses, pigs, women, and children scampered frantically to avoid becoming innocent victims of crossfires. White flags hung in silent capitulation from many windows. *Please spare this humble abode. It's not us you want, it's the real Nazis.* . . . These same windows often produced SS grenade launchers and machine gun fire.

Background terrain intermittently rumbled with rifle fire and artillery even when a particular unit was not in direct contact. No one could be sure where the Germans were, where or when they would decide to stand and fight.

Captain James Baker assumed command of Able Company after the Germans killed Lieutenant Huffman at Nieder-Schlettenbach. He sent out a recovery party when a big gun in a pillbox knocked out one of his tanks. All the crew except PFC Frank Jowers escaped. Jowers seemed to have disappeared, a probable KIA.

The next day, however, Able rumbled into a village along the march route where the black tankers were greeted by none other than Jowers and a 71st Infantry dough. They were the only GIs in town. They were the only *people* in town. Both soldiers sat rocked back in kitchen chairs in the middle of the street.

"Captain, sir," Jowers cracked. "Does this mean the town belongs to us? Can I keep it? Can I *sell* it?"

Everybody grabbed Jowers, hugged him, pounded him on the back. They thought he was dead.

"Naw," he said. After his tank was hit and he got separated

from the rest of his crew, he hid out until nightfall before he sneaked back to his disabled tank. The cannon still functioned. He fired seven shots into the pillbox before it blew up. A little payback. Then, not knowing where his unit had gone, he wandered around until he ran into a dough who was as lost as he. The two of them took over an abandoned village and waited.

"We," he boasted, indicating the white rifleman and himself, "are an occupying army."

Whenever possible, American soldiers either billeted in houses or kicked residents out of their apartments to allow men decent living conditions for a change. The Allies showed no hesitation in taking over an entire village. It was a simple process. The commander of the conquering unit spoke to the burgomeister and told him what was wanted. After all, if it weren't for the Germans, GIs would be back home in America living the good life. Clean featherbeds and nice furniture were often left irretrievably soiled after American soldiers moved on through.

Occasionally, the men caught a glimpse of General Patton as he rode by standing up in his Jeep, pearl-handled pistols and stars gleaming. He always had a pocketful of medals to pin on men who had earned them, regardless of race. Most of the other generals followed his example.

General William Miley, commander of the 17th Airborne Division, awarded a medal to Robert "Motel" Johnson before Motel's 105 tank rolled over and crushed him to death. General Miley had ordered him to fire onto a German bunker that was causing a problem. Motel slammed a single 105mm HE into it.

"You missed, soldier."

"No, sir."

Moments later, smoke started oozing out of the bunker. Jerries scurried out the back.

"Well, I'll be goddamned," General Miley exclaimed. *"One goddamned shot."*

He dug out a Bronze Star on the spot and hung it on Motel's dirty uniform.

It seemed a rare occurrence when a black soldier received credit like that. Generally, or so it seemed to Colonel Bates, his black tankers shouldered the blame when something went wrong and received little or no credit for what went right. He got hot under the collar when an infantry company commander charged that 761st tankers abandoned his men in a minefield. He stormed over to the infantry division's headquarters and confronted the officer in front of his general.

"This man's a goddamned idiot," he began. "What he's got is badly trained soldiers. Let me give you a lesson. We tell our guys that if they hit a mine to get the hell out of the tank as fast as they can. An artillery shell is going to hit because the Jerries want to burn the tank or explode it so it can't be repaired and used again. We beat into our tankers' heads to get out of the tank and get away by running in the tread marks, because any mines would have already been detonated.

"You know damned well there's going to be minefields when you go against fortified positions. If you had any sense you'd tell your infantry to go behind the tanks as a shield and walk in the tread marks. Don't blame my tankers. They did what they were supposed to do. You didn't tell your people what they were supposed to do."

The infantry commander hedged. "Well, you know, it's all right, sir. It's all right—"

"Damned right my guys are all right."

The enemy in Germany was not the same German the 761st had slugged it out with in places like Honskirch and Tillet. The current Wehrmacht *Soldaten* were mostly draftees and a conglomeration of Waffen SS survivors, reservists, and rear-guard types of extremely young or extremely old men drafted to fight a delaying action. Allied recon pilots reported German motorized columns moving east bumper to bumper as they retreated, clogging the roadways. Allied equipment and men took a beating simply pursuing the enemy.

Master tank mechanic Ernest Hill came across a crew stranded with a broken tank by the side of the road.

"The first general I see come by," the TC groused, "I am gonna stop him and ask how many more Germans do I have to kill before I can get a new tank."

Confused and caught off-guard, thousands of enemy troops surrendered and were herded into overcrowded containment pens. Others wandered about the countryside hustling for something to eat and hoping to be captured. Groups threw themselves at every passing American unit, hands on their heads, shouting, *"Kameraden!"*

Sergeant Crecy had little tolerance for them. "Get away from me, you bastard, before we blow up your asses more than we already did."

No one wanted to be saddled with POWs. They were a pain in the ass.

"See that road?" Pop Gates instructed, pointing. "Follow it. Somebody will take you in sooner or later."

"Food. Food?"

"Fuck you," someone snarled.

Young E. G. McConnell climbed down from his tank and distributed 10-N-1s. Some of the Germans looked no older than fourteen or fifteen. One appeared to be at least sixty.

"God bless you," E.G. said. "Now go on and don't try to fight no more."

That was what Moms would have told them.

E.G. turned away. "What kind of war is it," he mused, "when they come begging to be captured and we chase them off?"

88

I thank God that I have the privilege of being one of these amazing Black Panthers.

—CAPTAIN PHIL LATIMER

At staff meeting preceding the day's movement, Colonel Bates suggested Supply Officer Captain Phil Latimer go on ahead to a forward village and select a site for a battalion CP. Intel reported the village vacated by retreating Germans.

It was a bright morning. The mountains of western Germany had flattened out into hills green-tinged with spring around the warmer edges. Latimer looked forward to a perfect day of sightseeing while driving through the countryside.

"Mil," he asked his driver, Corporal Milton Dorsey, "do you feel up to occupying a town today?"

They hopped into Supply's three-quarter-ton truck. To Dorsey's surprise, Captain Latimer directed him to take off ahead of the battalion and its tanks.

"I thought you were kidding, Boss."

"Would I kid about taking over a Kraut town? That's why there are two of us."

Nothing marred an otherwise perfect day except for a few refugees walking the road, an occasional Allied fighter plane passing high overhead, and the far distant rattle of desultory rifle fire. The narrow improved road led past picturesque little farms that seemed to have survived so far with few scars.

Soon, they topped a hill and saw the village laid out ahead, actually a little town as pretty as the surrounding countryside. The war might have been a continent away. No fighting had damaged it. Red tile and yellow-brown straw roofs glowed in the sunlight. The macadam road turned to brickstone as it entered town. Oddly, there wasn't a soul in sight. Dorsey slowed the vehicle. White sheets, towels, even a large pair of white drawers hung from windows. A sigh would have echoed.

"Hold it!" Latimer said.

Dorsey hit his brakes. They sat in the middle of the narrow German street staring at a pillbox that occupied the other end of the street. The slits of its firing ports glared at them like evil eyes. The black barrel of an 88 Ripsaw stuck obscenely from one opening, like a primitive phallic symbol.

Terror froze them in the idling truck for what seemed hours but must have been not more than a second or two. They were afraid to move lest they alarm the occupants and cause them to open fire.

"Boss, I don't know if this was a wise thing to do."

"In hindsight, I'm inclined to agree with you."

"Why haven't they started shooting?"

"Maybe they want to surrender?"

"Maybe they expect *us* to surrender."

"I don't see anything moving. Real slow now, back out of here. It looks abandoned. We'll flank it and take a look."

Before they could put the plan into action, however, an elderly man and a girl unexpectedly appeared in a nearby doorway. Both waved white flags. The Americans looked at them, then looked at the pillbox.

"Boss . . . ?"

"Let's hold what we got."

The odd couple ventured out from the doorway and hesitatingly approached.

"*Guten tag. Wie geht en Ihnen?*"

Latimer replied with the little German he knew. "*Nein, ich spreche deutsch.*"

"What're they saying, Boss?"

"We gut little children?"

"Ask 'em about the pillbox."

"I don't speak German."

A young woman with some command of English was promptly produced. She shyly advised that the village was occupied by the enemy—a single German soldier left behind because he was wounded and couldn't travel. He did not want to fight. He wanted to surrender but was afraid to show himself.

"Tell him to come out," Latimer said. "We won't shoot him."

A call downstreet introduced a worn-looking young soldier who stuck his head out of a doorway. Seeing that he remained intact, he walked out with the assistance of a crutch fashioned out of a piece of table. He hobbled as quickly as he could up the street to present himself to his conquerors.

"He say he gladly prisoner of you," the interrogator said.

"Tell him we gladly he is prisoner of us. Tell him to wait here until troops arrive."

The soldier looked uncertain. "*Schwarze Soldaten?*"

"Yup. *Schwarze Soldaten*. Tell him they won't hurt him."

The new prisoner assured the Americans that the pillbox was unmanned, but they still had to check it out to be sure. Armed with carbines, they cautiously approached it while a group of German civilians and the soldier stood in the street and offered advice and encouragement.

Latimer peeked through one of the firing ports. There was no one inside. The big gun was unloaded. Relieved, Latimer leaned against the cold concrete and grinned. "We did it, Corporal Dorsey. We took this town without firing a shot."

Dorsey grinned back and shook out a K-ration cigarette. "Another day on the Western Front," he said.

89

*You thrust past huge roadblocks where the Germans
had hastily improvised defenses. Around these lie the
old familiar signs of another lost German battle.*

—SIDNEY OLSON, TIME/LIFE CORRESPONDENT

Unlike the remnants of much of the Wehrmacht the Allies encountered on the way into the Reich heartland, Hitler's 6th SS Mountain Division Nord would stand and fight. A ground force with its own chain of command independent of the Wehrmacht, it had not yet accepted defeat. Artillery and infantry of the 71st Infantry supported by tanks of the 761st encircled the unit of several thousand soldiers in the forests of Leisenwald, Waldenburg, and Eudlinger. Colonel Paul Bates distributed his battalion in various-sized elements throughout the 71st Division to aid in either capturing or decimating the SS, delegating his operational control and authority down to lieutenants, platoon sergeants, and even individual tank commanders.

"My men can handle it," he said.

Platoon leader Lieutenant James Burgess took one section of the Assault Guns Platoon to cover the forward movement of the 608th Field Artillery Battalion. Sergeant Richard Sparks with the second section reported to the commander of the 66th Infantry Regiment for what he thought was to be convoy duty. The commander looked at him and lifted a brow.

"Convoy, lad? Hell, we're going out to fight."

"Okay, sir. Let's go then."

Several minor clashes and skirmishes occurred during the cloudy but rain-free day as the SS division probed lines looking for a weak spot and a way out. Darkness approached with dusk beginning to settle like slow-falling ground fog over the forests and towns caught within the Americans' steel ring. An hour or so of daylight remained when German convoys attempted a break-out, hoping to bolt free under cover of darkness. More than four hundred Waffen SS mountain troops, two captured American Sherman tanks, two self-propelled antitank guns, eight Jeeps, and twelve deuce-and-a-half trucks, also formerly American, led the way southeast along the Nieder Mockstadt–Ober Mockstadt Road. Before the attempt, the Germans placed eight mobile artillery pieces on a hill to fire cover for the convoy.

In woods not far from the road, Captain Johnny Long stood on the turret of Baker Company's lead tank and listened to the unnerving rumble of the approaching movement. Shadows were growing long and purple. He had little time to act.

After a quick confab with infantry commanders, he opted to peel Lieutenant Harold Gary's platoon from the company and dispatch it to take care of the Kraut artillery pieces; they had given away their location by firing on infantry to the south. Gary's four tanks took off toward the north to circle around behind the hill on which the German artillery had dug in.

Doughs piled onto the rest of Baker's tanks like field hands onto trucks to go to town on a Saturday night. War wagons raced south at full speed, using old logging roads to parallel the route used by the SS convoy, jouncing across ditches and streams in an exhilarating effort to cut off the escaping enemy. Infantry held on and grasped each other in what was perhaps the most thrilling marathon of their lives. Some were even laughing from the excitement.

The tanks emerged from forest shadow and sped downhill across a clearing to reach and block the road ahead of the convoy. Someone shouted over the air, "Come Out Fighting!" The Black Panther motto.

A deep but shallow-walled ravine had cut its way across the clearing. Heretofore unnoticed parties of advance SS opened up with small arms as the tanks bore down on the ravine at full speed. Captain Long's tank reached it first. It shot over the lip and disappeared, reappearing almost immediately climbing up the opposite bank. It stopped to wait for the others. Infantry clinging to its sides and top flew off in all directions to lay down fire on the German advance party.

The bulk of Baker's tanks hit the gulch on-line like charging cavalry, taking it with a mighty reverberating roar of engines. At the bottom meandered a small stream clogged with tree stumps and mud. TC Billy Kitt's machine struck a stump with such force that a squad of infantry clinging to the hull dislodged and sailed through the air, completely clearing the creek before landing on soft earth. Uninjured, the doughs popped to their feet and scrambled up the opposite bank to join the firefight.

Two tanks got stuck in the mud and a third blew a track. Johnny Long jumped out of his wagon to direct the remainder of his tanks across. The crackle of the engagement rose to spiteful levels. Machine gun and burp gun bullets popped and slashed the air.

"The bastard's got balls," a dough exclaimed admiringly of Captain Long.

"You don't know the half of it, my good man," replied First Sergeant Purvis Easley, who was also directing traffic. "You can tell your grandkids you saw the Black Patton in action."

"I ain't ever going to have any grandkids at this rate."

A dough lieutenant shouted down from the top of the ravine. "Captain Long, that convoy's coming around the bend now."

Long climbed to the top. Sure enough, Sherman tanks appeared, flitting past growths of pine that lined the road. He had to tell himself that while they looked American, they were actually crewed by the enemy. If the convoy got past now, the bulk of the 6th SS would reorganize to cause mischief elsewhere. The convoy had to be stopped.

He vaulted to the turret of his mount and grabbed the radio mike.

Cats! Listen up. With me, let's go. Go! Go! Go! Give 'em hell. Give 'em everything we got . . .

Mud-mired and damaged machines stayed where they were in the creek. The remaining tanks scampered up over the edge of the embankment to confront the reckless and desperate German breakout attempt. Time went in crazy fast-forward mode as the iron predators stormed in a ragged line across the field, all guns roaring and blazing, trailing smoke in their wake. Let the doughs take care of the SS advance party; Long concentrated on the breakout.

Everybody zero in on the lead tank. It looks like ours, but it's not.

The road erupted in fire, smoke, dust, and death. The convoy piled up. SS storm troopers jumped out of U.S. trucks and formed defensive skirmish lines in the pines. Tracers crisscrossed the field like angry battling hornets as the tanks raced parallel to the now-stalled convoy, spitting HE from their main cannon and streams of tracers from machine guns.

It's coming from the left flank . . .

What is that red smoke . . . ?

Stay out. Don't go in close, but keep moving . . .

Damn! That one was close . . .

See the big gun behind the truck? Behind the truck, behind the other truck . . . ?

Lieutenant Gary's platoon had not yet reached the Kraut artillery. These big enemy guns joined the fray, bracketing and stomping in giant exploding footfalls around and among the attacking tanks.

I've been hit . . . !

The tank exploded and jumped completely off the ground, epicenter of a red-hot ball of flame. It crashed shuddering back to earth. Hatches flew open. Crewmembers abandoned it and took off for the ravine. Greasy black smoke boiled from every opening, the Ronson living up to its reputation.

A second tank whipped a ninety-degree turn to stay below

the crest of a slight rise, leaving only its turret and main gun in sight of the enemy. It knocked out a truck and a Jeep before taking a hit on its gun barrel. Once again, hatches flew open and black smoke poured out. The crew scrambled to safety, dragging a wounded tanker.

By this time smoke and darkness had reduced visibility to the point that one side could barely see the other across the field. Confronted with devastating artillery that had already disabled two of his tanks, Captain Long called off the assault.

Pull back to the creek. I repeat, pull back to the creek . . .

Did you say the creek, Johnny . . . ?

Yes. Damn it, the creek. Move . . .

Tanks veered off from the attack to rendezvous in the ravine, having sowed chaos and stopped the breakout. The Krauts would go no further, not tonight. Fires blazed here and there on the road. Doughs in the ravine, who had routed the SS advance party by this time, heard men on the road shouting and cursing in German as they attempted to reorganize, establish a defensive perimeter, and put out the fires.

The firefight, fierce at first, petered down to a desultory exchange now and then as both sides settled in to hold the stalemate. The doughs were running short on ammo anyhow. Their commanders issued orders to save at least three rounds per weapon—in the event of an emergency.

After a while, the night turned peaceful. Captain Long peered through the blackness in the direction of the trapped Germans. Not a sound came from their lines. He almost felt sorry for the poor sonsofbitches.

Sergeant Eddie Donald came up and stood next to him. There was no need to talk. They enjoyed the companionable silence of men whose bonds were forged by combat. Somewhere off in the distance, in a town whose name Long didn't know and didn't really care to know, something was still going on. A terrific explosion shook the ground. A ball of smoke, red-hot at its core, slowly rose above the town against the star-dotted horizon.

90

This was the happier type of fighting, the blitzkrieg style.

—AL HEINTZLEMAN,
AUTHOR OF *WE'LL NEVER GO OVER-SEAS*

U.S. armored and infantry units maneuvered under cover of darkness to close the ring not only on the trapped convoy, which still held out, but also on other major enemy pockets in surrounding towns and villages. With the German status quo rapidly weakening, the SS broke into smaller groups near dawn and attempted to escape on foot.

Lieutenant Gary's platoon wiped out the Kraut artillery responsible for providing cover to the breakout convoy, then chased a German command car fleeing on a secondary road. The fleet and nimble smaller vehicle quickly outdistanced the tanks, and the German general escaped.

"Damn! *Damn!*" Gary exclaimed, then compensated by destroying ten machine gun nests set up for a delaying action.

Captain English's Mosquito Fleet killed two hundred foot soldiers while performing screening and recon. Chico Holland led six tanks in capturing an enemy radio station and two fully stocked armored supply depots. Captain Pop Gates's Charlie Company joined Baker and squeezed in on the enemy's breakout convoy from the south and east to catch the SS as they began attempting to filter out of the trap.

By first light, hundreds of German soldiers were scattered all through the forest, rustling and darting about like a scourge of locusts in a cornfield. The only way to get them out was to blast them out.

"Gentlemen," Gates instructed his tank gunners, "raise your fire so it will explode in the treetops. That'll spread more shrapnel, knock down trees, and get those people out of the woods."

Tanks lined up and pounded the forest, kept pounding it. Fires broke out. Smoke roiled thick and heavy, cutting down available oxygen for the sonsofbitches trapped by it. But, sure enough, the tactic worked. Germans started staggering out waving white underwear or anything else white they could find.

"Stay in your tanks with the hatches buttoned," Gates ordered. "Wait until they get abreast of us and then direct 'em back to the infantry."

Surrendering Germans approached all across the company's front, staggering, coughing, tears rolling down grimy cheeks, uniforms scorched.

"*Kameraden!*" they called out, pleading. "*Kameraden!*"

One of the tankers, overcome with curiosity, made the mistake of springing his hatch prematurely and sticking his head out. The nearest Kraut stopped, stunned.

"*Schwarze Soldaten!*" he screeched.

The entire bunch, terrified, wheeled and bolted back toward the trees. Pop Gates bellowed an order.

Machine gunners, over their heads, stop 'em!

Guns ripped flame into branches above the fleeing soldiers. They stopped, threw up their hands again, and shouted more frantically than ever. "*Kameraden!*" Figuring they had better go along with the black soldiers after all.

A German officer who spoke English seemed puzzled over how black tankers could be in so many different places at once. He asked Captain Gates, "How many Negro panzer divisions *are* there?"

Gates laughed. "*Dozens,*" he said.

As the morning wore into full daylight, U.S. P-47 fighter-bombers screamed in low over the forests and hills to target German tanks and pillboxes, machine gun nests and artillery positions, infantry in the open, and occupied towns. Delayed fuses on the bombs gave the aircraft time to gain altitude after dropping their loads. The earth trembled as though from an earthquake, the noise enough to bust eardrums. Thirty-two-ton tanks shook, rattling the crews inside.

"Jesus God," Sergeant Walter Lewis moaned. "How much more can they take?"

91

War has made us numb and callous to feeling.

—SERGEANT WALTER LEWIS

The 6th SS lost Buches, Büdingen, and Waldenburg to the American advance. A doughboy private laying commo wire before the assault on Leisenwald spotted German soldiers with *Panzerfausts* setting an ambush for the four Able Company tanks assigned to the mission. He exposed himself to enemy fire in order to run across an open field to warn the approaching tanks.

The tanks eliminated the tank-killer ambush, then neutralized pillboxes on roads entering the town. Doughs stormed Leisenwald and engaged the SS in a bitter house-to-house battle that lasted well into the night before the surviving Germans started waving their underwear.

The sun rose to reveal Leisenwald as typical of towns east of the Rhine. Americans dubbed them "cow towns" because of the overpowering odors of manure. Thick stone houses crowded close against winding streets. Firewood in stacks lined the walls.

This morning, however, the stench of decomposing bodies masked the odors of manure. Dead German soldiers cluttered the streets. Firewood was strewn everyplace. Wounded Kraut soldiers being attended to by their medical specialists filled those houses left standing.

GIs herded a small group of SS prisoners out of an alley into the sunlight and urged them down the street. Black Panther Jonathan Hall was heating a canteen cup of coffee on a tiny fire built next to his tank. He looked up just as a captured German officer produced a straight razor and immediately slashed his own throat from ear to ear. Gurgling and pumping bright blood, he slumped to the cobblestone street. Hall and his crew watched dispassionately as the German slowly bled to death, writhing on the cobblestones.

Hall knelt and stirred his coffee. He tasted it before adding sugar. When he looked up again, the German lay still and the dough riflemen had gone on with the other prisoners.

92

If you fire your pistol in the air, a dozen Germans will come rushing in to be taken prisoner.

—A WEHRMACHT OFFICER

Allied casualties during the three-day action to destroy the 6th SS Mountain Division Nord were light, at least for the 761st. Not a Black Panther had been killed. Those few who suffered million-dollar wounds would not be permanently disfigured and were on their way home. Since Colonel Bates's return, the battalion seemed to exist in a protected state. Ole Hard Tack was a lucky charm.

Patton's Panthers continued their hard-charging drive through the Reichland. Sherman tanks cruised the autobahn, overrunning airfields and firing on enemy troops hidden in woods along the highway. Spring had definitely arrived. Days were warm and sunny. The Reich was a lovely green land if one ignored the shattered towns, the ever-present refugees, and the gaunt gray-suited soldiers who constantly appeared from nowhere to beg for food and the privilege of being captured. The frauleins were pretty too, even though shy and backward at first.

It was definitely the beginning of the end. Russians were squeezing the Reich hard from the east while Patton's army closed in on the west, collapsing the Reich as it went. Jerry was in full retreat. GIs advanced almost at will against broken armies. Germans surrendered in droves. Patton complained that his Third Army was held up more by the sheer numbers of surrendering enemy than by armed resistance.

Farm boys in the 761st knew the old wives' tale about the snake—that even if you cut off its head it would continue to twitch until the sun went down. The Third Reich was like that snake, dead, except it didn't know it yet and refused to accept it.

The Führer issued a "scorched earth" order that all industry and buildings in the path of advancing Allies would be laid to waste, burned, or otherwise destroyed. He decreed that captured Allied airmen, whom he blamed for destruction of German cities, would be executed. So would any German soldier accused of cowardice in the face of the enemy or suspected of being a deserter. Even *talk* of surrender was punishable by death.

The SS hanged six civic leaders in Lohr when they dawdled in defending the town. They machine gunned civilians who tried to flee from Aschaffenburg. Americans entering the town found a Wehrmacht officer dangling by the neck in front of a wine shop. A note was pinned to his tunic: "Cowards and traitors hang. Yesterday, an officer candidate died a hero's death destroying an enemy tank. He lives on. Today, a coward in officer's garb hangs because he betrayed the Führer and the people. He is dead forever."

While there were few battles like Morville, Honskirch, and Tillet, there were still Germans who, for whatever reason, did fight and fight hard, resulting in vicious clashes along country roads or in towns whose names were either never known or soon forgotten. Most resistance came from small bands of *Volksgrenadiers* or from occasional larger bodies of regulars making a last stand.

Weary tankmen helped seize Coburg, the ancient capital of Saxony where Attila the Hun had once established his seat of government. They ate dinner in the city square, in the shadow of a monument of a Dominican Negro friar who had been sainted centuries ago. They had fresh eggs and chicken and wine from a liberated winery. It was incredible how something as simple as hot food raised morale. There was even laughter as the tankers talked trash and horsed around with each other.

Someone interrupted a catch-as-catch-can football game with the news that President Franklin D. Roosevelt had died of a massive cerebral hemorrhage. Vice President Harry Truman took the oath of office at 1908 hours on April 12, 1945. No one was exactly sure what Roosevelt's death meant for the war effort; the war continued with hardly a bated breath.

Baker Company knocked out 15 machine gun nests, killed more than 100 soldiers, and captured 200 others at Kulmbach. Charlie killed 125 and captured two complete battalions and an attached company. Kulmbach fell quickly after that.

The warehouses in the city were crammed with treasures looted from countries previously occupied by Nazis. German civilians scurried joyfully through the streets, looting at will.

German regulars dug in at Bayreuth and on the outskirts and

prepared for a major battle. While the main body of the 761st was thus occupied, Colonel Bates cut out five light tanks from the Mosquito Fleet and two 105mm tanks from Assault Guns to accompany Task Force WEIDENMARK on a mad dash for the Czechoslovakian border. From the heights as the task force skirted Bayreuth, tankers saw dense clouds of rising smoke and the bright flickering of fires as more of Naziland was laid to waste.

The task force speared through miles of enemy territory and took town after town without firing a shot as it pushed to Czechoslovakia and the farthest east of any Allied forces. White flags popped into sight as soon as the armored vehicles appeared. Their greatest obstacles were hundreds of bedraggled, recently freed Russian POWs who clogged the roads in their tattered clothing, barefoot, bony, starving. Hollow, haunted eyes. Sunken whiskery cheeks. Ill and injured, with suppurating wounds. So frail and weak they could hardly walk without leaning on each other. Hands reaching for deliverance. Pleading for redemption. Begging for food and a kindly word.

"Amerikaneetskis! Amerikaneetskis!"

"Pitiful, just plumb pitiful," Sergeant Joe Tates murmured.

He hadn't seen anything yet. This was merely a preview of what lay ahead as the Allies snaked deeper into Adolf Hitler's land of Nazis and concentration camps.

93

There was nothing to be seen but mile after square mile of crumbled buildings, with here a wall or a tower standing and there a column of smoke rising. The fresh fires looked almost cheerful in the midst of so much desolation.

—Time/Life Correspondent Charles Wertenbaker

Patton's Panthers suffered their first KIA since Lieutenant Huffman died nearly a month ago. It occurred during the brief siege of Bayreuth, a key city along the Berlin–Munich autobahn. Baker Company's tanks had paused along the autobahn after a fierce engagement on an old farm, which cost the Krauts five panzers, seventy-five dead, and the loss of two hundred POWs. Baker had lost not a single man.

As the tankers took personals and checked on each other in a grove of trees alongside the highway, an 88 shell came out of nowhere and landed directly over the tank in which Corporal Fred Brown was a gunner. He was outside sitting on the deck plate at the time. Shrapnel shredded his body. He was evacuated and died somewhat later.

To the south of Bayreuth, ground troops of the 66th Infantry Regiment maneuvering in the woods toward the city unexpectedly encountered a large military airfield and an aeronautical school. Open fields more than two hundred yards across surrounded the strip, an obstacle as effective as a moat around a castle. The fields would have to be crossed during an attack. Not a tree grew on them, nor a blade of grass taller than ankle high.

"We are gonna run across *that?*" Pop Gates overheard an incredulous rifleman ask.

Charlie Company supported the assault. Captain Gates positioned his tanks in the woods with their big guns directed across the field at the buildings, fortified trenches, and other enemy positions around the airport. All the airplanes appeared to be gone, leaving only a considerable ground force as security.

Defenders held their fire, seemingly content to wait until the Americans started across the fields where they could get the most bang for their *reichmarks*. Infantry commanders positioned troops without interference for what, in effect, would be a World War I trench-warfare bayonet charge.

On a signal, tanks and the infantry's heavy indirect fire weapons opened up to prep the objective. Cannon muzzles flamed in long flickering lines, quickly generating a pall of smoke above the trees. Exploding shells on the receiving end plowed up the earth, tossed building materials about like matchsticks, and ripped off arms, legs, and other bodily attachments. Blood and flesh thickened the air and lent smoke a pinkish tint.

Then came the doughboys.

At first a thunderous roar erupted from hundreds of throats, a primordial gung-ho howl as they psyched themselves up. The roar went on and on endlessly. It took a lot of psyching to chase out onto that field and into the muzzles of enemy guns.

Long, weaving green lines surged from the newly budded trees out onto that damnable and interminable field. This time the Germans responded. Enemy machine guns whipped and lashed in streams of green tracers, tearing gaps in the green lines. Many doughs died on their feet, with their boots on, tumbling like rabbits picked off by hunters' shotguns.

Tanks and heavy weapons concentrated on locating and neutralizing machine gun emplacements. First Sergeant Bill Burroughs, gunner for Sergeant Crecy, jumped out to better locate a machine gun, since visibility buttoned up inside a Sherman was severely restricted. He had barely cleared the tank deck when a slug whacked him on the forehead. He collapsed in the grass.

Crecy went after him and dragged him back from the line of fire. His left eye hung from its socket on cords. The side of his face resembled freshly ground hamburger. He eventually lost his eye but kept his life.

Surviving doughs reached the airport and its security ring after what seemed like hours to support personnel and *days* to the men out there on that field. In a frenzy of rage and lust for payback blood, doughs swept across the airfield shooting everything that moved, setting buildings afire to drive out the defenders, and then cutting them down as they fled. It was one of the most savage exhibitions of raw human nature that Captain Gates had ever witnessed, as terrible in its own way as that night on the road from Silz when the battalion caught up with the convoy of fleeing Germans.

Why did the sonofabitching Krauts have to keep fighting? Didn't the bastards know when they were whipped?

Afterward, his tank guns now silent, the old man of the 761st sat wearily on the side of his tank, legs dangling, and looked out across the bloody field that had claimed such a toll in human life. Bodies lay everywhere, looking like clumps of old discarded clothing. Here and there medics were working on the wounded, whose combined cries and pleas seeped into the atmosphere in a universal sound of misery. Smoke eddied and whirled.

How much longer—*Lord, how much longer*—could it go on?

KIA (Killed in Action)
Corporal Fred L. Brown

94

*Being in an all-black outfit, I found my own experi-
ence with the black soldier was that he performed no
differently than white soldiers in terms of heroic
deeds.*

—SERGEANT EDDIE DONALD

Savage gunfire drummed from the trees ahead. A white lieutenant clearing some woods with his dough platoon came hustling back, bent over at the waist and running hard. Sergeant Johnnie Stevens had his head stuck up out of the hatch of his tank, waiting for news on the holdup.

"Looks like the white boys are having a little party up there," he cracked.

"If somebody's getting shot at," Corporal Joe Kiah the gunner said cynically, "then you can bet we are just about to get an invitation."

The lieutenant ran up to the tank, puffing hard, his face pale.

"We're pinned down in that field," he said, pointing.

Stevens's tank and its four-man crew, short an assistant driver, was the dough platoon's only supporting armor. They sat parked in the yard of a long-abandoned farmhouse. The roof sagged and webs of vine grew like wrinkles around its aged window eyes. Beyond lay forest. The infantry lieutenant pointed out the location of his men, what they faced, then said he had to get back to them. The crescendo of the firefight had risen to a steeper and more confusing pitch of fire and counterfire. The lieutenant hoofed off.

Stevens thought about it. He couldn't commit his tank in such terrain without knowing the situation. "Kiah, I'm going out there to see what's happening."

"Sarge, you crazy sonofabitch, don't go out there."

"Kiah. Cover me."

He stuffed grenades in his pockets, more as an afterthought than anything else, slung his .45 grease gun by its strap across his back, and took off past the abandoned house and into the forest. He worked his way cautiously toward the sound of firing until it seemed he might be right in the middle of it. He dropped to his belly and began crawling.

After another fifty yards, he came to the edge of a clearing overgrown with tall weeds. Muzzle flashes winking in the field confirmed that this was the location where the doughs were being held up. Oily blue rifle smoke hung in the air.

The grassland rose into a woodline to Stevens's left. Most of the hostile fire originated from it, close by.

Good enough. Here the good guys, there the bad guys. He lay resting a moment behind a rotted log while he visually scanned the most advantageous route for bringing up his tank and unleashing it. He was concentrating so hard on tactics that he failed to notice that he wasn't the only bear in the woods.

A Kraut machine gun cranked up next to him, not fifteen yards away, ringing his ears and causing him to almost jump out of his coveralls. Fortunately, although stunned and surprised, he was a veteran and too battlewise to panic. He hugged the ground, would have burrowed into it if he could. The realization of what he had done settled over him.

Somehow, without being seen, he had crawled upon an enemy machine gun nest. Would probably never have seen it until too late if it hadn't opened up on the doughs.

Sunshine bathed the clearing in bright golden light, but here among the trees lurked dark shadows and hidden places. Stevens looked around the end of his log.

Damn! Worse than he thought.

This wasn't *just* a machine gun nest. It appeared to be the flank of the enemy's defenses. The MG's muzzle flickered and danced in the dimness. Shadowy figures in Nazi helmets crouched around the gun. More figures—he couldn't tell how many—concealed themselves beyond.

What now, Mister Hero?

He looked around. There was the devil's own chance that he could crawl out the same way he came in. A snap of a twig, the rustle of clothing, the scrape of a boot on the ground . . . everything would be over for him except the shouting. It astounded him that he had made it in to begin with.

Anxious sweat beaded his face.

Let's see. He had four grenades stuffed into his pockets, the grease gun, and his .45 pistol. He had . . .

He had the doughs in the field. If he created a real ruckus, would the white lieutenant understand what was happening and send the platoon to his assistance?

What other choice did he have? He would have to chance it.

Ruben Rivers and Sam Turley had been heroes too.

He made up his mind. His heart pounded against the ground. Surely the Krauts must *feel* it vibrating through the earth.

He cautiously unslung his grease gun and eased back the bolt, since it fired from that position. He placed it ready for use next to his right elbow. He unsnapped the holster containing his pistol. Lastly, he took out the grenades. He arranged two within easy reach and kept the other two, one for each hand. He eased out the firing pins while gripping the spoon handles to prevent their detonating until he was ready.

He took a deep breath to calm the beating of his heart. He closed his eyes an instant and thought about home. He opened them again and drew in another deep breath filled with the scent of the rich earth. His final view of this old world, he considered with some sarcasm, was of rotting forest vegetation, a lichen-encrusted log, black dirt, and tree roots. He had never thought it would end like this.

Time to go to work.

He tossed the first grenade from where he lay, using a wide overhand swing. It was still in the air when the second joined it.

The near-simultaneous explosions crumped, banging with sharp flashes of light and smoke. Johnnie hugged the ground. Shrapnel whacked tree branches above his head.

He flung the other two grenades before the Jerries knew what was going on, before they could react and adjust. Unearthly screams of pain received them.

Stevens bounced to his knees, his little submachine gun stuttering and spitting as he sprayed volleys of heavy slugs into flesh and bone.

He had counted on the white lieutenant, and he came through. Relieved of pressure, doughs on the field jumped to their feet and charged the trees. When it was over, nine Kraut corpses lay mangled and torn around the machine gun and thirty-six more had the fight blasted out of them and gave up.

The lieutenant walked over to Stevens as his men led the prisoners away.

"That was some piece of work," he said.

The only thing Stevens wanted was to go lie down somewhere and sleep for a week.

"Another day on the Western Front," he murmured.

95

The same principle as a fire department. The troops were sent wherever there was a fire.

—REICHSMARSCHALL HERMANN GÖRING, ON HITLER'S STRATEGY IN 1945

Two platoons from Captain Pop Gates's Charlie Company and elements of the 66th Infantry Regiment attacked and occupied the town of Neuhaus on April 19. Few of the Nazis surrendered. Most withdrew toward the Veldensteiner Forest. Colonel Bates and his headquarters elements rolled into town behind combat lines to select and set up a new command post.

Lieutenant Ivan Harrison, commander of Headquarters Company, was checking out a house on the main street as a possible bivouac for his Service and Supply people when a German fighter-bomber, all that remained of Göring's Luftwaffe in the immediate vicinity, buzzed overhead and dropped a bomb several houses away. The concussion rattled Harrison's teeth and made a chair dance across the floor.

The lieutenant darted outside to check on his mess and supply trucks left parked in the street. None of them was damaged. Personnel had sought cover when they saw the plane dive.

A plume of gray smoke punctuated a section of street a block away. The warplane dwindled to a speck reflecting the red light of the westering sun. It wouldn't be back. It seemed to be high-tailing it for Berlin.

Captain Phil Latimer raised Harrison on the radio. "Ivan, are you going to stay put for a while?"

Puzzled, Harrison responded with, "Uh, Roger that."

"Roger your Roger. Out."

What the hell was that all about? The S-4 had been behaving strangely all day.

Harrison mulled it over. He stood on the cobblestone street and let himself feel transported back in time by the archaic atmosphere of the ancient town. Gothic was in the air. The medieval Veldenstein Castle glowered down on the town from its high green perch.

"Do you suppose that's Dracula's castle?" joked Corporal Billy Thompson from Supply.

"It was Göring's," Harrison said.

The reinforced stone walls and tunnels of Veldenstein Castle had stood for more than five hundred years high on its bluff overlooking Neuhaus. Hitler's commander-in-chief of the Luftwaffe, fat man Reichsmarschall Hermann Göring, claimed the castle when the Nazis came to power.

Like most high Nazi party members, Göring supported several houses, but it was at Veldenstein that he stored many of the priceless possessions he had scavenged from occupied countries during the successes of the blitzkrieg. He visited Paris four times in February and March 1941 after the fall of France to cart home loot stolen from private Jewish collections—paintings by Goya, Rembrandt, Rubens, Boucher, and others. When local German officials complained that this was illegal, Göring snapped, "The highest jurist in the state is me."

Göring abandoned the castle ahead of advancing Allies in 1945 and retired to Berlin along with Hitler and most of the Führer's staff, leaving a guard of SS to watch and protect his property.

A road wound up the steep side of the mountain toward the castle. Harrison watched as foot soldiers led by Charlie Company tanks ascended it. From this distance, the doughs resembled ants and the tanks some rare and exotic species of beetle. Darkness was closing in rapidly, but sufficient light remained to allow him to watch the drama play itself out.

The tanks belched smoke and pinpricks of fire. Sound rumbled like thunder. Shells bounced off the castle's stone walls or exploded in blossoms of flame without doing much damage.

Germans inside possessed little heart for a fight. They put up only a token resistance before scattering out the back like a bunch of field mice intent on joining their comrades in the forests. Tanks and doughs surrounded the castle.

Capturing the residence of a top Hitler Reichsmarschall reinforced in Harrison the belief that the war was almost over. He sighed.

The radio interrupted his reverie. It was Captain Latimer again. "Ivan, are you still there?"

"Negative. I'm *here.*"

"That's good. Out."

Black Panthers filled with awe entered Göring's castle high on the cliff. Seldom had they imagined, much less seen, such opulence.

Private Christopher Navarre's eyes widened with wonder over the master bedroom. It had marble floors, crystal chandeliers, Persian rugs, furs . . . Everything was trimmed in gold and polished silver. A giant gold and jade peacock with onyx eyes guarded the door. Bedside tables were constructed of solid polished onyx. Paintings of the Masters adorned the walls. The bed looked the size of a football field.

The bathroom was like a big Jacuzzi fashioned all in marble. Pornographic pictures depicting every imaginable sex act hung on the walls.

There was even an elevator in the dining room to transport Göring from floor to floor so the fat man wouldn't have to climb marble stairways.

"Them Nazi fellas lived real high on the hog," Leonard Smith observed. "What do you think, Father Christopher? Could you live like this or what?"

"Not if it was bought with the blood of other people," Navarre said.

The castle enjoyed the final rays of the sun while the purple of night spilled like ink over the town below.

Captain Latimer came up on the air again. "Ivan, stand by where you are. We're on our way."

The S-4 captain and his driver, Milton Dorsey, sped into town in their beat-up three-quarter-ton with the top back and the windshield down. Both men were grinning like possums. They jumped out.

"What's up with you—?" Harrison began.

Dorsey ducked around to the tarped back and returned carrying a case of champagne.

"Happy birthday, Ivan!" Captain Latimer sang out, laughing.

Harrison hadn't even remembered.

96

But I do nothing upon myself, and yet I am mine own executioner.

—John Donne 1572–1631

Captain Johnny Long's driver, Sergeant Fred Fields, was a big, awkward, dark-skinned kid from Dennison, Texas, with a fabled heart as big as that fabled state and as generous with his boss's possessions as he was with his own. He gave away his captain's liquor, cigarettes, and dry socks, and wore the captain's underwear. His personal loyalty to Long, however, as well as his dedication to Baker Company and the 761st, made up for any perceived shortcomings. Long trusted him without question. Only death would prevent his accomplishing any mission assigned him.

There was only one instance when Sergeant Fields so much as hesitated over an order. That was the day the Kraut sniper killed the medics and night demons took over Captain Long's sleep.

The 761st was settled into a bivouac for the night, placing out security and roving pickets, pitching pup tents, and warming Ks for supper. Colonel Bates toured the bivouac as he often did, stopping to chat, to share a meal or a cigarette, to talk about home and what the men would do when the war ended.

The colonel, Sergeant Crecy, Johnny Long, Fred Fields, Sergeant Holmes, and several other Panthers congregated around a small fire to talk and let down from the day. Everyone wanted to hear about how Crecy, the baddest Black Panther of all, had braved a hail of bullets earlier in the day to help Colonel Bates out of a disabled tank, thereby likely saving Hard Tack's life. Barely had the conversation touched on the matter, however, when ambulances brought in a load of white doughboys and black tankers from an ambush site and deposited their stretchers on the grass for the battalion surgeon, Doc William Bruce, to look after.

While Doc Bruce was on his way, several medics began working to stabilize the patients. They wore Red Cross vests with other Red Crosses prominently displayed on their helmets. Colonel Bates looked at the injured men, lowered his head without comment, and walked to his Jeep to return to battalion HQ. He limped slightly from his old wound as well as from sheer weariness.

Minutes later a single shot shattered the dusky stillness of approaching nightfall. A medic's helmet clanged sharply. It leaped from his head and spun through the air, the red and white colors of the cross flashing. The medic fell forward across his patient.

Bystanders instinctively hit the dirt.

A second shot rang out. A howl of protest and rage erupted in camp as another medic collapsed. The sniper was deliberately targeting medical people, violating a cardinal rule of modern civilized warfare.

Seven or eight Panthers managed to pinpoint the direction and location of the shooter. They grabbed carbines and grease guns and ran out to find the sniper and put an end to the evil bastard. They weren't gone long before weapons rattled and the men came back dragging a German shot through the thigh. He was slowly bleeding to death; his leg had already bloated to twice its normal size from blood leaking into the tissue. He needn't expect sympathy or compassion. Nothing but raw hostility and hatred greeted him.

"*Kameraden! Kameraden!*" he cried out.

"*Kameraden* my ass, you dirty Kraut. Fuck you."

Medics and the battalion surgeon weren't about to treat a man who had killed two of them and would have killed more had he not been stopped. Besides, they were busy elsewhere. They ignored the German.

Johnny Long turned to Sergeant Fields. "Shoot the sonofabitch," he said.

That was the single instance when the kid hesitated in obeying an order. His face turned the color of cold ashes. He fumbled for his sidearm.

Long realized immediately that he had issued an unfair and illegal order. He laid a gentle restraining hand on the sergeant's arm. He never asked a man to do something he wouldn't do himself.

"Fred, no. I'm sorry," he amended. "I'll do it."

Everyone stepped back from the German, who slumped to his hands and knees, unable to stand. He looked up with eyes the color of glacier ice. He had a thin face hardened way beyond its years. He emitted a sob when Captain Long drew his .45 Colt and he realized what was coming.

Long released the safety and, in the same swift motion, shot the man through the forehead. It was the first time he had killed close up, face to face. From that instant forward his nightmares would replay the moment the pistol cracked and blood spurted. He would carry with him always the image of that man's face and the glacier-blue eyes.

Captain Long and his driver never spoke of the matter again.

97

And bring the prisoners out of captivity.
—Prayer Book, 1662

Captain Johnny Long started toward his Jeep to run a quick recon of the area before his company and the battalion settled in a few nights after the sniper incident. Loyal as ever, like a faithful sidekick, Sergeant Fred Fields seldom ventured far from his boss's side.

"You don't have to go, Fred," Captain Long said. "I'm only going out a little ways to take a look."

"I'm with you, sir," Fields said, sliding into the driver's seat.

Not ten minutes later, a dozen Germans appeared out of the shadows to surround the Jeep as it slowed to negotiate a rutted logging road cut through thick, darkening forest, their weapons pointed and ready. Long immediately expected the same fate he had dealt out to the Kraut sniper. It was no secret that *Schwarze Soldaten* in tanks mopped up Jerries wherever they were, that while they took hundreds of prisoners they were also equally ready to oblige any who wanted to fight it out to the end.

Long slowly looked around. None of these guys wore the SS

Death's Head. Put that in the plus column; the SS were responsible for most atrocities. At any rate, SS or not SS, Long and his driver were outnumbered and surrounded and in deep shit. No use putting up a fight. They would be dead before they got off a single shot.

"Don't move a hair," Long advised.

Fields had already frozen. "Sir, I'm afraid I'm gonna wet my drawers."

"Are you wearing mine or yours?"

The first few minutes of a capture were the most critical, when emotions and adrenaline were supercharged. The chances of staying alive were good if you survived past that.

The Germans began yelling. They jerked the black men from the Jeep, disarmed them, threw them on the ground, and frisked them for hidden guns, grenades, papers, or anything else of interest. Fields trembled all over from fright. Dire thoughts ran through Long's mind.

What are they going to do to us? Kill us now or later? Do they know about the sniper I shot?

A boot nudged him in the ribs.

"You are prisoner to us. Come mit me. Do not please try escape or I am to shoot you in the arse. Do you understand?"

"Loud and clear."

They were bound hands and feet and tossed like old duffel bags into the back of a truck with two guards who forbade them to speak. They came to a town and stopped after a rough jarring ride that lasted about an hour. Guards dropped them out onto the street, untied their feet, and made them walk.

They were in some nameless cow town. Stacked firewood, winding cobbled streets, manure odor in the air. Rows of local German civilians, mostly women, turned out to shout insults and spit in their faces. Sergeant Fields was more scared than ever. He remembered when he was a child in Texas hearing about a black man being lynched. He understood now how the poor man must have felt just before they strung him up.

Guards took them to some kind of headquarters in a citadel called Walhalla at the other end of town. Brass bustled all over the place, but paid the prisoners little attention. Long and Fields were tossed into an empty room for interrogation by English-speaking noncoms.

"I am an officer of the United States Army," Captain Long protested, jockeying for time. "I refuse to speak to noncommissioned personnel."

If he died, he would die an officer and a gentleman, a credit to his unit, to the army, and to his race. Out of frustration, one of the German NCOs yanked Sergeant Fields to his feet and pressed the muzzle of a Mauser against his temple. Fields's eyes popped. Sweat dribbled off his chin.

"We will take him out mit us and shoots him in the head," the interrogator threatened.

Long died a slow death inside, but he figured they were going to be executed anyhow.

"Remember you are a soldier, Sergeant Fields," Long said in farewell to his driver and friend.

Fields stood there in the dingy room with his head up. "I'm with you, sir," he said.

The Germans dragged Fields out of the room, leaving Captain Long alone to wrestle with his despair and sense of loss and failure. He listened long agonizing minutes for a gunshot. When none came, he decided they must have taken Sergeant Fields out back where they wouldn't have to clean up the mess.

After about a half-hour, the locked door opened and a slender German general with Aryan eyes and blond hair walked in with one of the armed guards. Long figured it was his turn. He stood at attention, unblinking, his expression proud and defiant.

"What are you doing in Germany, you rich Americans?" the general began.

"Sir, I beg your pardon. Don't forget we found you in France."

A half-smile froze on the general's face. Then, to Long's surprise, he slapped his thigh and started laughing. That was the end of the interrogation. He turned and walked out.

Guards returned Fields a few minutes later. "Sir, they were bluffing," he pointed out.

Captain Long's tough personal armor cracked for a moment and he warmly embraced the driver he had never expected to see again.

While Long and Fields slept fitfully the rest of the night, all too aware of their uncertain future, a call went out back at 761st Battalion HQ for volunteers to search for the missing tankers. Everyone in the rear echelon—cooks and mess personnel, clerks and Supply, Colonel Bates himself—took up weapons and sallied forth into the surrounding woods. Only the battalion sergeant major remained at headquarters as "acting battalion commander." Someone found the Jeep, but there the trail ended.

The prisoners awoke at dawn and huddled together against the wall, softly plotting. Somehow, things seemed different at Walhalla from last night. A profound silence appeared to have settled over the old citadel and the town itself. Long eased over to the door and placed his ear against it.

"I don't hear anything," he reported. "I mean, I don't hear *anything*."

Still not daring to hope, the two men waited in the room several hours, afraid to try the door lest they be shot for trying to escape. Long's ear almost grew to the door. During all that time he heard not a single footfall.

"I don't think anybody's here anymore," he finally ventured.

Cautiously, he tried the doorknob. To his astonishment, he found it unlocked. He cracked the door an inch, bracing himself for a shot, and peered out into a hallway. Fields crouched close behind.

They saw nothing except the long, dark, stone, deserted hallway. Not a guard, not a soldier, not a soul in sight.

They slipped out of the room. After a while, when still not

confronted, they ventured out of Walhalla and into bright sunshine. The streets were deserted, the entire town seemingly abandoned. Even the women who had spat in their faces last night were all gone. That meant Americans were coming and the Krauts had bugged out before they got here.

A slow grin of relief spread across Fields's dark face. Captain Long slapped him on the shoulder.

"Shall we go?" he asked.

"Which way, sir?"

"Back to our own guys."

"I'm with you, sir."

98

We are constantly finding German camps in which they have placed political prisoners where unspeakable conditions exist. From my own personal observation, I can state unequivocally that all written statements up to now do not paint the full horror.

—GENERAL DWIGHT EISENHOWER

Almost immediately after his rise to power, Adolf Hitler began establishing concentration camps designed to incarcerate political prisoners, criminals, and those considered to be security risks. The "Final Solution" became official policy following the Wannsee Conference in Berlin in January 1942. From that point on, certain concentration camps were constructed with the express purpose of mass exterminating human beings, principally Jews. The most notorious of these camps were Auschwitz, Dachau, Treblinka, and Buchenwald. The Holocaust began.

The first major Nazi concentration camp to be uncovered outside Poland was at Natzwiller in France in November 1944. Members of the Free French found the camp, now abandoned, on top of a hill at the end of a road. Integral parts of the facility were a dissection room and autopsy table, a gas chamber and incinerator room for burning corpses, a storage room crammed with burial urns, and a small dark room with S-shaped hooks suspended from the ceiling where prisoners were hung by their hands while Zyklon-B gas was pumped in to kill them.

By the time of this discovery, indeed as early as 1943, Hitler's campaign of extermination known as *Aktion Reinhard* had already claimed the bulk of Jews living in the *Generalgouvernement*. As many as six million of Europe's eight million Jews had been slaughtered. The only Jews permitted to remain alive were those engaged in defense-related work in SS-run labor camps.

There was a clear distinction between the death camps and the labor camps, although in some sense the latter were merely slower death camps where thousands were worked to death while already succumbing to exposure, starvation, exhaustion, epidemics, disease, or execution for alleged crimes. Literally hundreds of labor camps were scattered throughout Germany.

It was inevitable that the Americans should begin encountering these on their rapid push across Germany in April 1945. Units of the 4th Armored Division of Patton's Third Army came upon the first camp containing both prisoners and corpses at Ohrdruf, a minor subcamp of Buchenwald. The dead and dying lay stacked in rows and heaps reeking of human putrefaction, piled up like cordwood ready for the fire. Half-dead men wearing filthy, ragged, striped prison uniforms crouched or wandered about the compound, moaning, trying to comprehend what was happening. This first revelation of the horror rendered by the Nazis upon their "inferiors" was about to be let loose on a world that had, until now, attempted to rationalize away reports of the Holocaust.

Sergeant Johnnie Stevens did not know the camps existed, had not even heard rumors of them, until the spring morning he paused his tank on a hilltop that overlooked a minor labor camp encased in high net and barbed wire. There had been fighting earlier, but only sporadically. The Germans had fled and now everything was quiet again.

The labor camp occupied a peaceful green valley in the woods outside a town whose name merged with the names of dozens of others through which the Allies had passed since crossing the Rhine. Stevens saw a large, long building, another high, white building, and several smaller ones inside the enclosure. Human figures, tiny and indistinguishable at this distance, moved slowly among the buildings. From afar, everything looked neat and orderly. It was only after he cranked up his machine and lumbered down for a closer look that the full horror and depravity sank in. Nothing prepared the tankers for what they were about to witness.

The atmosphere closed in dark and depressing as tanks drew up before the camp and stunned tankers climbed out for their first look at the results of the Nazis' most insidious efforts to build a Super Race and to eliminate those who did not belong. Sights, sounds, odors from some ether-filled Otherworld, some hell on earth, almost overpowered them.

People wearing crazy striped uniforms looked so mistreated that nothing remained of them but skulls attached to human skeletons. Gnomish apparitions with deep-set eyes, bald heads, legs and arms like sticks with huge bulging joints. Suppurating sores and boils, lice-infested, dying of TB, dysentery, and starvation. Holding on to one another, stretching out their bony, gnarled hands, hobbling with the excruciating slowness of large, lethargic insects.

Hobbling forward, sobbing and mewling at the sight of their liberators. Happy to be free but terribly ill and weak. Wanting to hug the Americans and kiss them, but tottering and falling with the effort. Dropping to their knees to grab GIs around the legs. Some cried, some laughed, and some sat and stared at the ground, every so often letting out a terrible animal scream.

A man held out his hands to Corporal Leon Bass. His fingers were webbed together with scabs and his ribs stuck out like those of a skeleton, with an unnatural light in eyes so sunken into his skull that he looked blind.

"My God, what *is* this?" Bass stammered. "This must be some kind of insanity. Who are these people? What have they done that could be so wrong to deserve this?"

These people were Jews and Gypsies, Jehovah's Witnesses, communists, unionists, homosexuals, anyone who failed to fit the ideal Aryan mold. The Nazis said these people were inferior and therefore segregated to avoid contaminating the perfect society while they worked themselves to death.

The Negro in America was also considered inferior and segregated—but nothing like this. Bass made the comparison, and he stood and looked at all these inferior people while tears ran down his cheeks.

"No more war, no more war!" one bony creature chanted with hysterical glee, staggering and clapping her hands. All her teeth were gone. It was hard to tell if she were young or old. Everyone appeared the exact same age—ancient.

It was enough to shake the sensibilities of even the toughest soldier. Johnnie Stevens would never forget the stench of discarded decaying flesh, burning bodies, piles of human excrement, sewer pits buzzing with flies.

Tough Captain Johnny Long watched inmates stumble about without direction or purpose until they spotted a dead horse recently stricken and killed just outside the now-opened front gate. Food! They tottered over to the bloating carcass as fast as they could and threw themselves upon it like starving jackals, ripping and tearing at the bloody thing with their bare hands as they ate the flesh raw.

The Panthers left all the food they could spare, not realizing that it might be too rich for the freed prisoners' shut-down systems. Many overindulged and began vomiting. Some even died.

After the camp, black men of the 761st saw the Germans in a new and more monstrous light. They were ready to go out and start shooting any and all Germans, no matter if they were soldiers or not.

99

I am going to fight in front of Berlin, fight in Berlin, and fight behind Berlin.

—ADOLF HITLER

On April 27, 1945, Radio Milan announced that Italian communist guerrillas had captured former Fascist Italian dictator Benito Mussolini and his mistress Clara Petacci. The next day, Radio Milan announced that Mussolini and his mistress were executed. Their unnamed executioner gave an interview on how it happened.

He said he persuaded the ex-dictator and his lover to accompany him from their shepherd's hut prison on the pretext that they were being rescued. Once outside, he pointed a Sten gun at them and ordered them to stand against a wall.

"Mussolini was terror-stricken. Clara Petacci threw her arms around his shoulders and screamed, 'He mustn't die!' I said, 'Get back in your place if you don't want to die too.' The woman jumped back. From a distance of three paces I shot five bursts into Mussolini. . . . Then it was Petacci's turn. Justice had been done."

By this time the Soviet Army had encircled Berlin and linked up with U.S. forces at Torgau on the Elbe River, cutting the Reich into two parts. Millions of German women and children choked roads in desperate attempts to escape the Soviets and avoid the rape and murder that their own armies had inflicted on much of Europe. Hitler himself was trapped, living underneath the Chancellery in an underground village known as the Führerbunker. He feared the same fate as Mussolini, the news of whose ignoble end seemed to affect him greatly.

Adolf Hitler was very sick, eyes bloodshot, breath ragged, unable to walk more than a few paces without gripping something for support, sleeping only fitfully with the aid of drugs. Although he decided that Berlin would be the decisive battle, that he would turn it into another Stalingrad, he was rapidly losing control. His staff began to desert. Göring fled to Berchtesgaden; Himmler attempted to negotiate a separate peace.

Eva Braun remained loyal and at his side, as Clara Petacci had remained loyal to Mussolini. On April 29, between 1:00 A.M. and 3:00 A.M., with fighting now only a few streets away, Adolf Hitler and Eva were finally married. The honeymoon lasted less than thirty-six hours.

At about 3:30 P.M. on April 30, Eva bit into a cyanide capsule. Hitler bit into another capsule while simultaneously shooting himself through the right temple with a Walther pistol.

The war continued. The snake had its head cut off, but it was still waiting until sundown to stop twitching.

100

Hitler had once said that no black or no Jew would ever set foot on his personal property. I had news for him.

—SERGEANT JOHNNIE STEVENS

The Germans were headless and on the run. Tankers of the 761st Black Panther Battalion, Patton's Panthers, had traveled more than 350 miles through enemy territory, rolling across the Reich toward a "destination unknown" but which was generally believed to be a meeting with the Russians in Austria. The black men of the 761st, who had been constantly on the front lines for some 180 days, who had lost good men in battle, and who had met and defeated the best of Hitler's armies, began to see the expected meeting with the Russians as some kind of closure. To them, that was the finish line, the end of things, without which the race and the war would never be over.

However, forces to prevent their reaching that goal were at work. The supply situation had become critical because of inadequate transportation facilities, long supply lines, and extremely heavy demands. Third Army needed gasoline and all types of rations. Commanders of all echelons were requested to use captured German food stocks as much as possible. General Patton imposed strict gasoline rationing. Gasoline was to be issued to certain outfits only, of which the 761st was not one.

Colonel Paul Bates, disappointed himself, made the announcement to his assembled battalion.

"It is with great pride that I review the accomplishments of the 761st Tank Battalion," he began. "You have more than lived up to the many indicators of battle success recalled in your training in the United States. Fighting in France, Belgium, Luxembourg, Holland, Germany, and Austria has required you to adjust to the requirements of a great number of different units. The courage you have shown in your tanks has been magnificently matched by truck drivers as they brought up supplies. Maintenance men have worked tirelessly to keep the armor going, doing without food and sleep and using every means possible to obtain spare parts. Medical personnel followed fearlessly and always cared for us regardless of enemy fire. Mess personnel, radio repairmen, clerks, all have performed in a superior manner.

"You have met every type of equipment in the German army—planes, V-bombs, bazookas, *Panzerfausts*, 88s, 75s, artillery, self-propelled guns, tanks, mines. All have hurt you. All have destroyed some of your equipment. But all are now behind you, useless, the German soldier defeated, his politicians silent, and you are victorious."

Sergeant Johnnie Stevens standing in ranks couldn't help feeling that this was the buildup for the hammer, that this was all okay *but* . . . there had to be a *but*.

Colonel Bates paused. Here it came. Here came the hammer.

"Equipment shortages and the great variety of equipment you have received have called upon you to continuously adapt yourselves to changing situations and conditions," he continued. "Now you are called upon to adapt a final time—to peace. Gentlemen, I salute you. Your war is over. I have received word today that no further gasoline will be issued to the 761st. We are to drive our vehicles as far as we can, at which time we are to settle in and wait for the armistice."

An angry and disappointed rumble rippled through the ranks. Sergeant Harding Crecy was one of the few who had had enough and was ready to stop. He had killed Germans, and kept killing Germans, hundreds of them, in revenge for the death of his friend Scotty. Further killing would not bring Scotty back.

"I want to go home now and be with Margaret," he said.

As for most of the others, it seemed they were ahead in the fourth quarter of the big game, two minutes to go, and their winning coach was throwing in the towel and simply walking off the field.

"What is it?" they demanded. "We run out of gas and we just sit out in the middle of nowhere and wait for the white boys to get the glory? That's what it's all about. Paddy didn't want us at the beginning and now he don't want us there at the end."

"Colonel Hard Tack, sir. If we can't ride, we'll *walk* the rest of the way. Sir, we can't stop now. We got to keep going all the way."

There was always a scrounger in every outfit who had a way of getting things when all other methods failed. Lieutenant Horace Jones of Supply satisfied that function for the 761st. He had little to say about the situation. Instead, he organized a convoy of deuce-and-a-half trucks and led it back to Kohlgrube where a Negro quartermaster unit operated an ammo and gasoline depot. A former first sergeant himself, Jones had become friends with the black first sergeant there.

"Sergeant, we have to have gasoline," he pleaded. "We're on our way to meet the Russians in Austria, but the white officers cut off our gas. We've come this far. We can't stop. We want black men to be there at the end."

The wily old first sergeant broke into a big grin and winked. "Sounds reasonable to me."

With the assistance of the quartermasters, Jones and his men liberated thirty thousand gallons of gasoline from the airfield.

"Just get there first," the quartermaster first sergeant said.

Colonel Bates was overwhelmed. "How did you manage it?" he asked Lieutenant Jones.

"If I tell you that, Colonel, you'll be an accessory after the fact."

Hard Tack slowly grinned. "Dismissed, Lieutenant. Let's get ready to roll."

Running on stolen gasoline, the 761st Black Panther Battalion reached Steyr, Austria, on the bank of the Enns River on May 5, 1945. The 71st Infantry Divisiion had negotiated for the surrender of one hundred thousand German soldiers who didn't want to be taken by the Russians. All day long they marched peacefully across the bridge to give up their vehicles, weapons, and equipment to Yank soldiers who herded them onto large fields, an amazing sight.

On May 6, 1945, Captain Richard English's Dog Company contributed ten tanks from his Mosquito Fleet to act as an honor guard while General Lothar von Rondulic, commanding general for the German Army South, signed surrender papers.

The war was over. Patton's Panthers had come all the way.

"What are you going to do now, Johnnie?" someone asked Sergeant Stevens.

"The same thing we're all going to do. Go home."

"Thank God," E. G. McConnell said, prayer book in hand.

Tanks of the 761st were lined up beside a small bridge for the surrender ceremonies when a Jeep waving a starred blue flag drove through between their lines. General George S. Patton, Jr., stood up in the Jeep, tall and straight, wearing his bright victory helmet, his riding britches, shined riding boots, and his pearl-handled pistols. The Negro troops of the 761st Tank Battalion stood at attention and saluted. He saluted back, sharply, and drove on. The great warrior wore a quiet, satisfied look on his face. He had asked for the best tankers, and, by God, he had gotten them. Patton's Panthers.

Afterword I

I know what my purpose in life was, and I did it.
—LIEUTENANT COLONEL PAUL BATES

The war was over. Most nurses in field hospitals, if not the hospitals themselves, consolidated with other hospitals or disbanded. Taffy found herself working in France at a general hospital waiting to be rotated back to the United States. She hadn't seen Paul since he crossed the Rhine with his tankers. He sent her a message and a map of where the 761st had settled in Steyr, Austria.

"I'm headquartered in the post office," the message said. "I'll try to get to you, but who knows when? You try to get to me."

That seemed a challenge. The Army Air Corps had built an airstrip of sorts on a field near the hospital, which accommodated mostly small single-engine Piper Cubs flown by recon and artillery observers. One of the young pilots had arrived overseas too late to get in on the war and his share of perceived glory. Taffy explained to him that her "husband" was commander of a tank battalion currently headquartered in Austria.

"If you can get me there," she bargained, "I'll make it worth your while."

"Well, what can you do for me?"

"I have some booze."

Officers received a ration of spirits. Since Taffy didn't drink, she saved her share for Paul to pick up for his tankers. He hadn't been able to make a pickup in weeks.

"What I'd really like," the pilot countered, "are some war souvenirs. I'll never get any now."

"It's a deal. I'm sure my husband has more war souvenirs than you can put on a ship."

Taffy had done it again—arranged to see her colonel against all odds.

The pilot and his passenger flew the Piper Cub from France and across the Alps to Austria, a rough enough flight to have Taffy sick much of the time out the window. The pilot studied his map and finally found Steyr, a small Alpine town surrounded by farmland but no airfield. He circled until he located a farmer's pasture sufficiently level and large enough for a landing.

"Hold on. This is going to get rough."

Every child in the town, summoned by the circling aircraft, rushed down to watch it land. When Taffy got out of the airplane, feeling much better now but still about a mile from her destination, she selected a twelve-year-old boy with a bicycle upon whom to practice her German.

"Do you know where the black soldiers are?" she asked him.

"Yes."

"Are they in the post office?"

"Yes."

"Can you take me there?"

He grinned broadly. Since Taffy was as small as she was pretty, weighing only about one hundred pounds, the Austrian boy patted his handlebars.

Colonel Paul Bates was coming out of the post office with his battalion staff after a meeting when he looked up and saw a blonde on the handlebars of a bicycle coming down the street. He froze with an unlighted cigar between his lips. The staff began roaring with laughter as Taffy hopped off the bicycle, kissed her young chauffeur on the cheek, and sauntered up to the colonel, who was still speechless.

"Taffy? Is that really you?" he finally gasped.

"It's me."

"Did you come all the way on a bicycle?"

"Paul, you'd better light that cigar before you burn your fingers. Are you going to marry me or what?"

Afterword II

*In thinking of the heritage of glory you have
achieved, do not be unmindful of the price you have
paid. Throughout your victorious advances, your line
of march is marked with the graves of your heroic
dead; while the hospitals are crowded with your
wounded.*

—GENERAL GEORGE S. PATTON, JR.

Staff Sergeant Johnnie Stevens received his Honorable Discharge from the U.S. Army at Fort Benning, Georgia. He was
waiting at the bus station wearing a chestful of medals on his
uniform when the bus pulled in. He started to get on with his
ticket to New Jersey and home when the driver barked, "Hey,
boy. You got to wait a minute."

Here we go again. Nothing had changed.

Patton's Panthers, the 761st Tank Battalion (N), had been in
combat 183 days continuously. During that time it had participated in four major Allied campaigns in six different countries,
and was attached or assigned to three separate American armies
and seven divisions. The Black Panthers inflicted more than
130,000 casualties upon the enemy. Eight enlisted men received
battlefield commissions, while 391 received decorations for
heroism: 7 Silver Stars for Valor (three posthumously); 56
Bronze Stars for Valor (clusters on three of them); and 246 Pur-

ple Hearts (clusters on eight).* Three officers and 31 enlisted men were killed in action, and 22 officers and 180 enlisted men were wounded.

And here one of the decorated veterans of that outfit was going to have to go to the back of the bus because he was a black man.

Eight veterans of the 26th Infantry Division with whom the 761st had fought in France were also waiting to board the same bus. A tough-looking white sergeant stepped forward and grasped the bus driver's lapels.

"Hey, don't you see those gawd damned medals on that man's chest?" he said. "He was with us in combat. Now he's gonna get on this gawd damned bus, and he is gonna ride up front with us. Got it? Sergeant Stevens, get on this gawd damn bus."

---

*In 1997, 53 years after sacrificing his life on the battlefield, Sergeant Ruben Rivers was posthumously awarded the Medal of Honor. In 1998, the 761st Tank Battalion (deactivated) received a Presidential Unit Citation, the highest award that a unit can receive.

Index